Gavin Hyman is Lecturer in Religious Studies at the University of Lancaster. He is the author of *The Predicament of Postmodern Theology* (2001) and editor of *New Directions in Philosophical Theology* (2004). His essays and articles have appeared in a variety of publications which include *The Cambridge Companion to Atheism; New Blackfriars; The Heythrop Journal; Literature and Theology* and the *Journal of the American Academy of Religion*.

'Gavin Hyman offers a much needed analysis and evaluation of the atheism that arose during the Enlightenment and extended itself into the modern and contemporary periods. He does so with a fairness and balance that illumines the subject rather than obfuscates it. Avoiding the supercilious polemic which has recently and regrettably marked the subject, Hyman's introductory history of atheism is honest in its assessment of the evidence and careful in its argumentation, taking up an issue that has preoccupied Western civilization since the ancient Greeks. The integrity of his inquiry and of his discourse have left us very much in his debt.' – ***Michael J. Buckley, S.J., Augustin Cardinal Bea, S.J., Professor of Theology, Santa Clara University, and author of* At the Origins of Modern Atheism**

'In this meticulous anatomy of modern atheism, Gavin Hyman pursues the idea that we get the atheism we deserve: that modern atheism is a function of the modern idea of God, and nothing more. Accordingly, as the author shows, the very idea of the "post-modern" spells trouble for the atheism that is built into modernity. The alternatives that post-modernity presents, Hyman argues, are whether to retrieve the pre-modern traditions of Augustine and Aquinas or to press on toward a thinking that moves beyond and displaces the distinction between theism and atheism. This is a lucid, engaging and astute work of historical and philosophical analysis.' – ***John D. Caputo, Thomas J. Watson Professor of Religion and Humanities and Professor of Philosophy, Syracuse University***

A Short History of

ATHEISM

Gavin Hyman

I.B. TAURIS
LONDON · NEW YORK

Published in 2010 by I.B.Tauris & Co Ltd
6 Salem Road, London W2 4BU
175 Fifth Avenue, New York NY 10010
www.ibtauris.com

In the United States of America and Canada distributed by
Palgrave Macmillan, a division of St. Martin's Press, 175 Fifth Avenue,
New York NY 10010

Library of Modern Religion, Vol. 13

ISBN: (PB) 978 1 84885 137 5
ISBN: (HB) 978 1 84885 136 8

A full CIP record for this book is available from the British Library
A full CIP record is available from the Library of Congress

Library of Congress Catalog Card Number: available

Designed and Typeset by 4word Ltd, Bristol, UK
Printed and bound in Great Britain by TJ International, Padstow, Cornwall

To my students in the Department of Religious Studies at the University of Lancaster, 1999–2010

Contents

Foreword

This book has been written for general readers and students, rather than for academic specialists. Scholars in philosophy, theology, religious studies and intellectual history will already be familiar with most of what appears in this book, simply because most of what is said here has been said before by others. I have tried to specify precisely who has said what in the text, footnotes and bibliography. At this particular juncture, however, it may be thought worthwhile to make these academic investigations accessible to a wider audience.

This is because the last few years have witnessed widespread interest in debates around atheism well beyond the boundaries of the academy. These debates have been conducted with passionate intensity by some and observed with a more detached curiosity by others. But what has been evident is that these discussions have largely been undertaken in ignorance of some important and pertinent work that has recently been done by academic specialists in the field. This is understandable because such work is often undertaken at an advanced and technical level, and is scattered widely in a plethora of books and articles that are not all easily accessible. Although understandable, however, such a situation is no less regrettable. This is because much of this scholarly work has direct implications for the conduct of public debates on atheism and the assumptions that underlie them. In particular, many of these debates seem to be trapped within a particular mental world-view that is a product of Enlightenment modernity. The assumptions and history of this world-view are rarely questioned or even acknowledged, with the result that the world-view itself comes to appear as a timeless given rather than as an historical product. Participants in the debate may thus be forced into positions and faced with alternatives that are dictated by this world-view, and deprived of the opportunity of exploring alternative approaches and ways of thinking.

A significant stream of recent scholarship has contended that the modern Enlightenment framework that so often encompasses contemporary debates between theism and atheism may not be the only one, nor indeed the most adequate one, within which to discuss these questions. Perhaps this framework produces conceptions of theism and atheism that are alike inadequate. Perhaps historical investigations will discern alternative intellectual approaches that widen horizons and create new opportunities for thought. Current public debates on atheism can often appear sterile and hidebound. Recent scholarship has suggested ways in which these debates may be opened up by their being exposed to wider vistas. But such scholarship has rarely penetrated through to the wider public domain. It is the aim of this book to make some contribution to the bridging of this gap.

My writing of this book has been made considerably easier by some ten years experience of being a university teacher. One of my own former teachers has said that 'teaching clarifies the mind' and I, in turn, have certainly found this to be so. Many of the formulations of ideas in this book were first aired in lectures delivered to undergraduates in the Department of Religious Studies at the University of Lancaster. I am particularly grateful to students who have taken the courses 'Modern Religious and Atheistic Thought' and 'Ethics, Philosophy and Religion' (on which I teach a section on 'Philosophical Conceptions of God'). Their responses, questions and requests for clarification have certainly helped me to shape many of the ideas expressed in this book. I dedicate it to them.

Much of this book was written during a period spent as a Visiting Fellow of Mansfield College, Oxford. I am very grateful to the Principal and Fellows for their generous hospitality. In particular, I should like to thank Robert Adams, Alex Brayson, Charles Brock, Tony Lemon, Peggy Morgan, John Muddiman and Tanya and Joel Rasmussen for their stimulating conversation and enjoyable company. Beyond Mansfield, although also in Oxford, I am grateful to Alastair Anderson, John Bishop, Stephen Bullivant, John Huber, Nick Kenworthy-Browne, George Pattison and Cornelia van der Poll for their welcome and hospitality.

Some of the ideas in this book have been given preliminary expression elsewhere. The material in the first four chapters was initially formulated in a much more succinct form in my essay 'Atheism in Modern History' in Michael Martin (ed), *The Cambridge Companion to Atheism* (Cambridge: Cambridge University Press, 2006). An earlier version of Chapter 4 was initially developed in Chapter 2 of my book *The Predicament of Postmodern Theology: Radical Orthodoxy or Nihilist Textualism?* (Louisville: Westminster John Knox Press, 2001), and a much briefer version of Chapter 5 appeared as an article written for Hans-Josef Klauck, Bernard McGinn, Choon-Leong Seow, Hermann Spieckermann, Barry Dov Walfish, Eric Ziolkowski (eds), *The Encyclopedia of the Bible and its Reception*, Vol. 1 (Berlin: Walter de Gruyter, 2009).

Introduction

The last few years have seen a remarkable surge of popular interest in the topic of atheism, both in the UK and the USA. Works by such writers as Richard Dawkins, Sam Harris, Christopher Hitchens and Michel Onfray, to name but a few, have figured prominently in best-seller book lists and have prompted widespread discussion in all sections of the contemporary media.[1] Few reading members of the Anglo-American public can have been unaware of the popularity of these books and of the ubiquity of these public debates on atheism.

In some ways, this has been a puzzling phenomenon. Rudimentary opinion polls and surveys, as well as sophisticated sociological analyses, repeatedly insist that atheism as a world-view remains a minority confession. As Charles Taylor has suggested in his recent book, *A Secular Age* (2007), most in the contemporary West seem unable to profess belief in the established religious orthodoxies, but neither can they rest content with the immanent certainties of an atheistic creed. Most seem destined to wander in an intermediate terrain, with little agreement as to what they are finding there.[2]

So why the sudden surge of interest in atheism? It is perhaps no coincidence that this has emerged at around the same time as a corresponding rise of interest in religious fundamentalisms of various kinds. Undoubtedly, this interest in fundamentalism has been to some extent politically motivated, arising in part from recent acts of terrorism by attackers who invoke religious rhetoric, predominantly, but not solely, Islamic and Christian. At a time of interest in religious fundamentalisms, it is perhaps to be expected that there would be a parallel interest in what some perceive to lie at the other extreme of the spectrum, and what others perceive to be a secular species of fundamentalism, namely, in both cases, atheism. Secondly, the occurrence of religiously motivated acts of violence only serves to feed the rhetoric of those atheistic apologists who see an indelible link between religion and violent intolerance. Indeed, a number of those writers mentioned above make precisely this link. Thirdly, in a situation in which people find themselves caught in a flux of uncertainty between religious orthodoxy and secular atheism, it is also to be expected that such 'seekers' will find themselves susceptible to exploring the writings of articulate, popular and persuasive evangelists, whether for religion or atheism, and even if they do so while reserving any final judgement.

But what is conspicuous about all these publications and debates on atheism is a certain lack of nuance and sophistication. It is not only that these atheistic evangelists often proffer crudely caricatured accounts of the religious beliefs against which they are reacting, although this is undoubtedly true at times. Neither is it only that they themselves unwittingly promote yet another version of dogmatic metaphysical belief in secular guise, although a case could be made that this is indeed so. But perhaps more important than either of these is a lack of awareness of atheism's own origins, of the historical, philosophical and cultural matrix out of which it emerged, of its own deep implication with the religion, or better, theism, against which it defines itself, of its own situatedness and cultural specificity.

It is the aim of this book to elicit and elucidate these complexities and, in so doing, to attain a richer understanding of the phenomenon of atheism itself. Central to this undertaking is the conviction that there is a deep and mutually implicated connection between three key terms: modernity, religion and atheism (particularly if we follow numerous scholars in seeing the term 'religion' as itself a creation of modernity). In effect, I shall suggest, it is impossible adequately to understand any one of these terms without an understanding of the other two. In terms of atheism, this means that its origin, definition and plausibility are inseparable from the 'modern' world-view out of which it arose, and the 'modern' form of religion against which it reacts and defines itself. Throughout the book, I shall draw attention to the various ways in which these three terms mutually reinforce and enlighten each other.

It should be said that it will not be the explicit purpose of this book to present a case *for* or *against* atheism. In that sense, it is not envisaged as a direct 'reply' to the writers and books on atheism mentioned above. Nonetheless, the arguments and analyses to be developed here may well have significant implications for the plausibility of the arguments which atheists themselves construct. In particular, if there is indeed a close connection between the three key concepts in the manner I have suggested, then certain recent developments may well have implications for atheism. For instance, if the world in which we live is no longer straightforwardly 'modern' in the way in which it once was, then the plausibility of atheism cannot but be affected. So too, if the distinctively 'modern' manifestations of religious belief are themselves being transformed into something else, this may well make the atheistic apologia less pertinent. But the primary aim of this book will be to bring readers to a better understanding of what I take atheism to be, even if this is an account that they themselves will ultimately wish to contest.

However, before proceeding further, it will be necessary for us to give some attention to questions of definition, particularly with regard to those key terms that I have identified as being central to this study. Disputes about what constitutes the 'modern' or 'modernity' have been long and tortuous and no definition will gain universal assent. The term 'modernity' derives from the Latin word *modo*, meaning 'just now'. It thus denoted the 'present', the 'contemporary' as opposed to the 'past' or 'historical'. More specifically, the modern defined itself in opposition to the 'ancient', the age of antiquity. Michael Allen Gillespie says that:

> The idea of the modern age or, as it was later called, modernity, was part of the self-understanding that characterized European thought from the time of Bacon and Descartes. This idea ... rested on a revolutionary notion of freedom and progress. Alluding to the discoveries of Columbus and Copernicus, Bacon, for example, argued that modernity was superior to antiquity and laid out a methodology for attaining knowledge of the world that would carry humanity to ever greater heights.[3]

In other words, at the heart of the notion of modernity was the conviction that the contemporary is intrinsically superior to the past because we have *progressed* from there to here. The modern way of thinking and acting is not simply an alternative way to that of antiquity; it marks a movement of improvement. As Gillespie goes on to say, what underlay this evaluation of modernity vis-à-vis antiquity was:

> not merely a new notion of knowledge but also a new notion of time not as circular and finite but as linear and infinite. Change was pictured as a continuous natural process that free human beings could master and control through the application of the proper scientific method. In this way they could become masters and possessors of nature and thereby produce a more hospitable world for themselves.[4]

Gillespie's comments here identify what we may well take to be the defining features of the modern world-view in all its various manifestations. What is central here is the conviction that the world – and time and change – is something to be *mastered* and *controlled*. Furthermore, the world is to be mastered and controlled not for its own sake, but in order that we may *progress*. Again, this progress is to be pursued not for its own sake, but so that human beings may produce 'a more hospitable world *for themselves*'. In other words, the world is to be mastered and controlled so that it may serve the needs of human beings. The human subject thus becomes the 'master' and the world itself becomes the 'slave', and the human subject exercises this mastery through the discipline of the application of reason and science. Through reason and science, the world may be manipulated, understood and thereby controlled.

But this, of course, was to enact a revolution in the understanding of the role and position of the human subject in relation to reality. When the human subject masters reality by means of reason and/or science, the self comes to understand itself as existing in a fundamentally *nominative* mode. That is to say, the self becomes the *subject* that applies the disciplines of reason and science to the world, which is thereby conceived to be the *object* of that activity. This was in marked contrast to the epistemological model that prevailed in medieval theology. There, human beings understood themselves as existing in an *accusative* mode. They, and the wider reality of which they were a part, were created by God and were therefore, in a sense, *objects* of God's creative activity. The only true 'subject', therefore, was God, the creator and 'author' of all known reality.

When humanity considers itself to be the only true subject, then everything else becomes an object in relation to it. This includes God, who now becomes an object of thought, like the rest of reality which is being mastered and controlled. When God becomes an 'object of thought' (rather than the source of all thought), then one would expect the resulting conception of God to be qualitatively different from that which prevailed before. Indeed, one of the central arguments of this book is that this was indeed the case. The advent of modernity brought with it a transformed conception of God, a distinctively 'modern' theism. When God is understood to be an object of thought, then God is created in the image of humanity. God comes to be conceived in human terms, his transcendence is domesticated and, in some instances at least, God increasingly takes on the characteristics of a 'big person'. In effect, God becomes a projection of the human subject. In what follows, therefore, I shall be arguing that this is what theism becomes in the modern period. This is what it means to speak of a distinctively 'modern theism'.

But how does all of this relate to atheism? Why is 'modernity' – and the modern form of theism that results – so indispensable for a proper understanding of atheism? For one thing, atheism is itself an intrinsically 'modern' disposition. The epistemological shifts that constitute the inauguration of modernity themselves open up the possibility of an atheistic world-view. Once the human self has been re-conceived as the knowing subject, atheism itself becomes a conceptual possibility in a way that it would not have been previously. When the task of humanity is conceived as being to master the world through rational and scientific means, then God becomes an hypothetical object in the world, the existence of which is, in principle, open to rational and scientific investigation. Atheism is an accomplice of modernity in that it shares its fundamental conviction that the truth of the world is, in principle, accessible to human beings through the exercise of their rational, experiential and experimental capacities.

Atheism is inseparably connected not only to modernity, but also to the theism against which it reacts and defines itself. Atheism is commonly defined as 'the belief (or conviction) that God does not exist'. Immediately, therefore, we see that atheism defines itself in terms of that which it takes to be denying. In this respect, atheism shares a structural similarity to the term 'postmodernism'. The term atheism itself 'positions the phenomenon as relational. [Theism] as that from which [atheism] is breaking away remains inscribed into the very word with which [atheists] describe their distance from [theism].'[5] Consequently, the meaning of atheism can be given positive content only if there is some definition proffered of the God that is being denied. In other words, if atheism is understood to consist in a denial of God, one first has to ask precisely what God is being denied. This is by no means an insignificant question, given that conceptions of God in the Christian tradition have varied so enormously in history. Does atheism arise as the denial of a *particular* conception of God? If so, what then becomes of the status of atheism in relation to *alternative* conceptions of God?

This question becomes even more pertinent if it could be shown that the origin, meaning and force of atheism are alike derived from the denial of a specifically *modern* conception of God. If modernity creates the conditions for the possibility of atheism, and if modernity also gives rise to a specifically modern rendering of theism, then it is to be expected that atheism would constitute and define itself as the rejection of this distinctively modern God. If, as I have suggested, theism mutates into something quite new and different at the advent of modernity, then it follows that it is *this* conception of God that modern atheism finds to be incredible and unsustainable. But where does that leave other conceptions of God, assuming there to be such alternative conceptions available in the contemporary world? Would the conventional atheistic critique have such force in relation to them?

So in the chapters that follow, I shall be arguing that atheism is inextricably bound up with modernity. This is so not only because atheism itself emerges out of and is made intelligible by a modern cultural and philosophical episteme. It is also because the plausibility and persuasiveness of atheism is sustained by the demise of a theism that is itself rendered in a distinctively modern key. The more that religion adapted itself to modern epistemological assumptions and procedures, the more vulnerable it became to an atheistic assault. It follows from this that the fate of atheism would seem to be bound up with the fate of modernity itself. In a time in which modernity is experiencing a crisis of confidence, one would hardly expect this to leave atheism undisturbed. My conclusion will be that 'modernity', 'modern theism' and 'modern atheism' are mutually defining and sustaining. The demise of one cannot but have implications for the other two.

If we are indeed currently witnessing the 'end of modernity', we would expect also to be witnessing the demise of (modern) theism. This is certainly so, not only in Western society more generally, but also in academic theology. In the latter there has recently emerged a theology more connected to its medieval past and more questioning of its Enlightenment inheritance. But we would expect also to witness a demise of atheism, as it loses not only its epistemological foundation, but also its antithetical foil, against which it defines and sustains itself. Clearly this conclusion (and this book as a whole) in no way constitutes a decisive argument against atheism. But it will, I hope, give the recent 'evangelists for atheism' pause for thought and will suggest that the truth and triumph of atheism may not be as unequivocal as they would have us believe.

Chapter 1

The 'Appearance' of Atheism in Modern History

In any discussion of the 'appearance' of atheism in the West, it is important to distinguish between two distinct spheres in which this occurred. On the one hand, it is possible to trace the emergence and development of atheism in modern thought as an intellectual phenomenon among writers, philosophers, artists and other elites. On the other hand, one may trace a parallel development of atheism in history as a cultural phenomenon, whereby atheism becomes a possible option, a viable world-view, whether for society as a whole or for groups or individuals within societies. To trace the contours of both these developments is to tell two quite distinct stories, each with their own beginnings and histories. There may be parallels and points of contact between them, but the time and manner of their respective developments are quite distinct.

It is also worth noting at this point that the story of the appearance of atheism is part of a wider story of the appearance of 'unbelief' in relation to Christianity. For, as we shall see, atheism is but one species of unbelief that emerged alongside, or in reaction against, other forms such as scepticism, 'free thinking' and, later, agnosticism. All these varieties of unbelief have their own distinct characteristics, but they are all part of a wider story of the gradual weakening of the hold of Christian orthodoxy on Western thought and Western society in general. As Charles Taylor has recently emphasised, there has been a remarkable shift in Western society, the revolutionary character of which is not always fully appreciated.[1] In a relatively short period (in world historical terms) of 500 years, we have moved from a situation (in around, say, 1500) in which it was almost inconceivable for an individual to take a stance of unbelief to one (in around, say, 2000) where unbelief has not only become a perfectly viable option, but a widespread and perhaps even the dominant one. This latter situation is the defining feature of what Taylor characterises as a 'secular age'.

His impressively detailed survey of the emergence of the 'secular' is undertaken to counter what he calls the 'subtraction' thesis of secularisation, the influence of which is remarkably widespread, even if not consciously acknowledged. This holds that 'secularism' is what is left, the remaining residue, once supernaturalism and superstition have finally been expunged. This, indeed, appears to be the underlying assumption of many of the contemporary popularisers of atheism, as discussed in the Introduction. On the contrary, argues Taylor, secularism is a positive and substantive intellectual world-view, the emergence of which is itself in need of explanation and which can be traced in terms of specific and contingent developments in Western thought and practice. Taylor himself acknowledges that his account is complementary to those of several other scholars who likewise dispute the notion that the emergence of the secular was somehow the result of a process of teleological necessity. Indeed, we shall be invoking some of these scholars in the chapters that follow, as their accounts likewise feed into my own, which contends that there is a deep connection between atheism, modernity and (modern) religion. But it is time now to turn explicitly to the question of the 'appearance' of atheism in modernity.

Although we have already noted the difficulties in identifying precisely where modernity 'begins', it is instructive to note that the term 'atheism' as an identifiable outlook is roughly contemporaneous with the birth of modernity itself. It has often been noted by scholars of antiquity that what we understand as 'atheism' would have been unintelligible to the classical mind. Certainly, there were disagreements on the nature of the gods or their activities, and sometimes even the denial of the existence of certain gods. But the notion, intrinsic to the modern understanding of atheism, of immanence – of the world existing quite free of any sort of transcendent realm – would have been almost unintelligible to them. As Jan N. Bremmer has said of Greek and Roman antiquity:

> [A]theism never developed into a popular ideology with a recognizable following. All we have in antiquity is the exceptional individual who dared to voice his disbelief or bold philosophers who proposed intellectual theories about the coming into existence of the gods without, normally, putting their theories into practice or rejecting religious practice altogether. If we find atheism at all, it is usually a 'soft' atheism or the imputation of atheism to others as a means to discredit them.[2]

Furthermore, Bremmer goes on to say that such 'soft' atheism as existed was constituted not by a resolute denial of a transcendent realm, but, rather, by a form of free thinking that ultimately sought to save the existence of the gods.

It is interesting, then, that Michael J. Buckley traces the first use of the term 'atheism' in England to the Greek scholar Sir John Cheke, who invokes it in a translation of Plutarch's *On Superstition*, undertaken in 1540. Indeed, the fact that the term was first used in this context is instructive. Cheke himself seems to be not entirely consistent in his use of the term. In his translation of Plutarch, the word is used as a form of accusation, directed against those who think there are no gods. But in his own essay appended to the translation, it denotes the denial of the specific doctrine of divine providence. What 'atheists' deny, in this usage, is the belief that the gods intervene in the world, guiding it in accordance with their own plans and purposes. Such varied usages of the term are also to be found in society more generally over the next century or so, leading Buckley to speak of 'the promiscuity of its definition and application'.[3] Thus, in this period, in both England and France at least, the term 'atheism' often denoted some form of heresy, although it increasingly came to denote an outright denial of theism as such. This former usage of the term, though different from ours, is still instructive for our purposes. For one thing, it shows how, in the period from, say, 1540 to 1630, the notion of a world-view that was entirely outside a theistic framework was only gradually becoming conceivable. The rebellious atheist was often one who questioned or denied certain central doctrines of the theistic world-view, and only later one who questioned or denied that world-view as such. On the other hand, this earlier understanding already prefigures our later one, in that, within this more limited context, it is already a negative and parasitic term, which defines itself in terms of that which it is denying. In this sense, the structural logic of atheism – as a denial of something else – is already in place, waiting potentially to be applied to the theistic tradition as a whole rather than to one specific element within it. If this structural logic of atheism had indeed already been established, then the real revolutionary turn was the one that allowed for the taking of an *external* viewpoint, casting judgement on the theological tradition as a whole from a position *outside* it. We shall consider in subsequent chapters precisely what it was that created the conditions for this revolution to occur.

By around 1630, however, at precisely the time that Western Europe was making its traumatic transition to modernity, this revolution had occurred, with the result that the meaning of the term 'atheism' had transmuted its meaning fairly decisively into a form that is now more familiar to us. This had occurred in reaction to the emergence of a group of individuals, small at first but rapidly growing, who were prepared to deny the truth of theism itself. Michel de Certeau has pointed out that in France:

> The 'atheists' who first occupy the polemic are the 'heretics' of every Church, the nonconformist believers and such. But soon the controversy centers on the existence of God. Around 1630 groups of 'libertines', erudite and skeptics [s]pring up; they will fade away around 1655 … before coming back around 1680. 'Atheism', which was never

> spoken of a hundred years earlier, becomes a recognized fact.[4]

Given that such a stance was barely conceivable a little over 100 years earlier, we should not imagine that the emergence of the new so-called atheists would have been observed with equanimity. On the contrary, they would have been regarded as a threat to the structure and stability of the whole world order. Furthermore, it can in retrospect be understood as one of several symptoms of wider and deeper intellectual and cultural shifts that we would now understand as constituting the birth of modernity. Old certainties and foundations appeared to be crumbling, and people had no clear idea of what, if anything, might take their place. Such shifts, insofar as they would have been consciously perceptible as such, would have been viewed less as an evolution and more as a degeneration, the imperative thus being to halt them at all costs.

Thus, as de Certeau points out, in early seventeenth-century France, the perceived danger posed by atheism becomes almost an obsession, as clear attempts are made to eradicate this dangerous and threatening other. Atheists became subject to official sanctions and restrictions, and, when these were violated, judicial sentences against them were duly passed. Public warnings against the dangers posed by atheism became widespread. It seems that atheism was perceived as a destabilising threat of the same kind as that presented by witchcraft and sorcery, the incidence of which was high throughout Europe in the early seventeenth century. Both atheism and witchcraft were perceived as being fundamentally malign in their origins and effects, and both were suppressed with the full rigours of the law. But perhaps the most significant difference between them was that whereas witches and sorcerers destabilised the dominant order from within by utilising the symbols and vocabulary of that order, atheists destabilised it from without by questioning the truth and intelligibility of the order as such. Thus, witchcraft and sorcery may perhaps be viewed as embodying an indirect and equivocal expression of a doubt in relation to Christianity that atheism proclaimed more openly and unequivocally. Indeed, this is what Michel de Certeau suggests in his study of the infamous case of demonic possession in the convent at Loudun in the early seventeenth century. As de Certeau points out, the first appearance of 'atheists' who deny the existence of God is contemporaneous in Europe with the sudden rise in the incidence of witchcraft. For de Certeau, both are manifestations of the doubt and uncertainty that plagued societies as the old edifice of medieval theology began to crumble and give way to something else. In this sense, the 'witch craze' of the sixteenth and seventeenth centuries was perhaps a transitional manifestation of the traumatic paradigm shift that was occurring at this time. The fading away of the witch craze at the end of the seventeenth century was perhaps a sign that this fearful crossing had been made.[5] Henceforth, religious doubt would be expressed in a clear and unambiguous guise, through an atheism that explicitly denied the existence of God.

If one development in the meaning of 'atheism' lay in the transformation from it carrying an internal 'heretical' connotation to it conveying an external and direct attack upon theism itself, then the next important development lay in the evolution of the term into one that could be adopted as a means of self-identification. For it has to be said that in the French context we have been discussing, and in other contexts too, the term was used primarily in the manner of an accusation or a term of abuse. In the public pronouncements, declarations, legal acts and court sentences of the time, the term 'atheist' was used rather in the way that such terms as 'nihilist' and 'relativist' were later used; namely, as a means to denounce others with whom one disagreed, rather than as a means of self-definition. The next major development, therefore, lay in attempts to reclaim the term as a respectable and acceptable one for atheists themselves, both in intellectual and social terms. The former was achieved before the latter, but both took some time to come to fruition. Atheism as a declaration of one's own belief (or lack thereof) does not really appear until the mid-eighteenth century, when it became increasingly widespread in the fashionable salons of Parisian intellectuals.

In particular, Denis Diderot (1713–84), whose statue stands in the Boulevard St-Germain in Paris, is widely recognised as being the first explicitly and self-confessedly atheist philosopher. As Buckley puts it: 'in many ways, Diderot is the first of the atheists, not simply in chronological reckoning but as an initial and premier advocate and influence.'[6] He was not always an atheist, for his thought was constantly evolving, and at certain periods of his life he would more accurately be described as a theist, a deist, and at other times as a pantheist. Indeed, even in this evolutionary movement, he was paradigmatic of the Enlightenment mind. Furthermore, he became editor-in-chief of the infamous *Encyclopédie*, an enormous undertaking and another quintessentially Enlightenment project in its scope and aims. As Buckley points out, Diderot 'argued his case not by repudiating the mathematical physics of Descartes or the universal mechanics of Newton but by bringing them, as he contended, to fulfilment'.[7]

He accepted Descartes's view of the universe as a single physical system, which is nonetheless dynamic in its obeying immutable laws which are assigned to matter in motion. But he believed that Descartes was not sufficiently faithful to his own foundational epistemology, making leaps and assumptions that were unjustifiable in its own terms. Likewise, he saw himself as freeing Newton from an urge to point beyond itself to non-mechanical principles. He saw the revolutionary character of Newton's discoveries for our whole understanding of the natural world and the way in which this had been advanced in an unprecedented way. But he saw that these had been achieved through a consistently empirical approach to the natural sciences, unhindered by extraneous presuppositions and beliefs. When Newton turned to his discourses on theology, he appeared to be setting these tried and tested methodologies to one side in a way that could only give rise to error and fantasy. Newton had discovered an indubitably successful methodological path; having done so, Diderot believed that it was his duty to follow it without deviation. Diderot thus passed the discoveries of Descartes and Newton through the purging fire of consistency. It was not that he denied their presuppositions or fundamental methodologies; on the contrary, it was precisely his commitment to these that led him to apply them in what he considered to be a more thoroughgoing, unflinching and logically consistent way. In so doing, he made 'the initial but definitive statement' of atheism: 'the principle of everything is creative nature, matter in its self-activity eternally productive of all change and all design.'[8]

But in making the 'initial but definitive statement' of atheism, he also thereby inaugurated the process of establishing 'atheism' as a respectable position that one could, with impunity, apply to oneself. Part of his efficacy in this respect was that he clearly could not be dismissed as a malevolent or frivolous mind. On the contrary, it was widely acknowledged that Diderot had been led to atheism as a consequence of his disinterested quest for truth, undertaken with intellectual integrity. Furthermore, he reached his atheistic conclusions by furthering and intensifying the insights of Descartes and Newton – the very thinkers upon whom Christians depended as modern defenders of the faith. Descartes was thought to provide a defence of theism using the weapons of modern philosophy, while Newton was thought to do so using those of modern science. Diderot's contribution in this respect was to show how clearly these weapons could turn out to be double-edged swords. Indeed, in the French context, atheism's ascent to respectability was crowned by the French Revolution. In socio-political terms, atheism was suddenly transformed from being an enemy of the state to being almost the official state creed. The newly-built Temples of Reason and the founding of the Cult of Reason bore witness to this in a particularly vivid and tangible way (although there has been disagreement amongst scholars as to the extent of continuing adherence to Christianity below the level of revolutionary officialdom).[9]

All of this was in marked contrast to the revolutionary experience of the then newly-emerged United States of America. It is often thought the American inauguration of the separation between church and state was one of its most significant contributions to the development of the modern polis, but the significance of this is often misunderstood. Certainly, it was a deliberate attempt to found a new political order as distinct from that of its former colonial masters. The founding fathers believed it to be essential to the new order that the state should not favour any one particular religion or denomination over others. But it should not be thought that this entailed the founding of a religiously 'neutral' state or, if it did, this was so only in a very specific sense. The new constitution did not envisage a public political space that was devoid of religion; on the contrary, it was saturated with it. But the point was that the religious dimension of the state should be limited to the tenets of 'natural' religion; that is, those elements of religion (and we were at this time, of course, talking exclusively of Christian religion) that were shared by all churches and denominations. Thus, the religious foundations of the state should be ones that could be shared by everyone, while the absence of an established church meant that everyone was also individually free to 'supplement' this natural religion with their own denominationally-specific religious beliefs and practices. This was the fundamental purpose behind the separation between church and state, rather than that the sphere of politics and government should be a religion-free zone.[10] Thus already, in the American and French Revolutions, we see the beginnings of what has become the notorious split between a 'secular' Europe and a 'religious' America. In the USA, there was nothing remotely resembling the anti-clericalism of the French Revolution. Consequently, the new USA was as inhospitable to atheism as France was the contrary.

But if the French Revolution made atheism officially respectable in France, it appeared to have precisely the opposite effect in Britain. The British reaction to events of the revolution was one of horror, and this was to be found not only among the aristocratic elites. Memories of Britain's own act of regicide were still relatively fresh, and the experience was not a happy one. In the British mind, the French Revolution was marked by violence, extremism, murder and immorality, however unbalanced such a characterisation was. The fact that many priests had perished with the peers loomed large in the public consciousness, and it was inevitable that an indelible connection would be made between atheism on the one hand and immorality, lawlessness and far-left revolutionary politics on the other. As a consequence, the old seventeenth-century usage of 'atheism' as a term of abuse and a marker of suspicion continued to echo throughout nineteenth-century Britain. This situation was further exacerbated by the fact that immorality and lawlessness emerged as the two great fears of the Victorian mind. These were to be combated at all costs as being detrimental, indeed fatal, to the health and well-being of society. Given that atheism inevitably brought these very things in its wake, this meant that atheism too was an evil to be combated, and this was further fuelled by the remarkable resurgence of religious belief and practice that Britain experienced in the Victorian era. As a result, the attempt to make atheism a respectable term of self-definition, which had made such strides in France, was one that still had to be fought by atheists in Britain throughout the nineteenth century in what must often have appeared to them to be a losing battle.

It was this that led many who were unable to subscribe to orthodox theism to coin new terms of self-definition, thus allowing them to remain uncontaminated by the stigma of atheism. George Jacob Holyoake, for instance, preferred to describe himself as a 'secularist', with the need to avoid being regarded as morally suspect being uppermost in his mind.[11] We see the same concern in other unbelieving writers in the later Victorian period. The novelist George Eliot, for instance, was both deeply influenced by and a translator of the works of Ludwig Feuerbach, and one of her chief preoccupations was to separate religion from morality so that the latter could be preserved independently of the former. It was partly this that motivated her quest for a 'religion of humanity' in later years. She too resisted any overt use of the term 'atheism'. But there were also other motivations for non-theists to find an alternative term of self-definition. The renowned naturalist Thomas Huxley, for instance, was unhappy with the term 'atheism' because he felt that it had now come to stand for a position that was too dogmatic. It made a definitive metaphysical claim about the nonexistence of God, for which Huxley believed there was insufficient evidence. In this sense, Huxley was among the first public figures to give prominent expression to a Humean metaphysical scepticism. Consequently, he believed that atheism was as guilty of metaphysical hubris as was theism. Furthermore, as we have already noted, memories of the

French Revolution resulted in 'atheism' being linked with far-left revolutionary politics, which further tainted the term in polite society. As Adrian Desmond has pointed out, 'Huxley's scientific civil service needed its own brocade banner. "Atheism" was out, there being no disproof of God; and anyway, it was a red republican flag, a political weapon to smash the spiritual basis of privilege.'[12] These concerns led Huxley and his associates to coin a new term, 'agnosticism', suggesting that the term represented not a new creed, but a metaphysical unknowing.[13] The term, of course, derives from the Greek word *gnosis*, to know. Thus, it did not denote a negation or denial of theism, but rather a negation or denial of (metaphysical) knowledge. That it was able to attain the respectability that still eluded atheism is suggested by Desmond, when he says that 'the word would push alienated intellectuals off the defensive for the first time since the French Revolution'. Henceforth, agnosticism would rival atheism as an alternative disposition for those unable to profess belief in God. Desmond even goes so far as to say (with perhaps a touch of hyperbole) that 'as the social axis shifted in late Victorian times, agnosticism was to become the new faith of the West'.[14]

We have observed that one of the reasons for the continuing stigma that attached to atheism was its connection with violent revolutionary politics, which had been vividly established by the French Revolution. But the developments of political philosophy in the nineteenth century reinforced this impression still further. In Karl Marx's thought in particular, revolution and atheism went hand in hand. It was not that atheism was a necessary precondition for revolution, but, rather, that revolution would necessarily bring atheism in its trail. For Marx, Christianity was an 'ideology' that emerged out of society's economic base; it both reflected and reinforced capitalism. When the economic base of capitalism disintegrated (as, for Marx, it inevitably would), then Christianity would simply fade away, so entirely was it a reflection of that base. For both would-be revolutionaries and those for whom revolution was their chief horror, Marx had reinforced the connection between left-wing revolution and atheism that had already been established in Western consciousness by the French Revolution.

The results were considerable and long-lasting. Not only would atheism be tainted with blood, violence and revolution, but also Christianity came to be regarded as inherently conservative and reactionary, an upholder of the status quo. It is significant, for instance, that when one of the pioneering British Christian Socialists, the scholar–clergyman F. D. Maurice, was being censured by his superiors at King's College, London, where he held a Chair, it was as much his left-wing political activities as his unorthodox doctrinal writings that perturbed them. One inevitably seemed to entail the other.

But in spite of atheism's growing connection with immorality, metaphysical presumption and left-wing revolution, there were still some who were committed to making it an acceptable and respectable outlook. One of the most prominent of these was Charles Bradlaugh, the first explicitly and self-confessedly atheist member of the British Parliament. He was able to take his seat in Parliament only after a lengthy and hard-fought battle of wills. To take their seats, members had to swear an oath of allegiance to the Queen, an explicitly religious oath sworn on the Bible, thus presenting what appeared to be an insurmountable barrier to atheists sitting in the British Parliament. Bradlaugh was first elected for the seat of Northampton in 1880, but his attempt to take his seat failed at the moment at which he was required to take the oath. He was re-elected in 1882 and again, with an increased majority, at the general election of 1886. Between 1880 and 1886, he was involved in various unsuccessful attempts to take his seat, each involving a personal appearance in the chamber of the House of Commons. There were also several court cases and appeals at which Bradlaugh pleaded his case, but which were ultimately futile.[15] The battle was one in which much was at stake. The British Parliament had ceased to be an exclusively Anglican body in 1828, when dissenters were admitted. In the following year, Roman Catholics were also admitted and the process of the religious pluralisation of Parliament culminated with the admission of Jews in 1858. Controversial though each of these concessions was, opponents were nonetheless still able to console themselves with the thought that, although no longer exclusively

Anglican, the British Parliament was still a 'religious' body. The admission of an atheist would end that final residual religious requirement for participation in the legislative arm of the state. Nonetheless, after the general election of 1886, the Speaker of the House of Commons bowed to what was increasingly appearing as the inevitable, and allowed Bradlaugh to take his seat. Atheists, secularists and free-thinkers alike hailed the decision as representing an historic turning point. But momentous though this undoubtedly was, of perhaps equal importance, albeit less dramatic, were Bradlaugh's various attempts to rehabilitate atheists as full and equal members of society. To this end, he conducted a number of public campaigns, the most prominent of which was his fight for the right of atheists to give evidence in court.[16]

If, by the end of the nineteenth century, atheism was finally beginning to rear its head as a respectable intellectual position, it was still far from widespread as a cultural phenomenon, and remained the preserve of the intellectual elite. This is not to say that all but the intellectual elite were filled with religious fervour. On the contrary, in Victorian England, for instance, the working classes were notoriously irreligious. This, indeed, was the main conclusion of Horace Mann's innovative religious census undertaken in 1851. Conducted on the day before the general national census, its purpose was to illuminate patterns of church-going on a national scale and, in addition, to determine the extent of the accommodation that was available nationally for religious worship. Mann himself concluded that

> the most important fact which this investigation as to attendance brings before us is, unquestionably the alarming number of the non-attendants... Nor is it difficult to indicate to what particular class of the community this portion in the main belongs ... while the labouring myriads of our country have been multiplying with our multiplied material prosperity, it cannot, it is feared, be stated that a corresponding increase has occurred in the attendance in this class of our religious edifices.[17]

Subsequent commentators have pointed out the limitations of Mann's figures and, in particular, have suggested that the incidence of working class religious observance was somewhat higher than he supposed.[18] Nonetheless, the general trend he identified cannot be doubted. What is open to doubt is how this non-attendance was to be interpreted. Did this mean that the British working-class population were predominantly atheists, secularists and agnostics? Mann himself addressed this question and suggested that

> the prevalence of infidelity has been exaggerated, if the word be taken in its popular meaning, as implying some degree of intellectual effort and decision; but, no doubt, a great extent of negative, inert indifference prevails, the practical effects of which are much the same.[19]

There was thus a prevalence of indifference which Mann characterised as an 'unconscious secularism'. The historian Owen Chadwick tends to agree, suggesting that contemporary priests and ministers confirmed Mann's general line of analysis: 'most slum pastors agreed that [the working classes] were free or almost free of infidelity. They found apathy and indifference and hostility, not unbelief.'[20]

A similar picture emerges if we look at the situation with respect to the working-class population of France. Although there was no national religious census comparable with that conducted by Mann, it is possible to get a general sense of the levels of active religiosity from statistics relating to Easter communicants and from contemporary accounts of priests and other observers. The abbé François Courtade undertook eight years of pastoral work in Paris from 1863, at the end of which he commented that '[t]he labouring population of Paris is on the way to becoming atheistic... The people of Paris are without faith and without God. The notion and the feeling of the divine seem to have entirely withdrawn from them.'[21] Commenting on this, Thomas Kselman says that 'Courtade's response was typical of the Catholic clergy, who complained of the rising wave of indifference throughout the nineteenth century, an indifference that could on occasion turn into hostility and violence'.[22] But Kselman goes on to argue that this impression is based too narrowly on statistics relating to church attendance, which may be an inadequate measure of assessing the 'religious' or 'atheistic' sensibilities of a population. He suggests that the situation in nineteenth-century France would better be characterised in terms of a process of religious 'pluralisation' rather than of 'secularisation', marked by an outright denial of theism. If he is right, then the situation may be regarded as being somewhat analogous to that in England. The comparatively 'indifferent' attitude of the working classes in England and France towards the church at this time does not necessarily indicate a positive avowal of atheism or unbelief. This in turn, however, raises the question of how this indifference should be interpreted. Was it the case that the working class consisted of predominantly theistic believers who were nonetheless suspicious and distrustful of (in England especially) a class-ridden and intimidating Church? Or was their indifference such that it amounted to a practical agnosticism? It may well be that both interpretations are, to some degree, correct, but either way it appears that, even among the notoriously irreligious working classes, the avowal of outright atheism was still comparatively rare; it could not be equated with the emerging secularism of Holyoake or the atheism of Bradlaugh.

As the nineteenth century turned into the twentieth century, however, the tide began to turn. Two prescient prophets, though unlikely soul mates, were Friedrich Nietzsche and John Henry Newman. Both were aware that a new spirit was stirring and, although people were scarcely aware of it yet, they knew that this new spirit would have far-reaching consequences. As Buckley observes:

> What Nietzsche and Newman foresaw was that religious impotence or uninterest would not remain a private or an isolated phenomenon, that it would increasingly characterize the 'educated intellect of England, France and Germany', and that its influence would eventually tell upon every routine aspect of civilization.[23]

And yet Nietzsche and Newman's prophecies did not come to fruition for at least another 60 years. What may be described as the 'age of atheism' (to borrow Gerhard Ebeling's phrase) did not become a reality until the last 40 years of the twentieth century. This has led some commentators to ask why the new spirit detected by Nietzsche and Newman took so long to come to birth. Stephen Toulmin, for instance, has suggested that the intellectual, psychological and artistic conditions for the emergence of the cultural *Zeitgeist* of the 1960s were already well in place by as early as 1914. But the turbulent nature of world historical events over the ensuing decades delayed the consummation of this world-view for a further 50 years.[24]

But whatever the explanation for the apparent delay, there can be little doubt that by the 1960s the predictions of Newman and Nietzsche were rapidly coming to pass. In the affluent West, at least, there emerged a 'radical godlessness' that was, by world historical standards, unique. As Buckley expresses this:

> It is critical to notice the historical uniqueness of the contemporary experience: the rise of a radical godlessness which is as much a part of the consciousness of millions of ordinary human beings as it is the persuasion of the intellectual. Atheisms have existed before, but there is a novelty, a distinctiveness about the contemporary denial of god both in its extent and in its cultural establishment.[25]

This raises the question of precisely how this transition was made; how a secular world-view of radical godlessness transformed itself into a general cultural condition over a period of 50 years or so from, say, 1950 to 2000. Indeed, this question has been the subject of a whole corpus of sociological literature, the task of which has been not only to provide some sort of descriptive account of this change, but also to develop an interpretative account of how this is to be understood and a predictive account of where this is likely to lead.

Needless to say, such studies have by no means produced a consensus. That there has been a precipitous decline in formal religious observance in the West is not open to doubt. What is in dispute, however, is the question of how this decline should be interpreted. Some, like Steve Bruce, have argued that the sociological data for church attendance and other manifestations of faith commitment have declined in so pronounced a way since the 1960s that the outcome for religion can only be fatal. In the absence of any evidence indicating an even partial reversal of this decline in the West, Bruce believes such a conclusion to be irresistible. He suggests that the time will come when people will no longer even define their beliefs negatively as a reaction against religion. Rather, the phenomenon of religion will become an irrelevant and distant memory.[26] Grace Davie, on the other hand, has argued that statistics relating to church-going and other overt religious activities are an unreliable guide to the 'religious' or 'secular' character of a population. She has developed a notion of 'believing without belonging', suggesting that many still maintain a residual sense of commitment to religious beliefs, but without manifesting them in the public way that was once common.[27] Still another line of analysis has been proffered by Paul Heelas and Linda Woodhead. They have suggested that although modernity has undoubtedly witnessed a turn from tradition-based religious commitment, this has not resulted in the widespread atheism that many had previously predicted. In fact, outright atheism remains a minority confession, and the modern Western world has witnessed the proliferation of alternative 'spiritualities' of various kinds, particularly what Heelas has gone on to characterise as 'spiritualities of life'.[28] Steve Bruce apart, it seems that many sociologists are convinced that many today are dissatisfied with atheism as an embodiment of the 'final truth' of the human condition. This would appear to qualify Ebeling and Buckley's characterisation of the contemporary condition as being an 'age of atheism'.

But this also raises the question of the extent to which our contemporary world has witnessed a transition from modernism to postmodernism. Could it be that current preoccupations with 'spiritualities' and the much touted 'return of the religious' are manifestations of this transition to a postmodernism that is somewhat more hospitable to religious concerns? This is to raise a complex question, not least because it has often been commented that spiritualities of life are as much modern phenomena as they are postmodern ones. But on the other hand, Mark C. Taylor and Graham Ward have both drawn attention to various aspects of the return of the religious in contemporary culture, a development that they both see as being bound up with a postmodern cultural turn. This phenomenon does not necessarily constitute a return to religious orthodoxy, but it does, they believe, indicate that the postmodern sensibility is one that is more open to the question of the religious than was the modern one, with its disguised or explicit commitment to immanence.[29]

I shall return to the question of the 'end of modernity' in more detail in Chapter 8. But for the moment, it does seem as though we are in a position to say something provisional about the link between atheism and modernity. For even on the basis of this very brief and sketchy historical survey, we have seen how closely linked atheism and modernity appear to be. The term 'atheism' was coined at precisely the moment that the birth pangs of modernity began to be felt: atheism as a direct and external challenge to the truth of theism emerged at the time that the modern epistemology and its sensibilities became explicit; atheism developed as an intellectual phenomenon, increasing in respectability and wider incidence as modernity itself developed. Both modernity and atheism seem to reach their 'high noon' in the mid/late twentieth century before they begin to crumble, giving way to something more nebulous and variegated as the twentieth century turns into the twenty-first. Already, it seems that the respective fates of modernity and atheism are intertwined. It could be, of course, that this parallel development was a coincidence, and it has to be admitted that the future development of cultural sensibilities and of atheism itself are still open to question. But in the chapters that follow, I shall argue that the link between atheism and modernity is far more than coincidental, suggesting that modernity itself is, at its heart, an atheistic edifice, even if this was something that only progressively came to light. I now want to look at the nature of this progression, and the movement by which modern thought passed from theism to atheism.

Chapter 2

The Development of Atheism in Modern Thought

To speak of the 'development' of atheism in modern thought is in some senses apposite and in some senses misleading. It is apposite in the most obvious way. Wherever the origins of modernity are located, atheism did not make an immediate appearance as such, but emerged through a long and gradual process of development. But talk of the development of atheism could also be regarded as misleading, in so far as such 'development' was really only a gradual realisation of a complete philosophical revolution that had been instantiated almost at once at the very outset of modernity. If this is so, then it could have radical implications for our view of the development of atheism in modern thought. In what sense, then, did atheism 'develop' in modern thought?

Already, in the Introduction, we have given some brief attention to the question of where the 'modern' might be thought to begin. When we turn specifically to the development of modern thought and, in particular, modern philosophy, we find that it has long been common to attribute the origins of philosophical and theological modernity to René Descartes. In Chapter 4, we shall look at some of the ways in which this claim has been questioned. But even if we accept that Descartes's philosophical innovations were only conceivable on the basis of shifts in thought that had taken place some centuries earlier, there is still a sense in which Descartes's philosophy enacts a major methodological break. For the Cartesian revolution was, in effect, the rejection of a specifically theological epistemology and methodology. It is unlikely to have been regarded as such at the time. Descartes's *Meditations on First Philosophy* (1641) was famously dedicated to the Faculty of Theology in Paris and, in his summary of its contents, Descartes gave the impression that it was a profoundly theological work, whose primary purpose was to ground belief in God and immortality of the soul on indubitable foundations, so that not even unbelievers would have any further grounds for their doubt. Descartes thus presented himself as a champion of theological orthodoxy and he would no doubt have been accepted as such by most of his contemporaries. Far from conceiving himself as inaugurating atheism, Descartes presents himself as its arch-enemy, upon which he will inflict a terminal defeat.

But already, in the very formulation of his self-appointed task, we begin to suspect that he has deviated very sharply from what had been thought to constitute theology hitherto. Talk of belief in God being indubitable, such that not even unbelievers would have grounds for doubt, would have appeared alien to a theological mind moulded by the medieval notion of a 'faith seeking understanding'. The quest for *certainty*, in particular, would have appeared misplaced. But perhaps more important than this were the grounds upon which such certainty was to be founded. For Descartes, such certain knowledge could only be secured on the basis of *reason*, and a reason that was unhindered by tradition or by any form of received knowledge that had not been tested by or founded upon a secure rational basis. For all its gloss of theological orthodoxy, Descartes's method was marked, above all else, by its quest for *certainty* on the basis of *reason*, and it was this that marked it out from all theology that had gone before.

But could it not be said that the great masters of medieval theology were themselves 'certain' of their faith and that they recognised an indispensable role for human 'reason'? Was Descartes really enacting such a radical shift? Certainly, Thomas Aquinas's faith was one in which he had a sure and unshakable confidence. But the notion that this faith was one that could be demonstrated beyond doubt by logical and publicly demonstrable procedures would have been an alien concept to him. Certainly,

Aquinas is known for having developed arguments for the existence of God, most notably his 'Five Ways' in the *Summa Theologiae*, but much recent scholarship has deemed it anachronistic to view the status of these as being rational demonstrations that lead to certain conclusions that are beyond doubt.[1] Such a conception is thought to be a retrospective post-Cartesian projection onto the medieval mind. Rather, it is said, the Five Ways should be understood as accounts of different ways in which philosophers, using natural reason, have been led to or drawn to the notion of God. But this experience of being 'led to' or 'drawn to' God does not amount to an indubitable rational demonstration. It is much more of the nature of a preparatory stage which then has to be supplemented and nurtured by faith, revelation and prayer. The 'arguments' constitute a preliminary opening onto religious possibilities, but are not to be regarded as sufficient in themselves.

Such an understanding of Aquinas's 'arguments for the existence of God' is intimately linked to Aquinas's understanding of human reason. Certainly, he accorded an indispensable role to human reason, but it was a role that was always to be exercised in the context of, and subject to the authority of, divine revelation. This was the assumption that underlay his well-known distinction between 'natural theology' and 'revealed theology'. In fact, there has been a great deal of scholarly discussion and disagreement on the precise nature of the relationship between reason and faith in Aquinas's theology.[2] But these debates mostly revolve around the extent to which Aquinas accords an independent validity to human reason apart from faith. But even if he does, almost all are agreed that human reason (natural theology) alone is insufficient and stands in need of supplementation by divine revelation (revealed theology). For Aquinas, this had to be the case, because human reason was, by its very nature, finite and limited, which in turn derives from his belief that human reason was creaturely, an effect of its Creator. This Creator, on the other hand, was neither finite nor limited, and it is this mismatch between finite creature and infinite Creator that saturates every aspect of Aquinas's theology. It means that human reason would always be 'drawn to' God on the

one hand, as betokening the indissoluble link between creature and Creator. But on the other hand, the very ontological distance between them meant that human reason would always 'fall short', would never be able to articulate more than a glimpse of truth and would always stand in need of the supplement of divine revelation. We shall see later that this understanding also underpins Aquinas's conception of the analogical nature of theological language, as well as his understanding of the nature of human reason.

Descartes rejected this centuries-old methodology in favour of an epistemology and theology on the basis of reason alone. Revealed or received knowledge, far from extending and perfecting human reason, was now thought potentially to lead it astray. It had thus become a stumbling block rather than a help-meet. Insofar as there was still a role for revealed knowledge, it would have to be a revealed knowledge that was itself grounded in the certain foundations of human reason. We thus see enacted a straightforward inversion. It is no longer the case that human reason is justified by the fact of its being created, by its participation in divine knowledge; on the contrary, it is now revealed knowledge that is justified by its being founded upon and justified by human reason. This inversion did not, of course, appear from nowhere and can be properly understood only in the context of the intellectual and historical context in which Descartes was writing.

When Descartes's *Meditations* was written, Europe was in a state of religious and political upheaval. The Reformation was less than a century old, and Christendom had not yet recovered from the resulting fracture. Central to Martin Luther's rebellion was his conviction that the only true sources of authority were the scriptures and the judgement of individual Christians. As he famously and dramatically put it at the Diet of Worms in 1521:

> Unless I am convicted of error by the testimony of Scripture or (since I put no trust in the unsupported authority of Pope or of councils, since it is plain that they have often erred and often contradicted themselves) by manifest reasoning I stand convicted by the scriptures to

> which I have appealed, and my conscience is taken captive by God's word, I cannot and will not recant anything, for to act against our conscience is neither safe for us, nor open to us.[3]

Commenting on this, Richard H. Popkin has said that

> in this declaration of Christian liberty, Luther set forth his new criterion of religious knowledge, that what conscience is compelled to believe on reading Scripture is true. To Catholics like [Johann] Eck, this must have sounded completely incredible. For centuries, assenting that a proposition stated a religious truth meant that it was authorized by Church tradition, by the Pope, and by Councils. To claim that these standards could be wrong was like denying the rules of logic. The denial of the accepted criteria would eliminate the sole basis for testing the truth of a religious proposition. To raise even the possibility that the criteria could be faulty was to substitute another criterion by which the accepted criteria could be judged, and thus, in effect, to deny the entire framework by which orthodoxy had been determined for centuries.[4]

But in challenging the age-old source of legitimacy and replacing it with another, Luther also prepared the way for his own source of legitimacy to be questioned in turn. In some ways, it was merely an extension of Luther's innovation to accept the primacy of conscience and, on that basis, to question the authority of Scripture. Indeed, it was not long before people were taking precisely this step. We saw in the last chapter that the 1630s were a period when France in particular was witnessing for the first time the rise of various doubters, libertines, sceptics and atheists.

Although these two challenges were distinct – Christian internal division was clearly of a different order to the development of an external atheism – we may nonetheless see them as two manifestations of a common underlying development; namely, the *pluralisation of legitimacy*. On the one hand, the

Reformation split was constituted by a disagreement over what constituted the sources of legitimacy for Christianity; on the other hand, the atheistic challenge was constituted by a disagreement over what constituted the sources of legitimacy for humanity. As Popkins observes: 'The Pandora's box that Luther opened at Leipzig was to have the most far-reaching consequences, not just in theology but throughout man's entire intellectual realm.'[5] The only solution would have appeared to be both obvious and irresistible. Some common source of authority and procedure would have to be found that would not rest upon Catholic or Protestant criteria (in order to mediate between the Reformation divide) and that would not even rest upon specifically Christian criteria (so as to mediate between Christians and atheists). Such a procedure, if it could be found, would thus appeal to Protestants, Catholics and atheists alike, cutting across these disagreements and resulting in a universal assent.

The phenomenon of the pluralisation of legitimacy gave rise to a situation in which the Western mind was awash with uncertainty. The challenge was to isolate an indubitable foundation for knowledge that could secure the holy grail of certainty. This could only be attained by ruthlessly questioning every received body of knowledge. Without such ruthless questioning, there was always the danger that such unexamined inherited knowledge might be mistaken and thus lead us astray. As is well known, such interrogation was enacted through Descartes's method of radical doubt. No body of knowledge or proposition was to be accepted if it could, in principle, be doubted. The fact that a proposition was open to doubt made it unreliable as a foundation for subsequent knowledge claims. In this process of radical doubt, theological knowledge was to be subject to the same procedure as was every other form of inherited knowledge. Having doubted everything that could, in principle, be doubted, Descartes finally arrived at his certain foundation, that which could not be doubted, the *cogito*. In the face of his self-imposed scepticism, he may well be drowning in a sea of doubt, but of one thing he can be sure: there is something doing the doubting. This is something he knows and experiences beyond question; there must be something that is doing the doubting. As Descartes puts it: 'I must finally conclude that this proposition, *I am*, *I exist*, is necessarily true whenever it is put forward by me or conceived in my mind.'[6] *Cogito ergo sum*: I think, therefore I am. Descartes had thus isolated his indubitable foundation on which certain knowledge could be built: the knowing subject, and he thereby also inaugurated what has become known as the 'age of the subject'. Herein lies also the source of the sudden and revolutionary inversion of Aquinas to which we have referred; if the thinking subject is now the foundation of all knowledge, this means that it also has to serve as the foundation of God, and not vice versa.

Discredited though Descartes's methodology was soon to be, there can be no doubt that the 'age of the subject' which he inaugurated was more long-lasting. It held sway over the Western intellectual world until it was dissolved philosophically by Friedrich Nietzsche and overturned theologically by Karl Barth. Indeed, the twin assaults of Nietzsche and Barth are not unrelated. However antithetical these two thinkers may appear, Barth thought that Nietzsche was quite correct, at least insofar as he exposed the only logical outcome to Descartes's method of radical doubt. He suggests that Nietzsche reaches the conclusion that Descartes should have reached if only he had 'seriously doubted and not just pretended to do so'.[7] Indeed, the question raised by Barth here is a pertinent one; namely, why was the *cogito*, in principle, not open to doubt? Why could my thinking that I am doubting not itself be an instance of my being deceived? Perhaps I am being deceived into thinking that I am doubting and, further, perhaps I am being deceived that there is an 'I' that is doubting. Taken to its logical conclusion, Descartes's method of doubt seems inevitably to culminate in a nihilism that Nietzsche finally brought to light. There is also here a related question as to the supposedly 'neutral' character of Descartes's epistemology. Given the 'inversion' of Aquinas's epistemology that Descartes enacts, we come increasingly to see the difference between them as being a difference between an epistemology that sees all legitimate knowledge as being derived from a *divine* source and a contrary epistemology that sees all legitimate knowledge as being derived from a *human* source. Presented in those terms, the 'neutral' status of Descartes's philosophy becomes increasingly difficult to credit: 'When fully developed, the Cartesian philosophy of the *cogito* leads to the "theory of the subject," which "lies at the heart of humanism" and forms the basis of humanistic atheism.'[8] By making the thinking subject the source of all knowledge, he appears, in methodological terms, radically to have broken with theology and sided with the atheists, against whom he claims to be writing. The apparently 'neutral' agenda is thus recast as a partisan (if disguised and unconscious) revolution.

It would be disingenuous, of course, to disguise the fact that Descartes's *Meditations* do make arguments for the existence of God and are intended to establish God's existence as being beyond reasonable doubt. But it is interesting to observe the part that this plays in Descartes's overall project. Having arrived at his certain foundation, the *cogito*, Descartes then found that he had secured the existence of the knowing subject, but was still uncertain about the existence of the external world. Although I may be certain that I am doubting, I am by no means certain that the external world actually exists. I appear to have experience of this external world, but these experiences could themselves be deceptions. Descartes thus needs some principle or being to serve as the guarantee of the reality of the external world, namely God. There can be no doubt, therefore, about the importance of the role played by God in Descartes's scheme. If Descartes had been an atheist, he would have established the certainty of nothing other than his own being as a thinking subject. But maintaining his prohibition on an appeal to unfounded revelation, he was obliged to establish God's existence on purely rationalistic grounds, rehearsing a decontextualised version of Anselm's ontological argument. The difference between Descartes and Anselm in this respect is quite striking. As with Aquinas's Five Ways mentioned above, recent scholars have argued that Anselm's argument works and is intelligible only within the context of faith.[9] The argument works as a preparatory meditation that shows how the mind is 'naturally oriented' towards the divine, but is not to be regarded as a neutral, stand alone demonstration of God's existence. But this is what it becomes in Descartes's hands. Understood in this Cartesian sense, the argument is a very precarious one, as Kant vividly demonstrated nearly 200 years later.

The point of Kant's famous objection that 'existence is not a predicate' was to claim that rational arguments such as this cannot tell us about anything outside the rational level at which they occur. In other words, such arguments may reveal to us something of the nature of reason or logic, but they cannot be supposed to establish the existence of anything external to these operations. But it is not only that the 'arguments for the existence of God' have now been transformed into rational proofs leading to certain conclusions; this transformation brings with it also a transformation of the concept of God that is being 'proved'. For some, the God that is proved to exist by means of rational argument cannot be said to be God at all. J. Hillis Miller has said that within the Cartesian framework

> [t]he ego has put everything in doubt, and has defined all outside itself as the object of its thinking power. *Cogito ergo sum*: the absolute certainty about the self reached by Descartes' hyperbolic doubt leads to the assumption that things exist, for me at least, only because I think them. When everything exists only as reflected in the ego, then man has drunk up the sea. If man is defined as subject, everything else turns into object. This includes God, who now becomes merely the highest object of man's knowledge. God, once the creative sun, the power establishing the horizon where heaven and earth come together, becomes an object of thought like any other. When man drinks up the sea, he also drinks up God, the creator of the sea. In this every man is the murderer of God.[10]

In light of all this, therefore, it may well be argued that Descartes had *already* inaugurated an atheistic framework, and that Descartes's invocation of God was an importation of an alien theological category into a secular rationalist framework. As such, it is an example of what Wittgenstein would later call a 'confusion' arising from improper distinctions between language games. That is to say, it entails the removal of a concept from its natural linguistic home in order to import it into a fundamentally alien linguistic framework. The result of so doing is to distort the meaning of the concept and, if the concept is sufficiently at odds with the framework into which it has been imported, to ensure its terminal demise. Ultimately, Descartes had already ushered in an atheistic epistemology, although it took some time for the implications of this to be brought explicitly to light.

In the late seventeenth century, Descartes's rationalist epistemology came under heavy attack from the English empiricist philosopher John Locke. For Locke, knowledge and truth were to be attained not through the exercise of reason, but through the founding of all knowledge on empirical sense data. For Locke, rationality, as a capacity of the human mind, is notoriously unreliable. It can lead us astray and can be mistaken in all sorts of ways, and does not provide the sort of solidity required to fulfil the function of a 'certain foundation'. In contrast, such a purpose may be served by the data of our empirical senses. For Locke, this was not simply a prescriptive philosophical methodology. It claimed to be, more fundamentally, a descriptive account of how our knowledge is, in fact, formed. Famously, Locke portrayed an image of the mind, in its pre-formative state, as being a *tabula rasa* (blank slate) upon which sense data leave their impressions. These impressions then serve as the 'building blocks' on the basis of which knowledge is formed. For Locke, rationality certainly has an indispensable role to play at the second-order level of reflection and in the production of 'ideas', but, in order for these processes to be legitimate, they must always accord priority to empirical sensations as being foundational.

The dispute between rationalism and empiricism emerged as a fault line in early modern philosophy, the epistemological implications of which were thought to be fundamental. But in retrospect the dispute appears more interesting for what the disputants had in common than for what divided them. Both were seeking a bedrock foundation which could secure certain knowledge; both located that foundation in immanent human capacities and both built their subsequent systems of knowledge in a foundational 'bottom-up' manner. In light of this wider commonality and in light of subsequent philosophical developments, the dispute over what the nature of this foundation should be appears to be relatively minor. Furthermore, like Descartes, Locke also attempted to force the theological concept of God into a framework in which it was ill at ease. There is, however, a case for saying that in Locke's case the incongruity between the concept of God and the framework into which that concept was being inserted was even more severe than it was for Descartes. For if God exceeds the bounds of the rational, even more so does God exceed the bounds of the empirical. Indeed, according to theological discourse, God not only exceeds the empirical, but is precisely that which is non-empirical. If, therefore, God has to be 'founded' on empirical grounds, the result promises to be even less propitious than it was for Descartes.

In the event, Locke develops a series of convoluted and tortuous arguments for God's existence on empirical grounds, developing in particular his own distinctive version of the cosmological argument. This was not, in many ways, surprising. If the *a priori* character of Anselm's ontological argument would have appealed to the rationalist Descartes, it was to be expected that the *a posteriori* character of Aquinas's cosmological argument would have appealed to the empiricist Locke. But Locke further argues that the concept of God can itself be arrived at within an empirical framework. He suggests that the attributes of God are all derived from '*Ideas*, received from Sensation and Reflection', and that these 'ideas' are then projected into infinity in order to reach a concept of God that would answer to the requirements of the concept that is called forth by his cosmological argument. As he puts it: 'when we would frame an *Idea* the most suitable we can to the supreme Being, we enlarge every one of these [simple *Ideas*] with our *Idea* of infinity; and so putting them together, make our complex *Idea* of God.'[11] Here again, we see an explicit, if not quite direct, inversion of Aquinas's epistemology with respect to God. For Aquinas, knowledge of God is reliable in so far as it relies not on human concepts and experiences, but on God's own self-revelation. In Locke's procedure, we find precisely the opposite approach. Knowledge of God is reliable the more that it can be traced back to and rooted within human empirical sensations.

There are several consequences of these attempts to transplant a theological concept into a fundamentally a-theological framework. For all that Descartes and Locke were attempting to develop conceptions of and arguments for God that would be invulnerable to external attack, the practical outcome of their endeavours, in fact, turned out to be precisely the opposite, and this is so on two fronts in particular. First, a thoroughly consistent rationalism or empiricism seemed to disallow any substantive knowledge of God, however much Descartes and Locke attempted to establish the contrary. Indeed, this has been one of the recurring themes in our brief discussion of Descartes thus far. We have already discussed Barth's observation that Descartes's method of doubt was inconsistent in that it seems to stop arbitrarily when it refuses to doubt the existence of the *cogito*. Descartes is unwilling to take his method to its seemingly inevitable conclusion. Furthermore, we saw in the last chapter that a similar argument (albeit from a different perspective) had already been made by Denis Diderot, whose contribution to the development of philosophy was to apply the thoroughgoing consistency to Descartes's method which the latter had conspicuously refused to do. Consistently applied, Descartes's rationalism seems to demand atheism and his method of doubt seems to demand nihilism.[12] We shall see how Locke was vulnerable to a similar attack in due course. But it appears that these rationalist and empiricist methodologies were almost pre-determined to secure an atheistic outcome from the outset.

Secondly, it should also be pointed out that insofar as conceptions of God were developed within these frameworks, the conceptions that were thereby produced were fundamentally different from those that had prevailed hitherto. This was particularly evident when it was recognised that the method employed for reaching God was intimately bound up with the conception of God that was actually produced. Thus, Descartes's God appears to be little more than an hypostatisation of rational concepts. Anticipating Kant again, we might express this in terms of the (illegitimate) projection of rational ideas into reality. Likewise, Locke's God appears to be little more than an hypostatisation of empirical realities. Anticipating Hume in this case, we may see this as the (illegitimate) projection of empirical realities into infinity, into the realm of the meta-physical. Indeed, when we look at the epistemological methods employed by Descartes and Locke and the conceptions of God produced thereby, the mechanism of 'projection' comes irresistibly to the fore. Again, this is entirely to be expected. Putting this very loosely, we may say that, when knowledge of God is located in divine revelation (as in Aquinas), the fundamental disposition of human beings towards such knowledge is that of *passive reception*. When this epistemology is inverted so that knowledge of God comes to be located in human (rational or empirical) sources, the fundamental role of human beings in the articulation of such knowledge is that of *active projection*. It should therefore come as no surprise that in the analyses proffered by later generations of atheists, the mechanism of 'projection' would play a central role. My suggestion, therefore, is that these vulnerabilities were built into these attempts to transplant a theological concept into fundamentally a-theological frameworks, however much the architects of those frameworks were unaware of the fact. But they were vulnerabilities that were to be brought into sharp focus by Hume and Kant (in relation to the disallowing of any substantive knowledge of God) and by Feuerbach and Marx (in relation to God as an hypostatisation of rational concepts or empirical realities). It is to these that I now turn.

David Hume's life spanned much of the eighteenth century, of which he was intellectually emblematic. Although he spent much of his life outside Scotland, he was Edinburgh's brightest intellectual star, as is attested by his statue which stands prominently on the Royal Mile in Edinburgh, between the Castle and Holyrood House. He published widely in his lifetime, by no means only in the field of philosophy, and was perhaps best known by contemporaries for his *A History of England*, the first volume of which was published in 1754. His *A Treatise of Human Nature* had been published in 1739, and he also published several works of religion, including *Of Miracles* (1748) and *Natural History of Religion* (1757). But what was to become his best-known work, the *Dialogues Concerning Natural Religion*, was not published until 1779, three years after his death. By this time, Lockean empiricism had triumphed over Cartesian rationalism, although Locke's version of the cosmological argument had been eclipsed by the even more explicitly empirical teleological argument as the favoured argument for the existence of God. In the *Dialogues*, empiricist metaphysics and the teleological argument were alike subjected to the coruscating acid of Hume's invective. The impact was scarcely mitigated by the fact that Hume's attacks were expressed through the voices of his dialogue characters, and his challenge was to have a devastating effect throughout the intellectual world of Europe. In effect, Hume performed the same philosophical service in relation to Locke as Diderot had done in relation to Descartes.

Indeed, the brilliance of Hume lay in the fact that he was willing to confront, unflinchingly, the implications of a thoroughgoing empiricist epistemology. He saw that if empiricism were adopted consistently, this would mean reasoning 'merely from the known phenomena, and [dropping] every arbitrary supposition or conjecture'.[13] The result was that one could have *knowledge* of nothing that was not derived from sense experience. As that branch of knowledge called metaphysics consisted, by definition, of that which was not empirical, this meant, for Hume, that one could have no knowledge of metaphysics whatsoever. Working with Locke's notion of the mind as a *tabula rasa*, on which sense impressions left their imprint, Hume deemed such impressions to be the only certain elements of knowledge. As soon as the mind begins to organise these impressions and to make claims on the basis of them, then we are immediately in the arena of psychological activity. That which the mind adds to the empirical experience is merely a 'belief' or construction, described by Hume as 'nothing but a peculiar sentiment, or lively conception produced by habit'.[14] The great error of so much historical philosophy has been to imagine that this activity of psychological 'construction' is the articulation of objective 'truths'. On the contrary, such activity may tell us something of the operation of the human mind, but it is a folly to suppose that they can tell us anything of the structure of the external world.

Understood in these terms, what counts as objective knowledge for Hume is startlingly minimal. Famously, he even claimed that such intuitive notions as 'cause' and 'effect' are likewise psychological 'fictions'. When we see something 'causing' something else to happen, what we really 'see' are two separate sense impressions, and these impressions are the only justifiable data of knowledge. In effect, the mind imposes the fictional notions of cause and effect onto these two elements of data from outside, as it were, in order to provide a subjective interpretation of the relationship between them. But it would be an illusion to suppose that the mind can somehow see or discover the operation of cause and effect as themselves being empirical facts. As he puts it: 'All reasonings concerning cause and effect, are founded on experience, and … all reasonings from experience are founded on the supposition, that the course of nature will continue uniformly the same.' But the uniformity of nature

> is a point, which can admit of no proof at all, and which we take for granted without any proof. We are determined by *Custom* alone to suppose the future conformable to the past… 'Tis not, therefore, reason, which is the guide of life, but custom.[15]

As Hume's use of the word 'custom' suggests, he was aware of the indispensability of such notions as cause and effect for the practice of everyday life. He was a pragmatist in the sense that he accepted the necessity of such notions as practical tools of negotiation, while maintaining a strict prohibition against supposing that they actually conveyed any metaphysical knowledge. This prohibition applied as much to the natural sciences as to anything else. All scientific discoveries, laws and theories were again viewed as being practical and necessary aids to progress, but in philosophical terms the status of such scientific laws was again that of psychological fiction in the sense that they go beyond what is strictly warranted by empirical data. Thus, we can see that this proscription against metaphysics extended to, but was by no means restricted to, theism. Furthermore, Hume's diagnosis of religion as fantasy was by no means straightforwardly atheistic in character. His epistemology was much more radically sceptical than was, for instance, Diderot's. Metaphysically, he would be more accurately described as an agnostic in the sense that he believed the theism–atheism question to be one that was *in principle* undecidable; both theism and atheism rested upon metaphysical presuppositions that he believed to be unsustainable. He was thus an agnostic before his time, the word itself not being coined until the nineteenth century, as we noted in the last chapter.

Hume had thus exposed the fact that both Descartes and Locke were attempting to do the impossible. They were both attempting to find a place for God within philosophical frameworks that seemed to rule out such a God from the outset. But Western philosophy was not yet willing to concede the last word to Hume, neither was it willing to dispense with God so easily. The seemingly impossible task of reconciling the irreconcilable fell to the great Enlightenment philosopher Immanuel Kant. His attempt to rescue metaphysics was all the stronger for its recognition of the strength and cogency of Hume's devastating attacks. Kant recognised that there could be no turning of the philosophical clock back to a time before Hume. Any serious and credible attempt to rehabilitate metaphysics would have to take direct account of the arguments of the thoroughgoing sceptic, and this is precisely what Kant sought to do. He said: 'I openly confess that my remembering David Hume was the very thing which many years ago first interrupted my dogmatic slumber and gave my investigations in the field of speculative philosophy a quite new direction.'[16] In particular, Kant accepted Hume's point that metaphysics had too often extended its reach beyond that which was philosophically warranted. The result was that philosophy had too often indulged in baseless speculation and fantasy and had consequently forfeited its status as a serious science. The only answer was for philosophy to reconsider its own first principles and for reason to engage in a self-reflexive reconsideration of its own capacities and limitations.

This task was undertaken in Kant's *Critique of Pure Reason*, which was as thorough a self-critique as one could want. The result was as significant for what it conceded to Hume as for what it withheld from him. Kant accepted Hume's insight that the human mind plays an active role in shaping empirical sense impressions, recognising that the mind actually plays a part in the creation of knowledge rather than passively receiving or reflecting it. But against Hume, Kant insisted that this activity was not a purely subjective psychological one, for the human mind was structured by certain organising categories or concepts that were universal and a priori. The universality of the categories is what saved the organising work of the mind from being purely subjective, and is what explains why objective agreement on certain truths may apparently be reached. Thus, it is possible to conclude 'objectively' that the sun heats the stone, because the two empirical impressions of the sun shining on the stone and the stone getting warmer are both filtered through the universal category of 'cause', such that every rational person would judge likewise. But again, Kant conceded to Hume that such universal truths are not quite objective reflections of the world as it is, independently of the mind. For Kant, such penetration through the world of appearances to the world in itself is impossible because all our experience and knowledge of the world is mediated through the organising activity of the categories. This world in itself was what Kant called the *noumenon*, which is, by definition, always inaccessible to us. All metaphysical truths, therefore, are only truths pertaining to the *phenomenal* world; that is, the world as it appears to us. If philosophy tried to claim more for itself than this, then it would indeed fall prey to Hume's attacks; but insofar as it recognised these self-imposed limits, then a role for metaphysics could still be justified and Hume could be confronted with impunity.

By the conclusion of the *Critique of Pure Reason*, Kant seemed to have rescued metaphysics (which constituted his refutation of

Hume), while also severely curtailing it (which constituted his concession to Hume). But with regard to God, Kant seemed to have advanced little further than Hume's own agnosticism. This was because God clearly could not be said to be a part of the phenomenal world. God does not appear to us in the guise of sense impressions that subsequently get filtered through the universal categories. In so far as there is a God, this can only be so in the noumenal world, in the world as it is in itself, independently of our perceptions of it. But given that Kant has placed a rigid prohibition on any human knowledge of the noumenal world, this appears to leave Kant with a strict agnosticism. His engagement with Hume had led him to see all too clearly that God would have to be placed *beyond* rather than *within* the limits of human knowing. The stark choice with which he was confronted was therefore between dispensing with God altogether (in the manner of Hume), or leaving God hovering agnostically beyond the limits of human knowing. He opted for the latter, the result being that the only thing that 'saved' God from a spectral existence of sheer possibility was Kant's invocation of his transcendental argument. It was this that he attempted to explicate in his 'second critique', the *Critique of Practical Reason*.

Practical reason, for Kant, pertained to that realm of reason that was an expression of morality. Central to this account was Kant's notion of the *summum bonum*, the highest good, the universal moral telos of all human life in which the highest degree of virtue is combined in equal proportion with the highest degree of happiness. In order to make rational sense of this universal human goal, he argued that it was necessary, on the basis of practical reason, to postulate three things that we would not be justified in positing on the basis of pure or theoretical reason. First, it was necessary to postulate the freedom of the will; that the will is free is not something that we can know in the phenomenal world. But without postulating that we are indeed free, the whole edifice of morality as we experience it would collapse. Our experience of the moral law, our duty to fulfil it and our quest for the *summum bonum* would all become meaningless without the supposition of human freedom. Secondly, if, for Kant, our pursuit of the *summum bonum* is not to become meaningless, it must be realisable; the universal pursuit of an unrealisable goal would transgress the dictates of reason. But given that few, if any, actually achieve the *summum bonum* in their mortal lives, it is necessary to postulate, secondly, an after-life in which the *summum bonum* will in fact be attained. Such an after-life, however, may be viewed as a necessary but not a sufficient condition for the realisation of the *summum bonum*; for it provides the conditions for, but not the guarantee of, its attainment. This is why the third practical postulate must be God, a being who has the will, the intelligence and the power necessary to ensure that the *summum bonum* will be attained.

So God was now a 'necessary practical postulate', required in order to make sense of the human experience of morality, but pushed into the realm of the unknowable noumenon. For Kant, we must *practically assume* that there is a God, but his actual existence is something that can be neither theoretically known nor rationally demonstrated. As Kant puts it:

> These postulates are not theoretical dogmas but presuppositions of necessary practical import; thus, while they do not extend speculative knowledge, they give objective reality to the ideas of speculative reason in general (by means of their relation to the practical sphere), and they justify it in holding to concepts even the possibility of which it could not otherwise venture to affirm.[17]

We must necessarily suppose that God is not mere possibility but actuality, even if this actuality can never be theoretically established within the realms of metaphysical knowledge. If this is theism, it is clearly a 'thin-line theism', and although he has been hailed as a 'saviour' of Christianity for the modern world, it has to be said that this is a very precarious salvation. Kant had seen – or Hume had made him see – that the respective philosophical frameworks of Descartes and Locke left no room for God. There could be no going back on that, as his trenchant critiques of all rational arguments for the existence of God made very clear. But he had ingeniously found a place for God beyond the bounds of metaphysical knowledge, and in a sense he had prolonged the life of the Enlightenment God for a little longer than might otherwise have been the case. Kant's long-term influence on Western philosophy should not be underestimated, and modern theology has likewise been sustained by a heavy Kantian influence. But ultimately Kant's defence of God – and his conception of God – was an uneasy and precarious truce that was inherently unstable. The ultimately atheistic character of modern philosophy would soon manifest itself explicitly, in spite of Kant's influential and ingenious attempt to disguise it.

Whether the atheistic character of modern philosophy was manifested in Kant's trenchant philosophical enemy, G. W. F. Hegel, is a nice question. The particular target of Hegel's censure was Kant's dualism, which may be seen as deriving ultimately from the latter's empiricism and its central division between the mind and the world. Hegel believed that such dualism artificially divided reality, leaving it permanently alienated from itself. Along with other early nineteenth-century philosophers, such as his erstwhile friend F. W. J. Schelling, Hegel sought to develop a philosophy of 'unity' wherein all dualistic oppositions would be shown to be epiphenomenal and would ultimately be overcome, including the ultimate dualism between God and the world. Hegel saw God as a religious pictorial image for the philosophical concept of Spirit (*Geist*). The world is not fundamentally separate from Spirit. Rather, the world comes to be through Spirit's positing of itself as 'other'. There is, therefore, a certain sense in which *Geist* and world are in a relationship of otherness, but this is only so in the context of their wider unity; the world *is* Spirit in its self-positing otherness. The world is not a place in which reason and matter are separate elements; the material world does not exist independently of the realm of rational consciousness. Rather, the material world is inherently rational and consciousness is in a state of constant and dynamic progression. The world, moving and developing through a process of dialectical progression, is itself a manifestation of the self-othering movement of *Geist*. This world comes to be through the self-negation of *Geist* as it abandons its primeval unity, pouring itself out into the world, which is simultaneously a process of self-negation, as well as of self-realisation. *Geist* has to negate itself as self-contained unity in order to come to full knowledge and realisation of itself. As Hegel puts it: 'Of the Absolute it must be said that it is essentially a *result*, that only in the *end* is it what it truly is; and that precisely in this consists its nature, viz. to be actual, subject, the spontaneous becoming of itself.'[18] Such self-realisation can only come about through a process of *Geist* encountering itself as other. For Hegel, these philosophical truths are represented metaphorically in the Christian religion.

Furthermore, Hegel's account has significant repercussions for the very nature of philosophy itself. He sees philosophical systems not as complete accounts of reality that are either 'true' or 'false', but as necessary 'stages' in the progressive process of *Geist's* unfolding. There is a sense in which each such stage is 'true' as a necessary step in the dialectical unfolding of *Geist*, but there is also a sense in which each stage is 'false' insofar as it is but a partial and transitory outlook which necessarily falls short of Truth itself. But this very movement, or dialectical progression, through these stages is itself the work of the revelation of Truth. This movement, Hegel says:

> can be regarded as the path of the natural consciousness which presses forward to true knowledge; or as the way of the Soul which journeys through the series of its own configurations as though they were stations appointed for it by its own nature, so that it may purify itself for the life of the Spirit, and achieve finally, through a completed experience of itself, the awareness of what it really is in itself.[19]

In this sense, Hegel claims to provide a total account of existence that encompasses the whole of history and all of philosophy.

It is because of this that Hegel has often been characterised as a thinker of 'absoluteness', 'totalisation', 'universality' and so forth. But Hegel's work is of such richness and complexity that these will always be inadequate characterisations. The universal dimension of his thought cannot be denied, but this is inseparable from his profoundly original insights into the nature of 'difference', the 'negative' and the 'other' which are likewise integral to his thought. This is why it has been possible for Hegel to be characterised as, simultaneously, the epitome of Enlightenment modernity and a harbinger of postmodern deconstruction. The same ambivalence applies in his relationship to theism and atheism. Even in his own lifetime and even more so soon after his death, theists and atheists were battling for the rights to his legacy. There continues to be much contemporary debate as to whether Hegel is ultimately a thinker of secular atheism or a thinker who allows for the recovery of Christian orthodoxy. On the one hand, his insistence that *Geist* pours itself out into the world's historical process, with which it is ultimately one, seems suggestive of a 'death of God' immanence that later thinkers have certainly developed, as we shall see in Chapter 8. On the other hand, he seems to register a protest against the kind of modern epistemology developed, albeit in very different ways, by Descartes, Locke, Hume and Kant, and which I have been presenting in this chapter as being covertly atheistic in its epistemology and methodology. Human rationality is no longer understood as having to 'justify' God, but is instead seen as being itself a manifestation of *Geist*. In this sense, it appears to open the door to more orthodox theological understandings. Because of this, Hegel appears as the black joker in the pack of thinkers we are considering in this chapter. He disrupts rather than participates in what I am presenting as the progressive self-realisation of modernity's intrinsically atheistic suppositions.

But he is important to our story, not least because of the way in which his thought was developed by some of his successors; most notably the so-called 'left Hegelians'. Drawing out what they perceived to be the implications of Hegel's philosophy of history, they developed some of the central elements of that system in an explicitly atheistic way. One of the most prominent of these thinkers was Ludwig Feuerbach, whose critique of Christian theism was unsparing. The nature of the relationship between his thought and that of Hegel is of particular significance. We have just mentioned that Hegel effected a kind of inversion of the dominant modern philosophical paradigms to date. For Descartes and Locke, God was a 'projection' (in a non-pejorative sense) from the foundational *cogito* or empirical sense data. Hegel reversed this so that, in an echo of older theological models, human subjectivity and rationality are manifestations or 'projections' of *Geist*. Feuerbach's deep Hegelianism notwithstanding, it is highly significant that it was this particular aspect of Hegel's thought that Feuerbach inverted, thereby re-installing the previous modern epistemological structure that Hegel had rejected. In this sense at least, it could be said that Feuerbach is profoundly un-Hegelian. Thus, as a result of Feuerbach's inversion, God becomes a 'projection' of human subjectivity. In one sense, this reinstates the models of Descartes and Locke, but with a crucial twist. For Descartes and Locke, the fact that the 'projection' emanated from foundationally reliable sources meant that the outcome of the 'projection' was epistemologically secure. In contrast, for Feuerbach, the self-reflexive awareness that the source of the 'projection' was human subjectivity meant that that object of the projection reflected nothing but its source.

Consequently, he reconceived theology as anthropology, regarding the traditional attributes of God as the best and highest attributes of humanity, personified and projected into infinity in order to produce what has become known as theism. Our doctrine of God, therefore, is really a disguised or coded doctrine of humanity. Furthermore, this process of projection exposes itself by the inconsistent manner in which it is put into effect. There is a projection of both human attributes on the one hand and human ideals on the other, and the resulting combination is self-subverting. He saw the Christian God as an incoherent amalgam of personal, active, quasi-anthropomorphic attributes on the one hand, and an impersonal ideal reality that is perfect, timeless and changeless on the other. For Feuerbach, such a conception of God was not only untrue but also gave rise to human alienation. For in projecting the best and highest aspects of humanity outside of themselves, humans thereby evacuated themselves of all that is good and valuable. The result is a human self-conception that is negative, worthless and sinful, in contrast to a God who is the opposite of these things and before whom human beings must abase themselves. As Feuerbach puts it:

> as what is positive in the conception of the divine being can only be human, the conception of man, as an object of consciousness can only be negative. To enrich God, man must become poor; that God may be all, man must be nothing.[20]

Human beings thus become divided and alienated from their own best natures and define their self-identity only in terms of their lower aspects.

The concept of alienation was to be central to another nineteenth-century post-Hegelian thinker, Karl Marx, whose own version of Hegelianism perpetuated Feuerbach's crucial inversion. If, for Feuerbach, theism was a projection of humanity, for Karl Marx, theism, as an 'ideology', was a projection of the economic base. This in itself represented a further and important shift. While Feuerbach sustained Hegel's 'rationalism', wherein the development of reason as such underpins and empowers the world historical process, Marx displaced it with his thoroughgoing 'materialism'. As a result of this displacement, historical change and development are determined not by reason, thought or ideas, but by material conditions and, specifically, the material conditions of economics. We saw that, for Hegel, historical development was empowered by a dialectical process whereby one system of intellectual thought suddenly becomes aware of internal rational inconsistencies, which cause it to crumble and give rise to its successor, its antithesis, which temporarily prevails until it too undergoes a similar experience.

For Marx, the development of history was understood in much the same way, but with the critical difference that the systems in question were not rational but economic. One particular economic system holds sway until it eventually becomes internally unsustainable, unable to fulfil its inherent economic purpose and thus giving way to its successor, its economic antithesis. But the common feature of all these systems is the existence of class antagonisms, based on the exploitation of one class by another. As with Hegel, this is not a process that continues indefinitely; rather, it is heading towards a final goal in which the dialectical process is itself overcome and economic stability is reached. Here, finally, class antagonism based on exploitation is finally overcome. This is, for Marx, the final communist utopia. But the economic base not only determines and drives the world historical process; it also determines, in a foundational way, every other aspect of a society and its supposed civilisation. In particular, a society's 'ideologies' are a reflection of its economic base. This includes its laws, ethics, customs and religion.

This meant that, for Marx, religion did not stand in a relationship of abrupt juxtaposition to the economic order, as many theologians had claimed. On the contrary, it was an intimate, if unconscious, accomplice. As Marx put it:

> the religious world is but the reflex of the real world. And for a society based upon the production of commodities, in which the producers in general enter into social relations with one another by treating their products as commodities and values, whereby they reduce treating their individual private labor to the standard of homogeneous human labor – for such a society, Christianity with its *cultus* of abstract man, more especially in its bourgeois developments, Protestantism, Deism, etc., is the most fitting form of religion.[21]

For Marx, religion (by which he means, in his context, contemporary Christianity) endorses the capitalist order by, for instance, teaching that all worldly authority is ordained of God and, as such, is to be respected and obeyed by humanity. The worldly hierarchy both reflects and participates in the divine hierarchy, with each person being divinely appointed to their appropriate position within this hierarchy.

Such an account was only partly at odds with Christianity's understanding of its own relationship with the secular, economic and political order. One strand of the tradition, formulated by St Augustine's account of the 'City of God', for instance, insists upon the heterogeneity of the relationship between the divine order and the human order. The latter is relativised and judged by the former, and the Christian is called to be in that human order but not of it. It is a tradition that finds twentieth-century expression in the dialectical theology of Karl Barth. But there is another strand – tracing its roots back to St Paul's exhortation to Christians to obey and honour the king – that seeks to efface that distinction. The medieval doctrine of the king's 'two bodies', one divine and one earthly, one spiritual and one temporal, established the monarch as the unique mediator between the two worlds, thus melding them together rather than keeping them apart. The idea persisted and, indeed, was enhanced, until well into the early seventeenth century. In Marx's own day, Christianity's complicity with the economic order seemed only too obvious. Perhaps the most often quoted expression of this is the stanza that appeared in the *Hymns for Little Children* of 1848, written by the future Mrs C. F. Alexander: 'The rich man in his castle, the poor man at his gate, God made them, high or lowly, And ordered their estate.' Such sentiments were representative rather than exceptional, and appeared to confirm Marx's analysis.

The other important aspect of Marx's analysis of religion, which is not unconnected with the first, was that it served as a compensation for those who occupied a lowly position within this hierarchy. Its rituals and consolations provided an amelioration of earthly suffering, as well as a compensatory offering of eternal bliss. It was this aspect of his analysis, of course, that gave rise to his famous characterisation of religion as the 'opium of the people'. But for Marx this aspect of religion had a dual aspect. On the one hand, it served the ideological purpose of keeping the oppressed classes reconciled to their condition, thus allowing the economic order to be sustained. But on the other hand, Marx also recognised its positive function in making life bearable and liveable for those whose lives would otherwise be without compensation and without hope. There could be no question of religion being 'abolished' while the economic conditions of capitalism still prevailed. This would in some senses be viewed as an act of cruelty to the oppressed and, in any case, every economic base will irresistibly produce its 'ideologies', which it would be a folly to suppress artificially. But for Marx, the collapse of capitalism would mean that there would no longer be any such functions for religion to fulfil, and so it would naturally and inevitably fade away. So wholly was Christianity a reflection and production of the economic base that there could be no question of its continuing independent existence once this base itself had collapsed.

For all their differences, what Feuerbach and Marx share is their conviction that theism is a projection or hypostatisation of empirical realities – whether human attributes or the economic base; for them, theism is an abstraction from such realities. The very acknowledgement of this process of abstraction is sufficient to expose theism for what it really is. It may well be said that their diagnoses seem all too pertinent if the theism in question is that represented by, for instance, Descartes and Locke. For I have been suggesting that Descartes and Locke inaugurated philosophical frameworks, the epistemological structures of which seemed to disallow, in advance, a place for God. Insofar as they did indeed attempt to force a concept of God into these frameworks, the respective epistemologies dictated that this could only be done by means of a projection – from rational or empirical realities. But this was always a transitory and unstable truce and, on the account being developed here, Hume and Kant demonstrated how their frameworks disallowed, in principle, any substantive metaphysical knowledge of God; and Feuerbach and Marx explicated the mechanism of projection that was involved in the conception of God that they attempted to produce. So it is important for us not to downplay the role of historical context here. The atheism of Feuerbach and Marx was directed against – and indeed is compelling in relation to – a specifically modern conception of God.[22] What this conception of God actually amounted to is worthy of further consideration, for it can hardly be supposed that the modern revolution in epistemology would leave the concept of God untouched. If Descartes and Locke were utilising a different epistemology to that employed by Aquinas, it is hardly to be expected that the resulting conceptions of God would have been the same. To understand atheism properly in modern history and modern thought, it is thus necessary to clarify what conception of God was dominant here. Precisely which God was modern atheism rejecting?

Chapter 3

The God that Modern Atheism Rejects

It seems commonplace to say that modern atheism rejected a modern God. But the implications could be considerable if it could be shown that a specifically modern conception of God was distinctive and marked a new departure from that which had prevailed hitherto. Many have claimed that this was indeed the case, to such an extent that the modern God was a 'thing' quite different from the pre-modern God. Indeed, to say that the modern God was a thing in many ways captures the distinction; for pre-modern theology, God was not a thing at all. In this chapter, I shall explore some of the ways in which this difference was manifested in both theology and philosophy, and also the nature of this transition from one conception of God to another.

It may well be objected that conceptions of God throughout history have been constantly evolving, and that this is to be expected. While there is a thread of continuity that links together all these conceptions, God is nonetheless understood and conceived differently in different times, places and cultures. It is therefore entirely natural that God would have been conceived differently in the thirteenth century to the way in which he was conceived in the eighteenth century, for instance. But this is no reason to suppose that we have witnessed a decisive and revolutionary shift, such that we would be justified in speaking of two quite heterogeneous conceptions of God here. In this chapter, however, I want to suggest that we do indeed witness such a radical break. We do, of course, have to be aware of historical change and development in theology, and we do also have to beware of the danger of constructing artificial 'breaks', 'ruptures' and exaggerated differences on to what might better be regarded as an evolving continuum. But my analysis in the previous chapter can already be read as presaging a significantly altered conception of God on the basis of the quite radical methodological shifts we outlined there. Indeed, the point of our tracing the development of atheistic thought in the last chapter was to suggest that we witnessed a radical epistemological break with Descartes, the full implications of which took some centuries to come into view. When they did finally come into view, it was suggested, the underlying assumptions of this epistemological break were shown to be fundamentally atheistic. Until this finally came to light, however, a place was still found for God, however incongruous, within the bounds of this new epistemology. Given that the concept of God was now being forced into a philosophical framework in which it was ill at ease, it was perhaps inevitable that this would have quite radical implications for this conception of God itself. In this situation, it was almost unavoidable that the very idea of God would undergo significant change in the early modern period. I now want to develop this suggestion further by showing how this was indeed the case.

It will perhaps be helpful to begin by identifying some of the most significant features of the medieval conception of God, as was manifested in the theology of St Thomas Aquinas. Not only did Aquinas produce one of the most ambitious works of medieval systematic theology, the *Summa Theologiae*, but the quality of his theological mind is also generally regarded as surpassing even that of his impressive predecessor, St Augustine. Furthermore, his status was confirmed in the eyes of the Roman Catholic Church by the official recognition of his status as that church's official theologian in the nineteenth century. If asked to identify the single most distinctive feature of Aquinas's conception of God, one might well reply that it lay in his high and constant emphasis on the *transcendence* of God. In all his work, this sense of distance between creator and creature, between the divine and the human, suffused everything else he said and wrote. This is not to suggest, of course, that this *distance* presented an insurmountable barrier. On the contrary, human knowledge may participate in divine knowledge, but only through God's own gracious initiative. As we saw in the last chapter, for Aquinas, knowledge of God comes through God's own self-revelation rather than solely through the exercise of human rational capacities.

For Aquinas, human attempts to encompass and 'capture' the divine constitute an ever-present temptation, against which one must be constantly on one's guard. Indeed, such temptation begins to exercise its allure as soon as one begins the very process of speaking about God. This is why Aquinas includes in his *Summa Theologiae* a lengthy discussion of how human beings may, with impunity, begin the process of speaking about God at all. When creatures begin even to speak of God, they immediately succumb to this temptation, or at least are in immediate danger of so doing. For when creatures speak of God – using, as they must, human language and human rationality – there is a constant danger of 'domesticating' God's transcendence, of turning God into a creature rather than respecting his status as creator.[1] All of Aquinas's theology, even when being expressed in a 'positive' mode, is underpinned by the imperative to guard against this ever-present temptation and to preserve that essential characteristic of God: his transcendence. In his battle to defend the citadel of divine transcendence, Aquinas had several weapons at his disposal. First, as we have seen, Aquinas emphasised the limits of human rationality with respect to God; we should beware of thinking that human reason can, unaided, take us into the realm of divine truths. Second, Aquinas had recourse to a 'negative theology' by which his 'positive theology' was balanced, and which had a long pedigree in the orthodox tradition. The negative theology has been spoken of as 'a set of doctrines, a temper of mind, and a style of spirituality' in which

> one of the most commonly recurring assertions runs as follows: it is certain that God exists, but the nature or essence of God is unknowable. The mystery may be invoked

> by speaking of it indirectly, or in negations, or by affirming symbolic 'names'; but in the end it is ungraspable by the mind, as the eye is dazzled by the sun.[2]

In many ways inseparable from this negative theology was Aquinas's third weapon; namely, his teaching on the analogical character of all theological language. Although Aquinas's teaching on analogy is well known, its centrality with respect to all his other teachings has not always been appreciated.

For Aquinas, the fundamental problem with theological language is that language in general has been developed by creatures to refer to creaturely things. It is therefore inadequate – and potentially misleading – when applied to God. It is, in essence, a finite, contingent, creaturely tool that is being used to articulate and convey an infinite, necessary, creator God. This fundamental mismatch between the tool and its object creates unavoidable dangers; there is a certain sense in which theological language *as* language fundamentally betrays God. One response to this would be to preserve silence and insist that nothing whatsoever may be said with impunity about God. Or, which amounts almost to the same thing, to insist that all language used of God is used *equivocally*; that is, to insist that all words used of God are used in a way completely unrelated to the way in which they are used in ordinary language. Whether one preserves silence or whether one insists that theological language is equivocal, the outcome is the same: a strict epistemological unknowing with respect to God. For Aquinas, this would constitute yet another betrayal, as it would cut God off from any human knowledge whatsoever. It is important to maintain the qualitative difference between creator and creature, but not at the price of cutting off the creator from the creature altogether.

It is in response to this dilemma that Aquinas develops his understanding of analogical language. If we are not to cut ourselves off from God, we must accept that some form of theological language is necessary. But in so doing, we must simultaneously recognise that our language can be applied to God only in a highly-qualified and provisional way. We cannot imagine that our language refers to God in the same way that it refers to things in the world. To imagine that it does would be to use theological language *univocally*, and this would involve us in the direct betrayal of God's transcendence. So if an equivocal understanding of theological language is to be avoided for betraying any human communion with God, so too a univocal understanding is to be avoided for betraying the transcendence of God. This twin conviction lies at the heart of Aquinas's teaching on analogy, which we might see as a kind of mediation between these two undesirable extremes. He said that whenever we use a word of God, we do so in a way that is *related* to the way in which we use it of finite things – and so it conveys some true knowledge – but as to the precise nature of that relation and as to what the word actually means when applied to God, we have to confess our ignorance. To use language in this way, with a constant awareness of this 'relation-in-difference', is to use language analogically. As Aquinas himself puts it: 'This way of using words lies somewhere between pure equivocation and simple univocity, for the word is neither used in the same sense, as with univocal usage, nor in totally different senses, as with equivocation.'[3]

Thus understood, theological language enables creatures to say and know something of God, but this 'something' is always tempered by a certain agnosticism or unknowing. And for Aquinas, *all* language predicated of God is analogical; from this linguistic usage, there is no escape if God's transcendence is to be preserved. Michel de Certeau expresses the logic of analogy when he says that: 'The weight of [God's] transcendence makes any proposition relative, even to the point that the statement "God exists" has to be followed by a denial.'[4] When expressed in this way, we begin to see why Aquinas's teaching on analogy is so closely connected to the tradition of the negative theology; so much so that we may understand analogical language as being one way in which the negative theology is expressed. Indeed, we see the two closely fused when Aquinas says:

> In this life our minds cannot grasp what God is in himself; whatever way we have of thinking of him is a way of failing

> to understand him as he really is. So the less determinate our names are and the more general and simple they are, the more appropriately they may be applied to God.[5]

Now it should be clear from this that an analogical understanding of theological language has profound implications for the way in which the God of which it speaks is conceived. It is not that analogy is a linguistic tool, quite separate and apart from the conception of God to which it refers. On the contrary, it is because God is conceived in a certain way that analogical language is thought to be the only appropriate way of expressing the divine. And, looked at from the other direction, it is because God can only be expressed in analogical language that certain ways of conceiving of God are prescribed and others proscribed. Thus, it can be known that God is, among other things, good, loving, perfect, simple and triune. But the fact that all such language is used analogically emphasises also that God is transcendent, mysterious, unknowable, hidden and beyond human comprehension. So Aquinas's teaching on analogy should be viewed as being inseparable from his negative theology, by which all his positive theology is always and necessarily qualified. All theological knowing is underpinned by a certain unknowing, and this unknowing is an integral part of Aquinas's faith, rather than an external negation of it. As David B. Burrell has observed: 'Aquinas displays his religious discipline most clearly by the ease with which he is able to endure so unknown a God.'[6]

From the birth of modernity, this understanding of the ubiquity of analogical language in all theology came to be lost. This is not, of course, to claim that talk of 'analogy' disappeared altogether. But it became marginal rather than central, and even where it did continue to be invoked as necessary, it was understood in a considerably less equivocal way than its Thomistic predecessor had been.[7] When we relate this back to some of the epistemological developments discussed in the last chapter, it is not difficult to see why this might be so. We saw there that what motivated modern philosophers from Descartes onwards was a quest for 'certain' knowledge, a quest that persisted down through to Kant, whose concern, we saw, was to establish philosophy as a 'certain' branch of knowledge, as a 'science'. In a philosophical episteme in which 'certainty' is so highly prized, it is not difficult to see why a doctrine such as Aquinas's on analogy would come to be regarded with suspicion. For it emphasised the necessary centrality of uncertainty, imprecision and the theological propriety of linguistic indeterminacy. To the modern mind, therefore, analogical language obfuscated rather than clarified, and inevitably came to be viewed as a hindrance to the quest for scientific certainty.

The shift that we see occurring at the outset of modernity is well expressed by Don Cupitt, when he says:

> Modern philosophy, having been to school with Hume, Kant and Frege, finds this old doctrine [of the negative theology] empty and foolish. The basic objection was clearly formulated by the deist John Toland: 'Could that Person justly value himself upon being wiser than his Neighbours, who having infallible assurance that something call'd *Blictri* had a being in Nature, in the mean time knew not what this Blictri was?' Toland is surely right. The affirmation that God exists has no content unless something can be said about what God is. From the modern point of view, Thomas Aquinas seems ... merely to be striving after vacuity.[8]

Indeed, similar sentiments are expressed by John Hick, when he says that 'a doctrine that can mean anything means nothing. So long, then, as we refrain from spelling out our faith it must remain empty.'[9] Cupitt goes on to make the point that such vacuity is not only viewed as being epistemologically problematic but also ethically undesirable, in that it subordinates us to what he calls the 'despotism of mystery'. In other words, appeals to mystery are not only likely to lead us astray philosophically, but they are also liable to undermine the integrity of human freedom, by enslaving people to a mystery beyond their control and beyond rational interrogation.[10] This point has been reinforced by Charles Taylor, who sees this as a major aspect of the modern mentality. It is seen first in the Reformation slogans against the Catholic Church, particularly in the rhetoric against transubstantiation, but is later directed against orthodox Christianity itself. He says that '[t]hese mysteries were branded as an excuse for what we would today call mystification; with the aim of holding Christians in thrall to usurped power... What Calvin did to the mysteries of the Catholic Church, Toland did to mystery as such.'[11]

Analogy and the negative theology, therefore, are now seen as embodying epistemological vacuity and moral servitude, with the result that Aquinas's delicate balance between positive and negative theology now gives way to a situation in which positive theology is unequivocally prioritised. Aquinas's insistence that *all* language of God is analogical came to be forgotten, and it was now thought that God shared with his creation at least some genuine predicates literally and unequivocally. This has been argued, for instance, by Amos Funkenstein, who refers to

> what may be called the transparency of God in the seventeenth century. I do not necessarily mean that seventeenth-century thinkers always claimed to know *more* about God than medieval theologians. To some of them God remained a *deus absconditus* about whom little can be known. What I mean to say is that they claimed what they knew about God, be it much or little, to be precise 'clear and distinct' ideas.[12]

To imagine that one can refer to God in precise, 'clear and distinct' ideas is clearly the antithesis of what is taught by the doctrine of analogy and constitutes, in effect, a rehabilitation of univocal theological language, the dangers of which Aquinas had never ceased to emphasise. If Funkenstein is correct, it does seem that there has been a major shift in the understanding of theological language here. But this linguistic shift would not be so significant in itself were it not for the fact that it carried with it a major revolution in how God was *conceived*.

That such a linguistic shift should have implications for the modern conception of God should not surprise us, given what we have already said about the close relationship between Aquinas's understanding of analogical language about God on the one hand

and his conception of God on the other. We have seen that, for Aquinas, these two conceptions were mutually implicated, and that his all-pervasive teaching on analogy was intended above all to preserve God's transcendence. With the abandonment or weakening of the commitment to analogy, it was perhaps inevitable that it would carry with it a dissolution or at least a change in the notion of what it means for God to be 'transcendent'. If language can now be predicated of God in the same unequivocal way that it is predicated of things in the world, the implication of this is that God is, in some sense, closer to things in the world; indeed, to such an extent, that he becomes a 'thing' himself. In other words, there is a qualitative change in what God is conceived to be.

One way in which this change was manifested was that God's 'being' came to be conceived no longer as an ontologically transcendent mystery, no longer as being related to but fundamentally different from worldly being. Rather, God's being came to be conceived much more in the manner of worldly being, such that God was thought to have a specifiable 'substance' in the world with an identifiable 'location'. Thus, there emerged a family of ideas that Funkenstein calls the 'body of God'. As the scientific elevation of precise, univocal, mechanical language came to infiltrate both philosophical and theological thinking, it became necessary to specify what sort of 'thing' God was.

Funkenstein says that one instructive example of this trend is that of Henry More. For More, the distinction between the creator and his creatures, or between the divine and the human, is best expressed in terms of a distinction between spiritual bodies and solid bodies. Undoubtedly, More conceives there to be a distinction between the two, but we also get the very clear sense that this is a distinction between two kinds of empirical realities. So, for instance, spiritual bodies are distinct from solid bodies in that they are penetrable and are able to contract and expand. In other words, the difference between spiritual bodies and solid bodies is not to be understood (as Aquinas would have understood it) as a difference between two heterogeneous kinds of realities, one empirical and one utterly non-empirical, but, on the contrary, as a difference between two species of empirical reality. That spiritual bodies are penetrable, and can contract and expand, distinguishes them from solid bodies, but in other respects, we get the impression that they are two species of 'substance' understood in a univocal sense. For More, God is the highest spirit, such that all other spirits are dependent on him. As a spirit, God is extended, but his extension is infinite; it is space itself.[13]

So what this apparently amounts to is the claim that God is undoubtedly an empirical reality within the natural world, but in order to maintain God's sovereignty over the natural world, he has to be virtually equated with the *totality* of that natural world, in a way that seems to prefigure pantheism. In effect, what More is trying to reconcile here is the conviction that God is an empirical reality within the world on the one hand, with the conviction that God must somehow transcend and have sovereignty over that same world on the other. With the decline of the whole tradition of analogy and negative theology, God must now somehow be conceived as an empirical worldly reality (the very thing Aquinas feared would happen if analogical observance were not maintained). The only way of maintaining transcendence in this worldly sense is somehow to see God as being an expression of that world's totality; he thus becomes an infinitely extended substance, virtually equivalent to space itself. Thus, far from being a spiritual reality that *transcends* space and time, God has almost become an *embodiment* of space and time. As Funkenstein puts it: 'More's concept of the divine amounts to the concept of a harmonious sum total of all mechanical and purposive forces in the universe.'[14]

More was by no means alone. Although modern theology (along with philosophy and science) was an arena of vigorous disagreement and debate, this was nonetheless conducted against a commonly accepted backdrop where the 'domestication' of God seemed to be taken for granted. Buckley, for instance, detects two major strands in the development of modern theism. One was a rationalistic and mathematical strand pioneered by Descartes and developed by Nicolas Malebranche. The other was more empirical and mechanical, deriving from Isaac Newton and pursued by Samuel Clarke. The resulting conceptions of God were quite distinct. But what they had in common was a conception of God as a 'thing' in the world, with a definable 'substance' and identifiable 'location' that could be referred to in much the same way as other things.[15]

We see this whole tradition being perpetuated in contemporary theology in the work of an analytical philosopher of religion like Richard Swinburne.[16] Indeed, it is possible to construct an account of his theology that makes it appear antithetical to Aquinas's in almost every important respect. Whereas Aquinas insists that all language about God is used analogically, Swinburne says:

> Unless there is good reason to suppose otherwise, clearly we ought to assume that theists are using words in their ordinary, mundane senses... When the theist says that God is 'good', 'good' is, I suggest, being used in a perfectly ordinary sense. The only extraordinary thing being suggested is that it exists to a degree in which it does not exist in mundane objects.[17]

As we would expect, this way of understanding the nature of theological language leads on also to a very specific understanding of the way in which God is conceived. Whereas Aquinas believed God's essence to be utterly 'simple', with the result that God is believed to be impassible, Swinburne believes that 'God is a personal being – that is, in some sense a *person*. By a person I mean an individual with basic powers (to act intentionally), purposes and beliefs.'[18]

Also, whereas Aquinas believes God to exceed rationality in a way that makes him beyond rational comprehension, Swinburne believes it to be imperative to provide an account of God that does not transgress the bounds of reason. Thus it is that, because Swinburne 'cannot make much sense of the suggestion' that God is outside time, he insists that God must be everlasting; that is to say, that although without beginning or end, God nonetheless exists *within* time.[19] It is difficult to imagine Aquinas reacting with anything other than abhorrence at such a suggestion. Indeed, this is exacerbated when we come to realise what further implications this suggestion has. Given that a God within time who has perfect knowledge of the future is, for Swinburne, rationally incompatible with the notion of human freedom, Swinburne is constrained to admit that God has no certain knowledge of the future. As he puts it:

> no one (not even God) can know today (without the possibility of mistake) what I will choose to do tomorrow. So I suggest that we understand God being omniscient as God knowing at any time all that is logically possible to know at that time. That will not include knowledge, before they have done it, of what human persons will do freely.[20]

Viewed thus, we can see just how different Swinburne's conception of God is from that of Aquinas. Indeed, the difference is nothing less than the difference between the medieval God and the modern God, which thus confirms our initial suggestion that once negative theology and its analogical conception of language falls away, this cannot but lead to a qualitatively changed conception of God. Furthermore, in each aspect of this change, we see Swinburne's conception of God moving away from Aquinas's in a 'domesticating' direction. In each respect, Swinburne's God appears more and more as a 'big person', which is far removed from the mysterious transcendence of divine simplicity alluded to but never grasped by Aquinas.

But if this is so, then how did modern theologians and philosophers pay obeisance to the 'transcendence' of God, as they were surely constrained to do? Theologians from More to Swinburne clearly did not deny God's transcendence, however much their 'domestication' of God's otherness seemed to suggest otherwise. In other words, what compensated for this process of divine domestication, such that God could still be spoken of as being, in some sense, 'transcendent'? We have seen how More grappled with this dilemma in a way that led him practically close to pantheism. But a common answer (of which More was, in many ways, an instantiation) was to stress God's quantitative difference from worldly things. So God's transcendence over the world came to be expressed as a *quantitative* distance from the world, rather than a *qualitative* difference from it. This meant that God's goodness differed from worldly goodness in the sense that it was much greater (in terms of quantity) rather than a different kind or quality of goodness, as Aquinas would have maintained. (Indeed, we have already seen this to be the case in Swinburne's theism, when he says that divine goodness is the same as human goodness, the only difference being that divine goodness 'exists to a degree in which it does not exist in mundane objects'.) Similarly, God's existence came to be understood to differ from human existence in the sense that it was infinitely greater (again, in terms of quantity), rather than a different kind or quality of existence. Thus, because God's 'being' was deemed to be of the same quality as human 'being' (so that an ontological transcendence was lacking), God's otherness instead came to be expressed by emphasising his quantitative difference from the world.

This is not to suggest, however, that an emphasis on a greater divine 'quantity' always had the same practical outcome in terms of the conception of God produced. Indeed, it is possible to detect two strands in particular that seemed to arise from this emphasis on the 'quantitative' difference between the human and the divine. On the one hand, as is the case with Richard Swinburne, to speak of God possessing 'being', 'knowledge' or 'goodness' to a much greater degree than human beings does not lead us to suppose that this makes God unduly 'hidden' or 'unknowable'. Accordingly, this strand of modern theism remains true to its founding moment, in which, as we have seen, attempts were made to overcome vacuity and mystification. On the other hand, there is another strand in modern theism in which the 'quantitative' difference between the human and divine is such that God becomes far removed from human knowing, without there being any analogical mediation between them. Although, in this strand, God remains ontologically continuous with the world, the quantitative distance is such as to move God further and further away, so that he ultimately recedes into an unknowable abyss. We see this strand being given its ultimate expression in Kant, for whom, as we have seen, God is placed strictly beyond the bounds of theoretical knowledge.

In this respect, it might be tempting to see Kant as taking a half-turn back to Aquinas and the negative theology, in that he seems once more to emphasise mystery and divine hiddenness and the way in which the existence of God cannot be established by theoretical reason. There is, indeed, a sense in which both Aquinas and Kant preserve a certain agnosticism with respect to God, emphasising the limits of human knowledge with respect to the transcendent world. But we should beware of being seduced by such apparent similarities. Theologians as divergent as Don Cupitt and John Milbank are agreed that there is a deeper and more significant difference between Aquinas and Kant that undermines and disrupts this apparent harmony. Don Cupitt expresses what he perceives to be the essential difference between them as follows: 'The old doctrine asserted that God's existence is certain but his nature unknowable'; whereas for Kant 'it is God's *existence* rather than his nature that is unknowable. God's *nature* is not mysterious, for we have a clear, unproblematic and *useful* idea of God immanent within our reason.'[21] This fundamental difference is reflected also in their strikingly different attitudes towards the concept of mystery as such. In this respect:

> what Kant is saying is strikingly different from the older negative theology, which had always been closely allied with mysticism. The Greek Fathers, for example, invoke a sense of the mystery of divine transcendence in order to awaken heavenly longings. Their language is designed to *attract*, whereas Kant's language is designed to *repel*. Kant wants us to renounce impossible and futile aspirations and be content with doing our duty... The old negative way was speculative and mystical, whereas Kant's purpose is to eliminate speculative and mystical theology.[22]

Although he expresses it in somewhat other terms, John Milbank in general agrees with this line of analysis. He says that Kant is totally agnostic concerning 'God-in-himself', but in a way dogmatic with regard to God's relationship to human beings, in the sense that he places an absolute prohibition on any human penetration of the boundary between the world of human phenomena and the divine noumenon. Aquinas, on the other hand, represents the antithesis of this in that he is less agnostic concerning 'God-in-himself', but more agnostic concerning the conditions of our relationship to God. Milbank therefore suggests that there is a kind of epistemological dogmatism in Kant that is lacking in Aquinas:

> far from being (like Aquinas) agnostically cautious about the extrapolation of categories from our material, finite, temporal existence, Kant was *metaphysically dogmatic* in affirming that they *do not at all* apply, precisely because he believed (unlike Aquinas) that he had direct cognitive access in practical reason to what the immaterial and atemporal is like.[23]

In other words, Kant's epistemological modesty was founded on a deeper metaphysical dogmatism; he recognised the *limits* of human knowledge precisely because he was *certain* of what the human mind could and could not know.

In any case, we can see that in spite of what might appear to be a common emphasis on the hiddenness of God shared by Aquinas and Kant, they nonetheless remain sharply divergent in a way that derives from their respective understandings of the negative theology and the role of analogical language. For Aquinas, God's 'existence' is of a different quality to human existence, and quite what God's 'existence' is cannot ultimately be specified in human language. But there is no insurmountable barrier between these orders of existence. Analogical language can mediate between these realms, albeit in a hesitant, halting and always uncertain way, such that 'knowledge' of God is always counter-balanced by an awareness of our non-knowledge of God, which is to say that positive theology is always counter-balanced by a negative theology. In Kant, however, God's existence is unknowable in rational terms and the noumenal–phenomenal barrier cannot be penetrated, whether by God's own self-revelation or by analogical language. Insofar as God can be known at all, this is only at the level of practical knowledge, by means of regulative ideals.

We are therefore now in a position to see that modernity conceived of God in a very specific and distinctive way, which differed sharply from the ways in which God had been conceived hitherto. In particular, we have seen the decline of the medieval tradition of negative theology and, in particular, its analogical understanding of theological language. We have seen that this development had very marked implications for the way in which God was conceived. In particular, the conception of God is 'domesticated' as the transcendence of God is downplayed, so that God can be referred to in the univocal language of 'clear and distinct' ideas, with the result that God is conceived in increasingly worldly and anthropomorphic terms. In order to compensate for this process of 'domestication', God's transcendence over the world comes to be expressed in quantitative terms, and it is at this point that we see the emergence of two distinct modern conceptions of God. One conception emphasises this quantitative difference, but without this having any mystifying implications in epistemological terms. The other conception pushes this quantitative distance to such an extent that God becomes theoretically strictly unknowable and pushed beyond the realms of human knowing. It is as though, once the insights of negative theology and its analogical conception of theological language have been lost, God must either be brought immediately before our eyes in a particularly vivid, personalist way, or else he recedes away beyond the sights of the epistemological horizon altogether.

It is my suggestion that modern atheism reacts against one or other of these distinctively modern conceptions of God. Indeed, more than this, I further want to suggest that both of these conceptions are particularly vulnerable to atheistic attack. In the case of the first anthropomorphic conception of God, it becomes all too obviously vulnerable to the charges of 'projection' in the way that we have seen Feuerbach and Marx in particular to have argued. Indeed, Nicholas Lash has suggested that once an analogical understanding of theological language is lost, then theology has no defence against the Feuerbachian charge. This is because

> we would be unable to discriminate between the 'models' of God that we fashion in metaphor and the discovered mystery signified by such constructions. All that we say of God, affirmatively, is indeed 'projected' from our human experience, is anthropomorphic in character, and we would have no way of showing the sense of such language to be other than 'merely' projective.[24]

But even if this were not the case, then it could still be said that when God is conceived as a substance who is accorded a place and function in the natural world, his days are already numbered. As the world becomes increasingly self-explanatory in scientific terms, a God with a specifiable body, place and function in the natural world comes to look increasingly redundant and unsustainable. Furthermore, when God's attributes (and limitations) become all too obviously the attributes of the human subject writ large, such a God comes to be seen as precisely that, a form of wishful projection revealing an infantile state of existence on the part of the humanity that does the projecting. Funkenstein expresses this well when he says:

> It is clear why a God describable in unequivocal terms, or even given physical features or functions, eventually becomes all the easier to discard. As a scientific hypothesis, he was later shown to be superfluous; as a being, he was shown to be a mere hypostatization of human rational, social, psychological ideals and images.[25]

Modern atheism, I am suggesting, constitutes itself in its rejection of this specifically modern conception of God. That this is so is illustrated by the fact that the only contemporary theologian discussed at any length by Richard Dawkins, in his book *The God Delusion*, is Richard Swinburne. Given that a whole host of contemporary theologians and philosophers, such as John Milbank, Rowan Williams, D. Z. Phillips and Fergus Kerr, to name but a few (and to whom we shall return in Chapter 8), would all regard Swinburne's conception of God as being incorrigibly modern and religiously impoverished, we begin to see just how limited and specific is the conception of theism which Dawkins attacks.

But the second distinctively modern conception of God fares little better. In Kant's philosophy of religion, and even more so in the work of some of his successors, God becomes a mere cipher, such that it is in danger of dissolving into nothingness. It is important at this point to recall those things which allow Kant to retain his residual commitment to theism. First, there is his conception of the noumenon, the world in itself as distinct from the world that we experience. Secondly, there are his transcendental arguments developed in the sphere of practical reason, which lead us to suppose the existence of God as a 'necessary practical postulate'. But it could well be argued that these are two of the most vulnerable and subsequently most frequently rejected aspects of Kant's philosophy.

First, his postulation of a noumenal world is weakened by his own insistence that we can know nothing of such a world. We have already observed how the modern episteme, as exemplified in the philosophy of John Toland in particular, is deeply suspicious of the postulation of anything that can be given no positive content. Such scepticism may be directed, as we have seen, against the pre-modern conception of the negative theology, but it could equally well be directed against Kant's conception of the noumenon. Indeed, such vulnerability is further exacerbated when the universal and *a priori* status of Kant's categories is itself called into question. Even philosophers sympathetic to Kant and generally accepting of the broad contours of his epistemology have been wont to reinterpret the status of Kant's categories as being contingent and culturally relative. In the philosophy of religion, for instance, John Hick has made precisely this point. Hick says that, in his own modification of Kant's epistemology, the categories

> are not universal and invariable but on the contrary culture-relative. It is possible to live without employing them; and when they are employed they tend to change and develop through time as different historical influences affect the development of human consciousness.[26]

The difficulty with this, of course, is that the universal status of the categories was what protected Kant from the scepticism of Hume, against which he was battling. Without them, we appear to be left with nothing but subjective experience, which in turn seems to imply that we are left with nothing but the phenomenal world of our experience, with no room for God or the noumenal world. (This is, of course, a conclusion which Hick wants to resist, although many critics have questioned the extent to which he can do so.)

As for Kant's transcendental argument for the existence of God as a necessary practical postulate, this is one which very few subsequent philosophers (again, not even those who are otherwise sympathetic to Kant) have felt moved to defend. The atheistic philosopher, J. L. Mackie, for instance, seems to have highlighted what many philosophers have regarded as the fatal weakness of Kant's transcendental argument, when he criticises Kant's assumption that 'ought' implies 'can'. This is seen to be at work, of course, when Kant argues that, because we feel an irresistible duty to achieve the *summum bonum*, this must therefore be possible. Mackie argues that there are no sound philosophical grounds for supposing this assumption to be true. As he puts it:

> the thesis that we ought to seek to promote the highest good implies only that we can *seek to promote it*, and perhaps, since rational seeking could not be completely fruitless, that we can to some extent actually *promote* it. But this does not require that the full realization of the highest good should be possible.[27]

If this point is conceded to Mackie, and given that Kant has himself ruled out any speculative knowledge of God, then it would appear that the Kantian defence of God immediately dissolves.

It can be seen, therefore, that the modern conception of God was in so many ways distinct from the conception of God that had prevailed in the pre-modern world. Arising out of the epistemological shifts outlined in the previous chapter, we see the emergence of a God whose transcendence is domesticated. Articulated in univocal or unequivocal theological language, God comes to be conceived in increasingly worldly or anthropomorphic terms. In some manifestations, God is conceived as an infinite 'person' who bears, in many ways, an uncanny resemblance to human persons, while in other manifestations he is reduced to a mere postulate or cipher beyond all bounds of human knowing. Modern atheism has found both conceptions to be equally unsustainable. As a 'big person', God is too obviously a crude projection, a hypostatisation of human realities, while as an ideal postulate God becomes increasingly superfluous and empty. With respect to such conceptions of God, the atheistic attack becomes all too pertinent and persuasive. But it should by now be apparent that the atheistic rejection of theism, persuasive though it may be, is so in relation to a specifically modern conception of God. Whether such arguments are also as persuasive in relation to other conceptions of God is another and open question. It is not my intention to pronounce on that here, but I do want to argue that modern atheism has, historically, defined and justified itself in relation to a specifically modern conception of theism. Nevertheless, theism as such is not exhausted by the distillation produced by this modern filter.

Chapter 4

The Theological Origins of Modern Atheism

We saw in the last chapter that modern atheism was constituted by the rejection of a specifically modern conception of God, a conception that was qualitatively different from ones that had prevailed hitherto. But this gives rise to the question of how God came to be reconceived in this distinctively modern fashion in the first place. Was this a secular corruption of an authentic theism? Was theology invaded by the alien powers of secular philosophy and science, giving rise to this quasi-philosophical and quasi-scientific God? Was theism forced to prostitute itself to these external attacks? Thus stated, such questions seem to imply that the advent of modernity is marked by the autonomous rise of a rational-scientific world-view that addressed the problematic of an anachronistic theism in its midst by first distorting it and then, ultimately, rejecting it. There is, however, a bold line of argument that questions such an analysis. Rather than envisaging an 'innocent' theology being attacked and undermined by a 'malign' secularism, it is argued that, within medieval theology itself, certain moves took place that both caused the nature of theism to change *and* laid the epistemological groundwork for an immanent, univocal and ultimately, therefore, atheistic world-view. In other words, atheism did not so much provide an *external* challenge to theism, but it is rather the case that atheism in its founding moment was constituted by a revolution *within theology itself*. This is to claim that the origins of modern atheism are ultimately *theological*.

We have seen that one of the chief characteristics of the theism against which modern atheism reacted was that God's attributes were believed to be of the same order or quality as human attributes, but that God possessed them to an infinitely greater degree. As a consequence of this, language could be applied to God univocally. If, as we have seen, this conception of theism contrasts with that which had prevailed hitherto, then we are led to ask where, when and how this distinctively modern conception of theism emerged. This is precisely the question that has been asked by the Swiss theologian Hans Urs von Balthasar and, more recently, by Éric Alliez, Catherine Pickstock and William C. Placher, among others. For these thinkers, the turning point comes as early as the fourteenth century with the Franciscan priest and theologian John Duns Scotus. For it was Duns Scotus who explicitly rejected the ontological difference between divine being and human being. It is this shift that I shall explore in this chapter.

Hans Urs von Balthasar says that in Aquinas's ontology:

> being (*esse*), with which he is concerned and to which he attributes the modalities of the One, the True, the Good and the Beautiful, is the unlimited abundance of reality which is beyond all comprehension, as it, in its emergence from God, attains subsistence and self-possession within the finite entities.[1]

The central point here is that 'being' is not something shared by God and humanity; rather, being only 'is' insofar as it emerges from and is created by God. Only thus is God's ontological priority preserved. If both God and humanity shared in the same quality or type of being, then God and creatures would alike be members of a common genus, which Aquinas vehemently rejects. He says that 'God is not a measure that is proportionate to what is measured; so it does not follow that he and his creatures belong to the same order.'[2] This is why, as we have seen, Aquinas insisted that all language predicated of God was used analogically. Only thus could the ontological difference between the divine and the creaturely be respected. It was this ontological difference that came to be dissolved during the fourteenth century.

Balthasar claims that the crucial turning point came with the rise of Averroism in the 1250s. At the time, Averroism claimed itself to be the only serious contemporary interpretation of Aristotle, whose great virtue was believed to lie in the fact that he was the sole 'scientific' philosopher. Crucially, Averroism attempted to discover how far human reason could go in the inquiry into the ultimate grounds of Being, independently of any revelatory knowledge. It may thus be viewed as an early anticipation of the epistemology of Descartes, in the sense that it did not presuppose or unquestioningly assume any knowledge on the basis of divine revelation. It thus placed philosophy above theology as the sole comprehensive science that could identify reality, rationality and necessity.[3] We thus begin to see that Descartes's epistemological revolution was not without precedent. I argued in Chapter 2 that Descartes's philosophical method was ultimately an atheistic one, even if not acknowledged or recognised by Descartes himself. This was because it embodied a method that was entirely immanent and God-less, and would thus ultimately lead to conclusions that were likewise immanent and God-less. The same may be said about the rise of Averroism. But what is of crucial importance here is that this immanent and God-less approach to philosophy was, in the fourteenth century, incorporated into theology itself. In the work of John Duns Scotus, Averroism was adopted by theology.

It is important to emphasise, of course, that Duns Scotus did not himself adopt an Averroistic methodology. He did not explicitly elevate a philosophical epistemology over a theological one. This radical move was not to happen until it was enacted by Descartes. But the influence of Averroism may be discerned in Duns Scotus's novel account of the relationship between God and being. Certainly, his account appears novel to many subsequent commentators, although it should be noted that Duns Scotus understood his own thought as being more continuous than discontinuous with that of Aquinas. He saw his task as being to refine Aquinas's thought and modify it in certain respects, but ultimately he saw himself as continuing rather than subverting the great theological work begun by his august predecessor. Many contemporary theologians, viewing his work with the benefit of hindsight, disagree. In particular, his conception of being as a single category, prior to the distinction between God and creatures, is seen by many as constituting a revolutionary departure. In Duns Scotus's own words, his fundamental contention was that 'being is univocal to the created and uncreated'.[4] The Averroistic legacy here is obvious; the aim is to conceive of being as a concept quite independently of any revelatory knowledge and independently of the divine-human distinction. Balthasar says that this re-conception arose out of Duns Scotus's concern to secure the place of 'reason' in the face of Christian theology. Reason is now able to posit 'being' as its foundational and universal concept, in such a way that it becomes prior to, and encompasses, the distinction between finite and infinite being:

> The concept has not only logical (expressive) universality, but also metaphysical universality, for it captures Being in its objective ('catholic') generality, so that *it can be univocally applied to infinite and to finite Being*, that is to God and the world, to substance and accidents, to act and potentiality.[5]

As a consequence of this, being was no longer something emerging from and created by God, but something in which God and humanity shared, even if God's 'share' in this being was infinitely greater than that of human beings. As Duns Scotus puts it:

> Whatever pertains to 'being', then, insofar as it remains indifferent to finite and infinite, or as proper to the Infinite Being, does not belong to it as determined to a genus, but prior to any such determination, and therefore as transcendental and outside any genus.[6]

With this move, the ontological difference between God's being and human being was destroyed and, for many commentators, this marks the fundamental turning point that laid the foundations not only for the distinctively modern conception of theism, as discussed in the last chapter, but also for the modern world-view itself. But we can also relate this back to the increasing epistemological distance between the divine and the human that we identified in the previous chapter. Now that the ontological difference between finite and infinite being had been lost, God's transcendence had to be articulated in quantitative terms on a single ontological plane. God transcends humanity only in 'intensity of being' and, again as we saw in the last chapter, analogical mediation between the divine and human realms is precluded. So, although there was an ontological continuity between God and humanity (the 'domesticating' move), this also installed an infinite metaphysical gap between them (the 'distancing' move). The 'distancing' move was intended to compensate for the domesticating move, but the combined effect of both was to turn God into an unknowable unfathomable abyss, which we saw to reach its apotheosis in Kant's conception of the noumenon. In effect, God's *ontological* transcendence became an *epistemological* transcendence.[7] As Éric Alliez says:

> In effect, once the *primary mover of continuity* (the Aristotelo-Thomist principle of universal analogy) has been abandoned to a universal conception of being giving no means to creatures to distinguish themselves ontologically from God by analogically drawing near to him, the distance between finite and infinite becomes infinite.[8]

What this means, therefore, is that Duns Scotus's univocal concept of Being both moves God closer to creatures *and* moves him further away. God is brought closer to creatures insofar as he exists in the same way as them (though with greater intensity), but is also moved further away from them insofar as they are now divided by an abyss that can no longer be crossed by means of analogical participation. As Catherine Pickstock puts it: 'the "same" becomes the radically disparate and unknowable'.[9]

We have seen that Aquinas's commitment to analogy was consequent upon his preservation of the ontological difference. It was precisely because of the ontological difference that language from one ontological level could not be applied univocally to the other. When the ontological difference was destroyed, therefore, it is only to be expected that this would have had a considerable impact on the doctrine of analogy. If Aquinas's conception of the task of analogy was to steer a precarious but necessary middle way between univocity on the one hand and equivocation on the other, in the wake of Duns Scotus, we see conceptions of analogy slowly shifting away from such a Thomistic middle way towards a more modern univocity. As William C. Placher has suggested, an important step in this process was enacted by Thomas de Vio, Cardinal Cajetan, in his work *The Analogy of Names* (1498).[10] As with Duns Scotus before him, Cajetan clearly believed his account of analogy to be continuous with that of Aquinas, and that he was merely 'systematizing and developing' it.[11] In recent years, however, the continuity between Aquinas and Cajetan in this respect has been increasingly questioned. David B. Burrell, for instance, has suggested that the perception of a fundamental continuity between Aquinas and Cajetan has been sustained by retrospectively and anachronistically projecting Cajetan's understanding of analogy back onto Aquinas himself. He says:

> Aquinas is perhaps best known for his theory of analogy. On closer inspection it turns out that he never had one. Rather he made do with a few vague remarks and that grammatical astuteness which I have suggested as a replacement for intuition. Others of course [especially Cajetan], organized those remarks of his into a theory, and that is what Aquinas has become famous for.[12]

Following Burrell's lead, Placher says: 'More than anyone else, Thomas de Vio, Cardinal Cajetan, systematized Aquinas' varied references into a "theory of analogy".'[13] According to Burrell and Placher, therefore, Cajetan betrayed Aquinas's original intentions by turning his unsystematic gesture into a systematic theory.

But in what precisely did this betrayal consist? To answer this question, we must look in more detail at Cajetan's specific understanding of analogical language. It is important to note that

Cajetan distinguished between what were at the time commonly taken to be three distinct forms of analogy: the analogy of inequality, attribution and proportionality. But he says that 'according to the true sense of the term ... only the last mode constitutes analogy, and the first one is entirely foreign to analogy'.[14] For Cajetan, the analogy of inequality is 'entirely foreign to analogy' because, for him, it is really a form of univocity. But more important for our purposes is the fact that Cajetan goes on to say that he considers the analogy of attribution to be merely a form of equivocation.[15] He defines the analogy of attribution as those things 'which have a common name, and the notion signified by this name is the same with respect to the term but different as regards the relationships to this term'.[16] As an example, he follows Aquinas in citing the adjective 'healthy', when it is predicated as an animal as a *subject* of health, of urine as a *sign* of health and as medicine as a *cause* of health. Here, he says:

> it is perfectly clear that the notion of health is not entirely the same nor entirely different, but to a certain extent the same and to a certain extent different. For there is a diversity of relationships, but the term of those relationships is one and the same.[17]

Whereas Aquinas cites this example as a classic usage of analogical language, Cajetan regards such a usage as merely a form of equivocation. Why? Because the term 'health' used in these ways has no 'definite meaning' common to all three usages, and the relationships between these usages is only implied in an 'indeterminate and confused way'.[18] It is because of this indeterminacy that Cajetan regards the analogy of attribution as being merely a form of equivocation and therefore not a genuine form of analogy at all.

On the other hand, Cajetan embraces the analogy of proportionality as 'analogy in the proper sense' and defines it by saying that 'those things are called analogous by proportionality which have a common name, and the notion expressed by this name is similar according to a proportion'.[19] Cajetan goes on to say that the analogy of proportionality may be divided into 'metaphorical' and 'proper' occurrences. Examples of the former may be found throughout Scripture, when it teaches of God by means of metaphor, referring to God as a rock, a king, a shepherd and so forth. These would all be instances of analogy of proportionality in its metaphorical occurrence. Of course, we may well wonder whether such a usage is in fact an instance of analogical language at all, for it appears to elide what so many have regarded as the necessary distinction between analogy and metaphor. Nicholas Lash, for instance, has suggested that those who assimilate the two ways of speaking turn out in practice to foreclose the way of analogy. He says that

> there are those who, in various ways, assimilate the logic of analogy to that of metaphor, using the two concepts more or less interchangeably. On this account, the 'way of analogy' is apparently open, but the appearance is illusory, because 'analogy' turns out to be either a sub-class of metaphor or the 'common heading' under which the 'family of metaphor' is subsumed.'[20]

In any case, Cajetan says that the analogy of proportionality occurs in its *proper* sense, when 'the common name is predicated of both analogates without the use of metaphors. For instance, *principle* can be predicated of the heart with respect to an animal and of a foundation with respect to a house.'[21] In other words, the word 'principle' is being used here in its proper analogical sense in relation to an animal and to a house; the word is being used to designate the *same idea* in both cases. Because we are talking of two quite different things – an animal and a house – it is inevitable that this 'same idea' will manifest itself in two different ways – as a heart and as a foundation – but the point of the analogy used in this way is to draw attention to sameness and unity, in which the difference is epiphenomenal or of secondary importance. But for Cajetan, this is precisely what makes this form of analogy preferable to others; it predicates perfections that are 'inherent in each analogate', whereas the other forms of analogy arise from 'extrinsic denominations'; thus he says that 'metaphysical speculations without knowledge of this analogy must be said to be unskilled'.[22]

With each step that Cajetan takes, therefore, we see his account of analogy becoming decreasingly equivocal and increasingly univocal. He elevates the analogy of proportionality over the analogy of attribution because the latter is too imprecise. Within the analogy of proportionality itself, 'proper' occurrences are less equivocal than 'metaphorical' ones, with the result that 'proper' occurrences are again preferred. The delicate balance between univocal and equivocal language seems to have tipped in such a way as to give ultimate priority to the univocal. Indeed, Cajetan himself says that his favoured analogy of proportionality is 'in a certain sense midway between what is analogous by attribution and what is univocal'.[23] Increasingly, therefore, we see the emergence of the conviction that it is possible to refer to God in 'clear and distinct' ways and without 'confusion'; indeed, that it is not only possible but desirable so to do. As Placher observes:

> Cajetan had moved a long way from Aquinas. Unsystematic references have become a systematic theory... Far from offering a series of reminders concerning how we cannot understand what we mean when we speak of God, analogy now functioned as a way of explaining just what we do mean.[24]

Francisco Suárez, a Spanish Jesuit, further developed this shift in the understanding of analogy, as is particularly evident in his *Disputationes metaphysicae* (1597). Balthasar makes it clear that Suárez 'has recourse to the Scotist notion of "univocal being", the *ens ut sic*, which as the simplest and most universal concept (*conceptus simplicissimus*) is the precise object of metaphysical enquiry'.[25] Discerning a tension between a univocal conception of being on the one hand, and an analogical account of being on the other, Suárez leaves us in no doubt as to which should be preferred. He says:

> we ought not to deny the unity of the concept in order to defend the analogy; rather, if we had to relinquish one or other of them, then this would be analogy, which is uncertain, and not the unity of the concept, which is based on *certain and demonstrable grounds*.[26]

Thus, analogy is downgraded because it is 'uncertain', while the metaphysics of being is preferable because it is based on 'certain and demonstrable grounds'. The anticipation of Cartesianism here is clearly evident, and it is because of these shifts that Jean-Luc Marion has spoken of a 'univocist drift that analogy undergoes with Suárez and others'.[27]

For Balthasar, what is of fundamental importance here is the fact that Suárez effaces the distinction between theology and metaphysics. Traditionally, the subject matter of metaphysics was the created Being of created beings, while the subject matter of theology was God. But once the ontological difference and the *analogia entis* have been sacrificed in favour of a single univocal concept of 'Being' shared by both God and creatures, then the distinction between theology and metaphysics is dissolved, and the way is thus opened for the modern metaphysics that was to follow. God becomes the object of metaphysics, and metaphysics itself proceeds on the basis of an immanent, worldly methodology. In this context, the revolutionary epistemological shift inaugurated by Descartes, which we have earlier characterised as being inherently atheistic, comes to appear much less surprising. Indeed, Descartes's methodological revolution appears to bring to final fruition tendencies that had been developing for several centuries in the thought of such figures as Cajetan and Suárez. If the significance of Descartes lay in the fact that he was the first to produce an a-theological methodological framework, it can be seen that the way was prepared for this by developments within theology itself. As Balthasar says: 'once freed from the external theological discipline of faith, and of the schools, what Suárez pursues with the complete naivety of the schoolman, becomes … the direct foundation for modern metaphysics from Descartes, Spinoza and Leibniz to Kant and Hegel'.[28]

As this would suggest, the theological shifts enacted by Duns Scotus and his successors had wide-ranging ramifications, which were felt far beyond the bounds of theology. For one thing, as Catherine Pickstock has pointed out, the dissolution of God's ontological transcendence gave rise to a 'desymbolization' of the universe.[29] Not only is God's 'existence' now understood in worldly terms, such that language may be used of God in a straightforwardly univocal way, but humanity's experience of the world itself is correspondingly 'flattened'. This is a process that has been extensively discussed by Charles Taylor.[30] He illustrates how the world was once a place that participated in all its aspects in a 'higher reality'. Time itself was not unilinear, but temporal time co-existed with and sometimes overlapped with, or at least drew closer to, spiritual time. In these and various other ways, our experience of reality came to be flattened. The world came to be understood as self-explanatory, as a place in which all was potentially open to view and in which time itself became unitary and linear. Furthermore, once a flattened, one-dimensional ontological world has been inaugurated, one can see how this would give rise to the modern philosophical mode of 'representation'. A world in which there are different levels of ontology and different modes of time cannot unproblematically be 'represented' in language. There are various modes of indirect communication, such as analogical language, liturgical performance, narrative and so forth, but none of these claims to provide a direct representation. On the other hand, a unitary ontological world is one in which a direct representation is much less problematic. God can be referred to in a direct univocal way, and if this turns out to be problematic, then the solution is not to find alternative ways of talking of God but, rather, to give up talking of God altogether.

And it is not only God who can be represented in univocal speech, but the world in all its aspects and, indeed, truth itself. As Alliez puts it: 'Politically, economically, from a public as well as a private point of view, *representation has become absolute*.'[31] When representation comes to the fore in this way, it brings into prominence that which is represented and that which represents, namely, the abstract concepts of subject and object. For if *ens* is, as

Duns Scotus says, 'the first natural object of our understanding', then this *object* has to be perceived by a *subject*. Herein lies the appearance of a neutral epistemological distinction between subject and object, *prior to any theological consideration*.[32] Such shifts are often taken for granted as being developments in a teleological process of human maturation. But we can see here how they arose directly out of contingent shifts within theology and the specific medieval move of overcoming the ontological difference. Such developments are what have led many contemporary scholars to come to regard Duns Scotus as being in some sense the 'founder' of modernity. Alliez, for instance, says that '[w]hat can be seen to be constituted … is a thought whose moving edges end up leading to that scientific revolution destined to make an "epoch" of our modernity'.[33]

Indeed, Alliez detects a line of continuity running from Duns Scotus to Kant, and thus deems Kant to be the 'last Scotist'. We have seen how Duns Scotus's dissolution of the ontological difference resulted both in God being ontologically 'domesticated' and in God being epistemologically pushed further away into an unknowable abyss. This abyss reaches its apotheosis in Kant, who deems knowledge of God to be beyond the reach of metaphysics; it 'ends up delivering the transcendental a priori of a God already so inaccessible to reason that the revelation functions as an object (*supplet vicem objecti*), a pure object of faith, a "thing in itself" and not one for us.'[34] Furthermore, if Duns Scotus initiated the break with Aristotle, then Kant brings that break to completion. He marks the temporal and brilliant end of this revolution:

> when the categorical diverting of the divine to which the dynamics of transcendence lent its voice is no longer anything but time, empty form,… no longer existing 'in itself' except within the relation between being and cognition, within the a priori foundation of the object of prefigured being.[35]

In summary, then, we can see that with the inauguration of a single level of ontology, the foundations of an 'immanent' world-view are being laid, within which an immanent reality may be neutrally observed and 'represented'. The world is no longer perceived as participating in a higher ontological order, but is self-sufficient and self-explanatory. In such a world, analogy, poetry, narrative and rhetoric become superfluous, dangerous even (as far as epistemology is concerned), and representation, observation and the scientific method become epistemologically privileged. It is not difficult to see how, in such a world, atheism becomes inevitable. As there is only a single level of ontology, God cannot be seen to transcend the ontology of this world, but must somehow be fitted in – given a function and location – with the ontology of this world. As such, God becomes a 'thing' (albeit a supreme thing) among others in this world. But such a God is not only liable to become incredible or unbelievable (a 'big thing' that soon becomes too obviously a projection of 'ordinary things'), but also, as the world becomes more self-explanatory and self-sufficient, increasingly superfluous. In such a world, atheism becomes almost irresistible.

It should be noted that not all commentators wish to lay the blame (or credit) for these innovations solely at the feet of Duns Scotus.[36] But the identification of the specific innovatory figure(s) is less important than the fact that there is a widespread conviction that the origins of modernity and, by implication, atheism itself, lie within theology. As befitting a negative and parasitic term, 'atheism' did not arise autonomously as an independent mode of thought, but emerged as a result of certain intellectual moves within theology and resulting changes in the prevailing conception of theism. Modern atheism was the rejection of a specific form of theism, a form of theism that can be understood only in the context of the ontological and epistemological shifts we have here been discussing. Furthermore, our discussion has helped us to come to a greater understanding of certain observations we noted at the outset. It is now easier to see why atheism and modernity are so deeply linked. In the light of the analysis here presented, we can see why each is almost inconceivable without the other. It is also now easier to see the significance of 'atheism' being a negative and parasitic term; we have seen why it is almost impossible to understand the modern (or any) form of atheism without having a proper understanding of the particular form of theism against which it is reacting.

What does all of this imply for the contemporary debate between theism and atheism? Is there any sense in which the foregoing analysis, in this and previous chapters, constitutes an argument 'against' atheism? I shall return to this question in more detail in Chapter 8. But for the time being, it is sufficient to note that I do not believe this to be so. I think it is perfectly possible to be persuaded by the broad contours of the analysis that has been developed here without it necessarily resulting in a rejection of atheism or a conversion to theism. On the other hand, I do think that our analysis, if accepted, cannot but weaken the force of a certain *kind* of atheism and a certain *kind* of argument in defence of atheism. Those analyses that proceed on the basis of it being taken for granted that a 'modern' theism is the only kind of theism there is or has been, and advance their arguments as though those arguments are themselves without a history and without a context, are, I believe, the kind of analyses whose force would be weakened by the line of interpretation developed here. Furthermore, we have seen that modern theism and modern atheism share far more than their devotees often credit (a common definition of God, a common understanding of truth, a common epistemological procedure). What our analysis has exposed, I believe, is that these shared assumptions themselves are contingent, have a history and may be called into question. When they are indeed called into question, this cannot but have detrimental effects for *both* modern theism *and* modern atheism. This is to raise a much bigger question of what, potentially, might come after both of them. But this is to anticipate a discussion that will, for now, be deferred.

Chapter 5

Atheism and the Rise of Biblical Criticism

In the preceding three chapters, we have been examining the philosophical origins of modern atheism. We have traced the birth of atheism in modern thought, identified the specific modern conception of theism that atheists believed themselves to be rejecting, and located the origin of this modern conception of theism as lying within theology itself. But however much the conceptual foundations of atheism were laid in the medieval period, and however much an atheistic epistemology was enacted in the early modern period, we now need to examine the processes by which such latent atheism came to be made explicitly manifest. When examining the ways in which atheism as such was brought into light, we find ourselves turning to intellectual and cultural developments in the nineteenth century in particular. Although we have seen that sceptics, libertines and atheists certainly existed before then, it was not until the nineteenth century that atheism – and religious doubt more generally – became a central and inescapable feature of the cultural landscape. This was the century in which Feuerbach and Marx developed their atheistic explanations of religion; Nietzsche announced the 'death of God'; religious doubt became a recurring theme of poetry and literature; atheists were given official recognition by the state in many European countries and were for the first time admitted to the British Parliament; the new term 'agnosticism' was coined and its 'creed' developed; and John Henry Newman saw the first stirrings of a radical godlessness. In all these ways, therefore, the nineteenth century provided the setting for the explicit emergence of atheism as a visible cultural phenomenon.

Nineteenth-century historians are generally agreed that there were three developments in particular that were perceived as contributing to the decline of religious belief and the growth of atheism and agnosticism: moral considerations (arising from the perceived immorality of theological teachings on, for instance, everlasting punishment); the rise of science and a perceived clash between scientific and theological truths, not least in regard to accounts of creation; and the rise of historical and critical approaches to biblical interpretation. It is these three factors that I want to consider in this and the following two chapters. At the outset, however, it is important to note that these challenges should not be understood in isolation from the developments we have been tracing up to this point. On the contrary, we shall see that moral considerations, scientific discoveries and biblical criticism were damaging to theism, *precisely because of* the modern Enlightenment form of theism that was then dominant and which we have thus far been elucidating. Had theism not taken this distinctively modern turn, it is unlikely that these three factors would have been as damaging to theism as in fact they were. Indeed, it is the burden of this and the following chapters to argue precisely that.

With this in mind, therefore, I shall begin by considering the specific challenge presented by the new critical approaches to the interpretation of the Bible, which became so prominent in the nineteenth century, and which did so much to shake the citadel of faith. In doing so, however, I also want to consider a question of at least equal importance; namely, how it was that, by the modern period, the Bible had come to be interpreted in such a way as to be so vulnerable to the rise of biblical criticism. For we shall see that there was nothing intrinsic to biblical criticism that made it necessarily an enemy of faith. It was rather that a distinctively 'modern' interpretation of the Bible meant that the results of biblical criticism were more destructive for faith than they might otherwise have been. There is therefore a close link, I shall suggest, between the origins of a modern reception of the Bible and the origins of atheism itself, and the primary purpose of this chapter is to examine the nature of this link.

In order to understand the nature of the challenge to theism presented by biblical criticism, it is necessary to appreciate the particular way in which the Bible had, by the nineteenth century, come to be interpreted, read and understood. To that end, we need, in turn, to illuminate the way in which biblical hermeneutics was related to the epistemological shifts that we have identified and discussed in our earlier chapters. We have seen that the new philosophical epistemology that emerged at the advent of modernity was marked by two characteristics in particular. First, as we observed in Chapter 2, there was an epistemological shift away from tradition-constituted forms of knowledge to ones that were, on the contrary, free from 'contamination' by traditional sources. There were, as we have seen, disagreements as to the sources of this neutral, tradition-free knowledge. Some believed that it resided in the exercise of reason (as exemplified by Descartes in particular), while others maintained that it lay in empirical sense data (as exemplified by Locke in particular). But in many ways, what united them was more important than what divided them; namely, that they were both concerned to free epistemology from any 'inherited' or 'received' knowledge. This came under suspicion primarily because it was 'uncertain', 'unreliable' or 'imprecise'. This did not in itself constitute a rejection of tradition or of religion as such (both Descartes and Locke were theists), but it did mean that tradition and/or religion had to be grounded in and justified by 'certain' knowledge, and thus had to be independently verifiable.

This leads on to the second major characteristic of modern epistemology, namely, its quest for 'certainty' and 'precision', which increasingly marks modern thought in all fields of endeavour. In this respect, Stephen Toulmin has argued that modernity had two separate and identifiable beginnings. The first was a literary and humanistic form of modernity, as embodied in the writings of Montaigne and Shakespeare, which began a century or so before a second philosophic and scientific modernity, as embodied in the work of Descartes and Newton. For Toulmin, modernity could potentially have developed in either direction, but, as it happens, the philosophic and scientific manifestation of modernity eclipsed and triumphed over the literary and humanistic form of modernity. He says that there were historical reasons as to why this was so, but the practical effect was a generalised elevation of the permanent over the transitory. This was embodied, Toulmin says, in four transitions: from the oral to the written; from the local to the general; from the particular to the universal; and from the timely to the timeless. Furthermore, disciplines and modes of linguistic practice that were amenable to the development of certainty and precision were elevated above those that were presumed not so to be. Thus, logic, science and mathematics came to be prized above poetry, rhetoric and narrative. As Toulmin observes: 'It is no accident that diagnostics and due process, case ethics and rhetoric, topics and poetics, were sidelined and called in question at the same time.'[1] In general terms, the sciences came to be prized above the humanities and, furthermore, the humanities themselves came to be conducted in an increasingly scientific way.

It may be thought that such an intellectual climate was uncongenial to religion. One might envisage a situation in which a cultural regime prizing logic, science and mathematics pits itself against a religion stubbornly clinging to its discourses of poetry and narrative. But scholars such as Amos Funkenstein and Michael Buckley have argued that the modern contribution to the demise of religion was more indirect than this. They have shown how religion itself adapted to this new episteme by transposing its own discourse into a propositional, scientific and mathematical key. So much so that the distinction between theology and science became blurred. Funkenstein speaks of 'a peculiar idiom, or discourse, in which theological concerns were expressed in terms of secular knowledge, and scientific concerns were expressed in theological terms'.[2] Furthermore, in this 'fusion' of theology and science, it was clear that science was accorded methodological priority. In many ways, this was inevitable given the trend identified by Toulmin, with the downgrading of poetry, rhetoric and narrative, and the elevation of logic, mathematics and science. So theology now had to be justified in scientific terms (neutrally, rationally), and theological statements themselves took on a 'scientific' character (i.e. they became empirical propositions or hypotheses). Thus, as Christian doctrine came increasingly to be understood as being straightforwardly propositional, God came increasingly to be referred to by means of 'clear and distinct' ideas, and theological language in general became increasingly univocal, a development traced in more detail in the last chapter.

But there were also some very significant implications for the practice of biblical hermeneutics. In particular, one result was that the Bible came to be interpreted in an increasingly historical, scientific and mathematical way. In the early modern period, the Bible came to be seen as being an embodiment of 'literal' truth, and this meant that it was viewed as being historical in all its parts. So much so, in fact, that the historical truth of Scripture was widely accepted as being a *sine qua non* of Christian faith. Furthermore, it was widely assumed that this had always been so. Christians believed the Bible to be 'true', and to the modern mind a true narrative was one that described events that had actually happened in an historical sense. It occurred to few that such an understanding of what it meant for a text to be true was actually of relatively recent origin. In fact, it represented a striking departure from earlier understandings, most notably those of the Early Church fathers. Among the few who did recognise this was the then Bishop of Exeter, Fredrick Temple, who, in his Bampton Lectures of 1884, pointed out that the Early Church fathers had a much more complex and variegated account of what it meant for the Scriptures to be true. Five years later, Charles Gore, in his *Lux Mundi* essay, made a similar point.[3] It will be worthwhile for us to give some consideration to these earlier understandings of scriptures, not least because it will help to elucidate the ways in which the modern emphasis on the 'historical' and 'literal' sense of scripture was a distinct and novel development.

As J. N. D. Kelly has emphasised, the approach of the Early Church fathers towards scripture was replete with complex forms of hermeneutical exegesis. In particular, he identifies two forms which were frequently employed – typology and allegory – and it is important to understand something of the distinction between the two. In the case of allegorical exegesis, Kelly says:

> the sacred text is treated as a mere symbol, or allegory, of spiritual truths. The literal, historical sense, if it was to be regarded at all, plays a relatively minor role, and the aim of the exegete is to elicit the moral, theological or mystical meaning which each passage, indeed even each word, is presumed to contain.[4]

Augustine was a prominent, although by no means the only, practitioner of such exegesis.

In contrast, typological exegesis worked along quite different lines:

> Essentially it was a technique for bringing out the correspondence between the two Testaments, and took as its guiding principle the idea that the events and personages of the Old were 'types' of, i.e. prefigured and anticipated, the events and personages of the New. The typologist took history seriously; it was the scene of the progressive unfolding of God's consistent redemptive purpose.[5]

While this was by no means a straightforwardly literal way of reading scripture, it can be seen that this approach nonetheless carried a stronger emphasis on the 'historical' nature of scripture, as Kelly again makes clear:

> typology, unlike allegory, had no temptation to undervalue, much less dispense with, the literal sense of Scripture. It was precisely because the events there delineated had really happened on the plane of history that they could be interpreted by the eye of faith as trustworthy pointers to God's future dealings with men.[6]

Thus there was no doubting that the stories of Moses and his dealing with the people of Israel, for instance, were historically true, but in a typological reading the main concern was to elicit the ways in which these stories prefigured those of Jesus and his dealings with God's people. This exegesis was applied throughout the whole of the Old Testament, so that all these books had to be shown to be in some sense an anticipation of the truth that was later revealed fully in Christ.

Kelly says that of these two approaches, typological exegesis was the one that was most characteristically Christian, not least because of its distinctively Biblical view of history. But it would be a mistake to view the relationship between these two methods of exegesis as being mutually exclusive. Frequently, they were combined, so that in a particular instance it was less a question of whether an allegorical or a typological method of exegesis was being employed and more a question of which method was dominant. From what has just been said, it should be obvious that, in instances where an allegorical approach was dominant, there was a tendency for the literal or historical meaning of scripture to be relegated to a position of only secondary importance. Perhaps the most well-known practitioner of a predominantly allegorical approach to scripture was the third-century biblical scholar Origen:

> An admirer of Philo, he regarded Scripture as a vast ocean, or (using a different image) forest, of mysteries; it was impossible to fathom, or even perceive, them all, but one could be sure that every line, even every word, the sacred authors wrote were replete with meaning. Formally he distinguished three levels of signification in Scripture, corresponding to the three parts of which human nature is composed: the bodily, the psychic and the spiritual. The first was the straightforward historical sense, and was useful for simple people; the second was the moral sense, or the lesson of the text for the will; the third was the mystical sense with relation to Christ, the Church or the great truths of the faith.[7]

Although Origen appears to employ a somewhat different classification in practice, it is clear that in his scheme the literal or historical meaning is of least theological significance. Indeed, he is even open to the possibility of taking a step further than this, arguing that in certain instances a literal reading of scripture is positively to be avoided in cases where

> it would not be proper to take literally a narrative or a command unworthy of God… His rule for determining whether the literal or the figurative sense was the more correct was that whatever can be shown to be inconsistent, if taken literally, with propriety of life or purity of doctrine must be taken figuratively. In a general way he thought that no interpretation could be true which did not promote the love of God or the love of man.[8]

It has to be admitted that Origen was one of the most promiscuous practitioners of the allegorical method, and it has also to be admitted that there was a reaction on the part of the Antiochenes against allegorism in general in the fourth and fifth centuries. Nonetheless, if other exegetes were more cautious in their approach than was Origen, it is still evident that, in the Early Church, there was a complex and multi-levelled approach to the interpretation of Scripture that was clearly something other than straightforward literalism. For the Early Church fathers, the typological, allegorical and spiritual meaning of the text was more important and carried a more profound level of truth than did the literal meaning. Indeed, this was a point that Charles Gore emphasised in the aforementioned essay in *Lux Mundi* (1889). Although he was by no means disposed to adopt Origen's hermeneutical methodology in its entirety, he was very clear that the church had not

> committed herself to any dogmatic definitions of the meaning of inspiration. It is remarkable indeed that Origen's almost reckless mysticism, and his accompanying repudiation of the historical character of large parts of the

> narrative of the Old Testament, and some parts of the New, though it did not gain acceptance, and indeed has no right to it (for it had no sound basis), on the other hand never raised the Church to contrary definitions. Nor is it only Origen who disputed the historical character of parts of the narrative of Holy Scripture. Clement before him in Alexandria, and the mediaeval Anselm in the West, treat the seven days' creation as allegory and not history. Athanasius speaks of paradise as a 'figure'… From this, it cannot be denied that the mystical method, as a whole tended to the depreciation of the historical sense, in comparison with the spiritual teaching which it conveyed.[9]

If such approaches had been carried over from the medieval into the modern period, it is interesting to speculate as to whether the advent of biblical criticism would have had quite the disturbing impact that it in fact had.

But such approaches did not survive, and we have already considered some of the developments that would explain why they did not. Following Funkenstein, we have seen how the rapidly developing scientific method in the early modern period was scarcely distinguished from theology; rather, the two were 'fused' into one seamless discourse. Furthermore, we have seen that, within this seamless discourse, precision and certainty were deemed to be of paramount importance. The equivocal, imprecise, figurative and mystical were all distrusted as being liable to lead one astray. When such a mind applied itself to the study of scripture, it was inevitable that symbolic, typological and allegorical readings would be distrusted as being imprecise, vague and arbitrary. In the interests of precision and certainty, it would have appeared quite proper to read the texts in a literal and historical way. Furthermore, with the 'fusion' of theology and science, it would have seemed natural to read the bible in much the same way as one would a scientific treatise; namely, as the straightforward recording of empirical fact. Such a development was given further impetus by what Charles Taylor has called the 'homogenization of time' in modernity, whereby time comes to be conceived in a linear and one-dimensional way. As we noted in Chapter 4, the medieval world held to a conception of time, wherein there were different 'orders' of time corresponding to secular, sacred and other dimensions of being. So it was possible for scriptural events to have 'happened', to be 'historical', albeit not necessarily within this order of time or this order of being. Within this structure of ontological difference, the scriptural reader was spared the straightforward antinomy between literal truth or falsehood. As Taylor points out, once time is homogenised, biblical events had either happened literally/historically or they hadn't happened at all.[10] So in a modern episteme that prized precision and certainty and distrusted the analogical and mystical, it was inevitable that the exegetical approach of the Early Church fathers would be superseded by an alternative one in which the 'literal' meaning of the text was all-important.

As is well known, the most notorious manifestation of this shift came in the person of James Ussher (1581–1656), distinguished scientist, scholar and Archbishop of Armagh. He was perhaps the most egregious example of one who saw fit to interpret the Bible in the manner of a mathematical and scientific text book. In *The Annals* (1650–4), in particular, Ussher elided the distinction between the scientific and astronomical on the one hand, and the scriptural and theological on the other, and thus calculated that the world must have been created in the year 4004 BC.[11] Ussher was a respected scholar of distinction, and his calculations were taken seriously as something akin to a revelation. That this was so is indicated by the fact that English translations of the Bible from this point onwards frequently included Ussher's dating of the event of creation as an editorial interpellation. Charles Darwin confessed that for many years he was ignorant of the editorial status of this dating, assuming that it was actually a part of the scriptural text.[12] Even among those who did not labour under this misapprehension, Ussher's calculations were believed to be almost as authoritative as the scriptural texts on which they were based. This was to have important repercussions, not least with respect to nineteenth-century discoveries in geology, as we shall see in the next chapter.

But the significance of this for our purpose here is to show how much more is now at stake in the literal and historical truth of scripture. Intrinsic to faith is a belief that its scriptural texts are literally and historically true in all their parts. Religion, it seems, now has to stand or fall on the literal truth of its scriptural texts.

The scene is now set for an understanding of why the rise of biblical criticism in the nineteenth century came as such a devastating blow to the faith of the religious, and why it was such an important factor in the growth of atheism. The birthplace of this new critical approach was in what is now known as Germany, and some of the earliest practitioners were such figures as Johann Gottfried Eichhorn, Ferdinand Christian Baur and Julius Wellhausen. Their work was slow to penetrate the domain of English scholarship. The young Edward Pusey visited Gottingen in the 1820s and acquainted himself with some of this work, but he was exceptional and he by no means emerged as an apologist for the methods of German biblical criticism. By the time *Essays and Reviews* was published in 1860, several of the essays examined the approaches of the German critics and thus brought them to a wider audience. Gradually, translations of their works began to appear. Particularly influential was Wellhausen's *Prolegomena to the History of Israel*, an early version of which was published in Germany in 1878, followed by a revised version in 1883 and an English translation in 1885. The underlying principle of this and other approaches was to treat the Bible in the same manner as any other object of scholarly inquiry. In the infamous words of the Victorian English theologian, Benjamin Jowett, the central precept was to 'interpret the Scripture like any other book'.[13]

But when this precept was followed, all sorts of discoveries were made which conflicted with what had by now become the assumptions of orthodoxy. It is not our purpose to develop a detailed narration of these discoveries; it will suffice to note that they resulted in revisions to the date of authorship of many books, the discovery of composite rather than single authorship of other books and, in some cases, the questioning of the identities of the authors themselves. Furthermore, these discoveries carried implications for the historicity of many of the narratives contained therein. For instance, in cases where the dates and authorships of books were vastly different from what had previously been assumed, one result was that it now appeared highly unlikely that many of the narratives of those books could be strictly historical. They were written too far away from the events themselves and by individuals who could in no sense be thought of as eye-witnesses. Furthermore, such objective critical approaches revealed internal contradictions within the texts themselves, thus further undermining their historicity.

This may have mattered less to readers of the Bible who were well versed in the exegetical methods of typology and allegory, but to the nineteenth-century mind, the 'truth' of the Scriptures had come to be equated with the historical veracity of its narratives. Some contemporary theologians were well aware of the folly of this equation and attempted to undo it. Indeed, this was the burden of Benjamin Jowett's contribution to *Essays and Reviews* (1860), and his underlying motive was well expressed when he said:

> as the time has come when it is no longer possible to ignore the results of criticism, it is of importance that Christianity should be seen to be in harmony with them. That objections to some received views should be valid, and yet that they should be always held up as the objections of infidels, is a mischief to the Christian cause. It is a mischief that critical observations, which any intelligent man can make for himself, should be ascribed to atheism or unbelief. It would be a strange and almost incredible thing that the Gospel, which at first made war only on the vices of mankind, should now be opposed to one of the rarest and highest of human virtues, the love of truth.[14]

In expressing such views, Jowett was swimming against the contemporary tide, as the hostile and high-profile reactions against *Essays and Reviews* testified. Nonetheless, Jowett's gentle but penetrating efforts were soon to be eclipsed by those of a much less subtle exponent of a similar line of analysis.

John W. Colenso was an Anglican African missionary bishop. In a previous incarnation, he had been a mathematical scholar at Cambridge and a Fellow of St John's College. His *Colenso's Arithmetic* had established itself as the standard school mathematical text book and was widely used throughout the country. As well as being a mathematician, however, he was also an ordained Anglican clergyman. On marriage, he was obliged to resign his fellowship at St John's (fellows of Oxford and Cambridge colleges were then required to be unmarried in a remaining echo of the colleges' monastic origins). As was common, he then became rector of a parish church, the patronage of which belonged to his college. It was not long, however, before he was called to high clerical office, and in 1853 he was chosen to be Bishop of Natal and thus to lead a new missionary diocese in southern Africa. Although there were some reservations expressed at what some perceived to be Colenso's sympathies with the controversial theology of F. D. Maurice, this hurdle was duly negotiated, and Colenso and his family departed for Natal later that year. In many respects, Colenso was a tremendous success as a missionary bishop. He developed a great affection and respect for the Zulu people among whom he worked, and acquired a deep knowledge of their language and culture. He produced the first Zulu–English dictionary and also translated the Gospels into Zulu. He undertook his missionary activity sensitively and argued, controversially, that the requirements of Christian morality ought to accommodate Zulu traditions and customs. Although regarded with suspicion by many of the white settlers and colonial authorities, he was highly regarded by the Zulu people, who bestowed upon him the title of Sobantu ('father of the people').[15]

None of which suggested that he was to become one of the most notorious controversialists in the field of biblical criticism. But it was his work among the Zulus that indirectly brought this about. As Colenso himself explained:

> While translating the story of the Flood, I have had a simple-minded, but intelligent, native – one with the docility of a child, but the reasoning powers of mature age –

> look up, and ask, 'Is all that true? Do you really believe that all this happened thus...?'.

Being acquainted with recent geological discoveries, he went on:

> I felt that I dared not, as a servant of the God of Truth, urge my brother man to believe that, which I did not myself believe, which I know to be untrue, as a matter-of-fact historical narrative. I gave him, however, such a reply as satisfied him for the time, without throwing any general discredit upon the general veracity of the Bible history.[16]

In this, of course, Colenso was sharing in the widespread disquiet felt by many educated clergyman in the late nineteenth century, as was given expression in the passage written by Benjamin Jowett, from which we have just quoted. There was a feeling that clergymen were being placed in a morally intolerable position in being asked to profess with their lips what they did not believe in their hearts. This was likely to lead not only to moral and psychological anguish on the part of these clergymen themselves, but also to the alienation from Christianity of educated men and women who could not assent to what orthodox belief appeared to require of them. If orthodox Christianity demanded of the faithful that they believe every word of the Bible to be literal truth, then this was something that they were simply unable to believe. Colenso said that unless these issues were addressed directly, such people would drift into 'irreligion and practical atheism'.[17] For the sake of clerical integrity, intellectual credibility and the witness to Christian truth itself, it therefore became increasingly clear to many that the truth of Christianity on the one hand, and a commitment to the literal and historical truth of the Bible on the other, would have to be uncoupled.

In this conviction, Colenso was at one with many other clerics and theologians of the time. But it was the manner in which he sought to give practical expression to this conviction that set him apart from the rest. In principle, of course, there were numerous ways in which such a conviction might be apologetically promoted.

It might have been pointed out that such biblical literalism was quite at odds with the exegetical approaches of the Early Church fathers, as we ourselves have just noted. It might have been argued that undue literalism gave rise to a spiritually impoverished form of faith, such that divine truth was being occluded. It might have been argued that historical, textual and exegetical research rendered literalist readings of scripture implausible. But Colenso decided to emphasise none of these. Although his own approach did incorporate elements of the last, his chosen methodology revealed a prioritisation of a blend of empirical–scientific–mathematical presuppositions. For Colenso evidently believed that the strongest line of argument was to show, mathematically and beyond doubt, that many of the narratives recorded in the Bible – especially in the Old Testament – could not *possibly* be true. In such an approach, Colenso showed himself to be a product of the very mindset against which he was battling. In other words, his primary aim was not to show that theological truth was best expressed through means other than that of literal history (although this was something with which he undoubtedly now agreed); rather, his aim was to show that if one accepted the historical-literal approach, the Bible would be rendered nonsensical. He wanted to demonstrate, with *certainty*, that the Bible could not possibly represent literal truth; and then, having demonstrated that, proceed to consider ways in which the Bible *may* be seen as a vehicle of divine truth.

In this, he now brought his mathematical skills to bear on the biblical texts in *The Pentateuch and Book of Joshua Critically Examined* (1862–4). His aim was to demonstrate – on the basis of their own internal evidence – that these scriptural books could not possibly represent literal truth. On the basis of the facts and figures contained therein, he claimed that the accounts were mathematically self-contradictory. It will suffice to quote just one passage to get a sense of Colenso's distinctive mathematical approach to biblical criticism. On the basis of the following: first, the requirements laid down by the Law for the fulfilment of the priestly function; second, the number recorded of those who participated in the Exodus; and third, the record that there were three priests at the time of the Exodus, Colenso asks:

> Yet how was it possible that two or three men should have discharged all these duties for such a vast multitude? The single work, of offering the double sacrifice for women after child-birth, must have utterly overpowered three Priests, though engaged without cessation from morning to night. As we have seen,… the births among two millions of people may be reckoned as, at least, 250 a day, for which, consequently, 500 sacrifices (250 burnt-offerings and 250 sin-offerings) would have had to be offered daily. Looking at the directions in *L*[eviticus] i, iv, we can scarcely allow less than *five minutes* for each sacrifice; so that these sacrifices alone, if offered separately, would have taken 2,500 minutes or nearly 42 hours, and could not have been offered in a single day of twelve hours, though each of the three Priests had been employed in the one sole incessant labour of offering them, without a moment's rest or intermission.[18]

The three volumes of Colenso's *Pentateuch* were filled with calculations of this sort, leading many to perceive his methodological approach as being somewhat akin to that of Ussher. But whereas Ussher had accepted the results of his calculations as being true, Colenso's calculations were conducted precisely in order to show that they could not possibly be so. As Owen Chadwick has remarked: 'It was the ancient school of biblical calculation topsy-turvy, used to confute and not to prove.'[19] But although his route was laboured, his destination was clear, and in his expression of it he was unequivocal:

> From the above considerations it seems to follow, that the account of the Exodus of the Israelites, as given in the Pentateuch, whatever real foundation it may have had in the ancient history of the people, is mixed up, at all events, with so great an amount of contradictory matter, that it cannot be regarded as historically true, so as to be appealed to, as absolute, incontestable matter of fact, in Church formularies. For, let it be observed, the objections, which have been produced, are not such as touch on only one or

> two points of the story. They affect the entire substance of it, and, until they are removed, they make it impossible for a thoughtful person to receive, without further enquiry, any considerable portion of it, as *certainly true* in an historical point of view.[20]

Although Colenso undertook his work in order to save the well-informed from falling into atheism, for as long as the central connection between the truth of Christianity and the historical veracity of its scriptures remained intact, then it inevitably appeared to some that Colenso and other biblical critics had 'disproved' the Bible and, indeed, Christianity itself. But the real difficulty, of course, lay in Christianity having come to accept an historical and quasi-scientific understanding of its scriptures in the first place. The great paradox was that Christianity had become a victim of its own adaptation to the prevailing cultural and intellectual episteme. We have seen how this was the case with the concept of God. When Christianity adapted itself (however unconsciously) to a specifically modern epistemology, this entailed the development of a 'domesticated' idea of God as a 'being' that the modern world itself would later deem to be untenable. A similar process was enacted in relation to biblical hermeneutics. Another aspect of Christianity's collusion with the prevailing mentality was a shift towards an increasingly literal-historical understanding of scripture. Again, however, far from securing its position within the modern episteme, this shift turned out fatally to weaken Christianity when the tools of modern rationality and critical scholarship exposed such an understanding of scripture to be untenable. In other words, collusion with the prevailing cultural and intellectual milieu had damaged rather than buttressed Christianity.

But this is to raise the question of how decisive a factor biblical criticism was in the rise and development of atheism. There were clearly other important factors at play, most notably those that we shall discuss in the following two chapters. But it seems likely that, for at least some individuals, the impact of biblical criticism would have been decisive in their profession of atheism. As Owen Chadwick has observed, in the early 1860s, 'a young man like

Leslie Stephen thought he must either believe every word of the Bible or not be a Christian'.[21] It is difficult to determine the extent to which Stephen was, in this respect, representative of others. Writing elsewhere, Chadwick himself appears to qualify the extent to which Stephen's attitude was emblematic of a wider intellectual trend, and further suggests that his attitude was perhaps more nuanced than has often been portrayed. He says that Stephen

> is sometimes represented as losing his faith because he could no longer believe in a universal flood. He did this during the 60s when for thirty years most educated men had ceased to believe in a universal flood. From Stephen's own descriptions we sense a more subtle attitude. It was less a question of intellectual dissent than of moral repudiation. Here was he, a clergyman who did not believe in stories in the Bible, placed by his Church in a situation where the liturgy compelled him to read such stories as though they were true. He could do it no longer. He could not assume, as his successors could assume, that the congregation would not for one moment suppose him to take the story of Noah to be history.[22]

Chadwick seems to be suggesting that it was not so much the case that Stephen thought the non-historicity of the Bible to be incompatible with Christianity; rather, he felt that the fact that he did not believe in the historicity of the Bible was incompatible with his position in a church which seemed to expect him to speak and behave as though he did.

Such quandaries and intellectual agonies now belong to a bygone age. It is undoubtedly the case that, in the twentieth and twenty-first centuries, biblical criticism and doubts about the literal truth of scripture are much less likely to be cited as a factor in the confession of atheism. To a large extent, this is because neither theist nor atheist wishes to regard a commitment to the historical accuracy of scriptures as being an essential requirement of Christian belief. In this respect, the efforts of Temple, Gore,

Colenso and others appears to have borne fruit. Within theology itself, there has been an increasing awareness of its own historical error in adapting to modern epistemological procedures, including its commitment to the literal and historical truth of its scriptures. For many contemporary theologians, the historicity or otherwise of particular scriptural narratives has become something of an irrelevance. What matters is the power of the scriptural narratives to convey spiritual truths, not whether the events narrated therein actually happened.

This is not to suggest that there is a consensus in contemporary theology that the scriptures should be regarded as true in only a metaphorical sense (although some theologians undoubtedly do think this). It is rather to point out that theologians have been drawing attention to the ways in which modernity saw an impoverishment of the 'literal' sense of scripture so that it came to be understood solely in terms of historical description. Gerard Loughlin, for instance, has written of a 'general diremption of the literal sense in the modern period: between the literal-as-written and literal-as-historical'.[23] Once the literal comes to be understood in so monochrome a way, it then becomes possible to contrast the 'literal' with the 'metaphorical' as two separate and alternative readings between which one must choose. But for pre-modern theologians, as we have already intimated, this was to be forced with a false dichotomy which could only lead to an impoverished view of scripture. Rowan Williams has pointed out that for Aquinas,

> the literal sense [of scripture] is not dependent on a belief that all scriptural propositions uncomplicatedly depict real states of affairs detail by detail; it can and does include metaphor within the literary movement that leads us into the movement of God with the time of human biography. In this way, Thomas [Aquinas] sketches an understanding of the literal that allows for a plurality of *genres* within it; it is the failure to see and to develop this insight that has led to those narrow and sterile definitions of the literal sense against which recent hermeneutics has so sharply reacted.[24]

So for Williams it is a mistake to suppose that readers of scripture are confronted with a straightforward choice between an historically literal reading and a merely metaphorical reading. Rather, a literal reading of scripture is attentive to the genres of metaphor, allegory and typology within it, and by no means entails that its narratives are historical descriptions.

To delve further into these suggestive comments would be to take us into the more complex terrain of contemporary biblical hermeneutics. But even these brief quotations give us some sense of the direction in which contemporary theology has been moving. It appears to be taking a half-turn back to the church fathers and their practices of typological and allegorical exegesis as being more revelatory than 'mere' literalism-as-history. This is not simply because it has been forced to do so by the impact of biblical criticism. As the comments of Loughlin and Williams show, there is a conviction that more nuanced readings of scripture are more theologically rewarding and revealing, and are more in line with the orthodox tradition itself. In this sense, the reading of scripture as 'literal history' can be seen to be a temporary aberration, but an aberration that brought with it many damaging effects. Not only did it lead to a more sterile rendering of faith itself, but it also made that faith vulnerable to atheistic attack when biblical criticism showed such a reading to be untenable.

So while there may be seen to be an intimate link between atheism on the one hand and biblical criticism on the other, we may conclude that it was a link that was manifested in a specific historical period – that of modernity – was relatively short-lived and has certainly now waned.

Chapter 6

Atheism and the Rise of Science

At some point in history, a seed was planted from which would sprout an indelible mental connection between 'atheism' and 'science'. Although the strength of this connection has weakened in recent years, it has by no means been entirely dissolved and to some lesser extent lives on still. As to its origin, there can be little doubt that it both made its appearance and also reached its zenith in the second half of the nineteenth century. Observing that 'doubt' was a much more widespread phenomenon (in Britain at least) in 1885 than it had been in 1855, Owen Chadwick says that

> in 1885 many persons, whether they doubted or affirmed, blamed 'science' for this change in opinion. Some of them talked as though 'science' alone was responsible. And among those who blamed science, some fastened upon the name of Charles Darwin as the symbol, or centre, or intellectual force, of an entire development of the sciences as they came to bear upon the truth of religion.[1]

What had given rise to this situation? In some senses, it was a puzzling phenomenon, for science was hardly new. However revolutionary and influential were Darwin's discoveries and hypotheses, he himself can hardly be credited with the creation of science as such. Furthermore, in the already long history of the natural sciences, there had been very little portent of the conflict that was to come between it and theology. On the contrary, the relationship between theology and science had long been held to be one of harmonious amity. This amity was perhaps given its most symbolic expression in the figure of the eighteenth-century scientist *par excellence*, Sir Isaac Newton. No one doubted Newton's stature as a scientist; indeed, his discoveries had ramifications that were nothing short of revolutionary. At the same time, however, few thought that his work served in any way to undermine theology. Certainly, they led some to reconsider inherited conceptions of divine activity and notions of divine providence, but these were generally seen as theological as well as scientific advances. Many saw Newton as having, in a way, furthered the reach of divine revelation; he had exposed the rules by which God decreed that the world should be governed, and the wonder of them was seen to redound to the credit of divine genius. In this sense, Newton was seen to have enhanced the sense of awe and wonder with which the faithful worshipped God. To a great extent Newton shared this conception of his work and, it should be remembered, for all of his scientific endeavours, he still found time to write substantial books of theology. However much the verdict of posterity has decreed otherwise, Newton himself was inclined to regard his theological works as being on the same level of importance as his scientific works, at least in terms of their intrinsic integrity, if not of their wider disciplinary ramifications. Although his work in these two spheres proceeded by means of differing methodological procedures, there was seen to be a fundamental continuity between them, deriving primarily from the conviction that they shared a common object, albeit viewed from different perspectives. As John Hedley Brooke has commented: 'There would be a degree of artificiality in asking how Newton reconciled his "science" and his "religion", if he saw himself pursing a form of "natural philosophy", in which the two interests were integrated.'[2]

This sense of fundamental harmony between science and religion was further confirmed by the fact that in Newton's day and, indeed, well into the nineteenth century, most of the leading scientific pioneers were themselves ordained priests of the established Church. A prime example of this was the eccentric but pioneering geologist, William Buckland, whose professorship of science at Oxford was combined with his being a clergyman and Canon of Christ Church Cathedral.[3] But however exceptional he was in other respects, in his dual status as a scientist–priest, he was wholly typical. When the relationship between science and theology was perceived as being as harmonious and continuous as it was perceived to be by Newton, it seemed entirely natural that a scientist should also be a priest. It is interesting to compare this with the contemporary outlook, which has a tendency to regard a figure such as John Polkinghorne as an interesting and anomalous curiosity precisely because of his dual role as a scientist and a priest. Such an assessment would have been entirely unintelligible to the pre-Victorian mind, where the two vocations were perceived to be two manifestations of an harmonious whole.

So how did it come about that, within the space of but a few decades, the relationship between science and religion was transformed from amity to enmity to such an extent that science was being blamed for the decline of religion, and scientists and priests were perceived as being perpetually at loggerheads? The transformation and the speed with which it occurred are alike remarkable. But before proceeding to probe this question, it is important to remember the character of the harmonious accord that prevailed between science and religion in the eighteenth century. As we saw Amos Funkenstein to have argued, the early modern period was indeed marked by a 'fusion' of scientific and religious discourse. Far from being perceived as distinct spheres of thought, each with their own methodology, grammar and criteria for truth, they were, on the contrary, perceived as operating on a methodological continuum. Scientific questions were imbued with theological language, and theological truths were expressed in an explicitly scientific way. But we also observed that this apparent unity and harmony was in some ways misleading. For, as we saw Michael Buckley to have argued, the harmonious accord between science and religion had, in fact, been achieved by the methodological surrender of religion to science. We saw, of course, that this 'surrender' was unwitting and unconscious rather than one that was explicitly acknowledged. But Buckley's argument, we saw, was that the surrender was no less real for that. Religious truths were seen to be legitimate insofar as they could be shown to accord with empirical, scientific assumptions; religion itself thought it entirely natural to justify and defend itself on empirical, scientific grounds. As Buckley says 'Science now grounds not only philosophy but theology.'[4]

If this is so, however, then it does cast some considerable light both on the nature of the earlier amity between science and religion and also on the process of its rapid collapse. For what it does suggest is that, however secure and entrenched the accord between science and religion appeared to be, it was in fact utterly precarious in the sense that it depended entirely on science not in any way contradicting religious teaching, something that could not be indefinitely guaranteed. The fact that religion and science had been 'fused' into one seamless whole meant that there could be no mutual accommodation between two distinct spheres of discourse. The continuity between them meant that the two had to be entirely compatible and in accord within a single system of logic. It so happened that Newton's discoveries did not in any way seriously question theological teachings – other than in some of the ways we have already mentioned; and these potential disputes were easily resolved by theological adjustments that theologians themselves were only too happy to concede. But given the advances that science was continually making, it was perhaps to be expected that more serious clashes than this would arise and that when this happened – given the methodological victory that theology had, in principle, already conceded to science – theology would inevitably have to give way. Although this was, in effect, what happened in a very dramatic way with Darwin's discoveries in particular, there were already signs that such shifts were subtly beginning to occur.

For instance, it appears that many university dons (who were, until the late nineteenth century, almost all Anglican priests) were willing to reinterpret belief or even reject outright certain religious doctrines where these conflicted with their scholarly researches, scientific or otherwise. In this respect, Leslie Stephen paints a vivid picture of the 'average Cambridge don of my day' (he was ordained as a deacon in 1855). He describes such a typical figure as

> a sensible and honest man who wished to be both rational and Christian. He was rational enough to see that the old orthodox position was untenable. He did not believe in hell or in 'verbal inspiration' or the 'real presence'. He thought that the controversies on such matters were silly and antiquated and spoke of them with indifference, if not with contempt. But he also thought that religious belief of some kind was necessary or valuable, and considered himself to be a genuine believer. He assumed that somehow the old beliefs could be 'rationalized' or 'spiritualized'. He could accept them in some sense or other but did not ask too closely in what sense. Still less did he go into the ultimate questions of philosophy. He shut his eyes to the great difficulties and took the answer for granted.[5]

This important passage is significant for several reasons. For one thing, it suggests that the intellectual and psychological process of 'accommodation' or 'adaptation' of beliefs in the light of emerging scientific knowledge was well under way, at least among the educated elites, some time before the Darwinian and other high-profile scientific discoveries were revealed with such explosive force. Secondly, however, and more immediately pertinent to the point under discussion, it also reveals something of the character of the process of accommodation itself. There were potentially, of course, various forms that such accommodation could take. In the twentieth century, influenced by certain more-or-less explicitly Wittgensteinian insights, it was common to accommodate science and religion by referring to them as two distinct 'spheres' of thought, each with their own logic and distinctive grammatical rules, thus removing the force or even possibility of any direct conflict between them. But in the nineteenth century, with, as we have seen, its inherited 'fusion' of religious and scientific discourse, such a recourse was not yet available. Instead, whenever direct clashes were perceived as having occurred, some compromise or even surrender would have to be admitted, and for most educated people it would almost invariably be religion that would have to give way. This is what is vividly evoked in Stephen's depiction of 'the average Cambridge don', who seems willing to discard any number of theological doctrines where these are seen to be incompatible with emerging knowledge. While such priestly dons considered themselves to be genuine believers, there was in principle no clear boundary that would set unambiguous limits to this process of doctrinal sacrifice. For some, it was to be expected that doctrines and teachings would be sacrificed until there was nothing remaining that could meaningfully be called religious, a process that was ultimately to be undergone by Leslie Stephen himself.

As we saw in the last chapter, however, Leslie Stephen's own loss of faith was to at least some extent determined by his loss of faith in the literal truth of scripture. It is important at this stage to note the extent to which the challenge of 'science' was bound up with the challenge of 'the Bible'. We saw in the last chapter that the discoveries of biblical critics need not, in and of themselves, have been damaging to faith. What made them so was the fact that the Bible had, in the modern period, come to be understood in a literal, scientific and mathematical way. Biblical criticism showed such an understanding of scripture to be untenable and, given that this was, for many, the only way of understanding scripture that was available, this appeared to entail the abandonment of scripture in its entirety. A similar sort of process can be seen to have been at work in the whole phenomenon of the challenge of 'science'. With respect to most of the scientific discoveries that were at issue, few had negative implications for religious belief as such. As Darwin himself always insisted, there was, in theory, nothing incompatible between his evolutionary hypothesis and theism, neither did the acceptance of evolutionary theory make theism either more or less likely. But for many the true malevolence of evolutionary theory was the doubt it cast upon the veracity of scriptural accounts of creation. In other words, the challenge of science was logically and practically akin to the challenge of biblical criticism: they both cast doubt upon the literal truth of scripture. As David Newsome has observed:

> If the impact of Darwinism after 1859 was to rock the boat of orthodoxy more alarmingly than anything encountered before, it was because the revelations of the *Origin of Species* came at a time when the accepted authority of the Scriptures was already being challenged – ironically, by the calling into question of that very aspect of Victorian religious teaching that had been so confidently regarded as the most essential message to be absorbed and put into practice by all Christians: the moral content of the Word of God in Scriptures.[6]

It would be a mistake, of course, to reduce the challenge to theism represented by advances in scientific knowledge to the blow that it dealt to biblical literalism. As science, particularly geology, advanced its frontiers of knowledge and as the evolutionary hypothesis gradually came into view, there was clearly, as we shall see, much more at stake for religion than the question of whether its scriptures could continue to be read as representing historical and literal truth. But as far as the emergence of atheism is concerned, the connection between them is an important one. Independently of science, biblical critics had cast doubt on the historical veracity of scriptures. Independently of the biblical critics, scientists advanced their own reasons for reaching similar conclusions. The cumulative force of the evidence was such that fertile ground was already prepared for doubting minds to be receptive to the various other ways in which scientific advances seemed to challenge theistic accounts of truth.

However much the challenge presented by science to religion is associated with the name of Charles Darwin, there can be little doubt that the challenge was already considerably developed by the time his monumental book was published in 1859. Robert M. Young has argued that 'Darwin and Darwinism have become clichés for a much wider movement' which, he suggests, began in the 1790s, and proceeded through several distinct stages. He identifies the first as being the publication, in 1798, of a work by Thomas Malthus, a priest and economist for the East India Company. Entitled *Essay on the Principle of Population*, it questioned the basic assumption – so widespread during the Enlightenment – that nature was harmonious and humankind benevolent. Young summarises its central arguments and the implications for religion as follows:

> God would not provide food for all the mouths but more than enough mouths for all the food; charity – either private or state – would worsen the lot of the poor. The impact of Malthus' theory was heightened by its apparent mathematical force; in successive generations population could be increased geometrically (2, 4, 8, 16, 32, 64, 128) while in the same time food supplies could only be increased arithmetically (1, 2, 3, 4, 5, 6, 7). The difference between 128 mouths and food for seven represented a potential gulf between unrestrained population growth and man's efforts to provide food. Not only was nature niggardly, but vice, misery, war, famine, and death were inevitable consequences of nature's laws, unless man could restrain his sexual appetite.[7]

At the time, its implications were felt most keenly in the political realm, rather than in those of science and religion. It provided succour to the Whig government then struggling to introduce the New Poor Law, which set public policy in a direction away from intervention and welfare provision. But the logic was such that it obviously prefigured Darwin's conception of the dynamic that would drive his theory of 'natural selection', as Darwin himself acknowledged.

The second stage in the movement identified by Young takes us directly into the field of geology. In the early 1800s, important discoveries were being made in relation to fossils and the relationships between the various strata in which they were embedded. But geology was doing more than this; it was also 'a science of violent crustal movements, wrenching strata, and mountain thrusts'. It asked questions about the nature of the natural world as it appears to us, whether it had always existed thus, whether it had developed and, if so, by what means. One of the most significant of the nineteenth-century geologists was Charles Lyell. Although a lawyer by training, he was independently wealthy and was thus able to live off his capital and devote himself to his geological studies. These studies bore fruit in his *Principles of Geology* (1830–3), the first volume of which was read by the young Charles Darwin during his geological voyage of discovery on the *Beagle*. In the words of Darwin's biographers, Adrian Desmond and James Moore:

> Lyell pictured a world constantly and slowly changing, with the past no more violent than the present – so that today's climates, volcanic activity, and earth movements are all we need to explain the ancient world. Crustal movements balance one another: land rises in one area as it falls in another, not cataclysmically … but gradually.[8]

So landscapes were formed by a developmental process of slow and steady change. Lyell famously refused to apply this developmental principle to life and animal forms, but nonetheless his arguments in relation to the appearance of the world's landscapes already laid the foundation for some sort of evolutionary hypothesis. Darwin's observations on the *Beagle* seemed to confirm what Lyell proposed, and already he 'started to view the world as slowly and gradually changing'.[9]

The next step in the emergence of an evolutionary hypothesis came with the publication in 1844 of an anonymous work entitled *Vestiges of the Natural History of Creation*, the author of which, it emerged some 40 years later, was Robert Chambers. In effect, this argued that the principles Lyell applied to the history of the earth, according to which it developed in accordance with unvarying natural laws, could not consistently be withheld from the development of life itself. Furthermore, he drew on the phrenological work of George Combe to support his contention that the principle of 'transmutation' according to universal laws should be applied to human life, including, specifically, mental life. It was not well regarded by the scientific establishment; it was written by an amateur for the consumption of the general public, and professional scientists were appalled by the standards of scholarship employed by the author. Adrian Desmond has described it as a piece of

> brilliant journalism, pot-boiling synthesis of the fringe sciences. It was cleverly crafted to unite the secular factions under the banner of 'Development'. But the science was second-hand and [Thomas] Huxley loathed the book's blundering pretension. It was also visionary, sweeping from the coalescence of planets, the first 'chemico-electric' generation of living globules, through the fossil fish and ancient reptiles, the 'vestiges' of the title, to the perfection of man.[10]

If it was intended for a wide readership, it certainly succeeded in this goal, having sold over 25,000 copies by 1860, and 100,000 copies by the end of the century. (In comparison, Darwin's *Origin of Species* had sold 47,000 copies by 1895.[11]) But however much the scientists disparaged it, there could be no doubt that their own researches were moving in a similar direction, the ramifications of which promised to be considerable. Chambers himself brought out what was undoubtedly the single most significant implication when he said:

> It is hardly necessary to say, much less to argue, that mental action, being proved to be under law, passes at once into the category of natural things. Its old metaphysical character vanishes in a moment, and the distinction usually taken between physical and moral is annulled.[12]

This quotation, which was considerably and several times modified in the numerous editions of the work that appeared, already portended that there was more at stake for religion in scientific advances than the mere question of biblical literalism. Much orthodox theology rested on the assumption that there was a qualitative difference between humankind and the rest of creation. Humankind, uniquely, was created 'in the image of God' and the salvation wrought by Christ was a singularly human benefit. The religious sensibility itself and the receptivity to truth that this brought was one that was uniquely possessed by human beings. Insofar as science threatened to undermine this qualitative distinction in favour of some sort of immanent continuum between human, animal and vegetable, it now came to appear to be distinctly threatening to religious sensibilities. The harmonious marriage between religion and science, which had constituted their relationship a century earlier, now appeared to be undergoing a process of dissolution.

Meanwhile, Charles Darwin continued with his painstaking work of piecing together the various elements of his evolutionary hypothesis. It was common at the time, and sometimes subsequently, for critics to complain that Darwin presented as scientific fact that which was only a 'theory' or 'hypothesis' for which there was no direct 'evidence'. It is true that evolution was not a scientific 'discovery' unearthed in the manner in which other such discoveries are made on the basis of empirical experimentation. But Darwin's hypothesis was of a different order to scientific discoveries such as the law of gravity, for instance, and it is difficult to know quite what would, in principle, constitute irrefutable evidence for the 'truth of evolution'. This is not to say that Darwin's work consisted of wild speculations, unfounded fantasy or wishful thinking. On the contrary, his work was based on almost 20 years of painstaking observations and the gathering of indirect evidence in the fields of botany, geology and other fields of endeavour in the realm of what was known as 'naturalism'. He proceeded cautiously and was unwilling to let his work loose on the world until he was satisfied of its scholarly and scientific solidity; so cautiously, indeed, that he came to fear that all his originality would be 'smashed', when, in the summer of 1858, he discovered that Alfred Russel Wallace had independently reached similar conclusions. They presented their findings jointly at a meeting of the Geological Society in that same year, and this galvanised Darwin into setting out a full exposition of his entire evolutionary thought and the evidence on which it was based. Working with remarkable speed, the book was published in the following year, and *The Origin of Species* was finally released to a waiting world.

Darwin had long anticipated the publication of his book with ambivalence, but certainly with a degree of apprehension. He may have stated towards the end of the book that he saw 'no good reason why the views given in this volume should shock the religious feelings of any one', but this statement was undoubtedly defensive rather than predictive. Inevitably, initial reactions were mixed and were by no means entirely polarised. Shortly before publication, Darwin had been immensely cheered by a letter of endorsement which he received from the Christian Socialist priest Charles Kingsley, who found it 'just as noble a conception of Deity, to believe that He created primal forms capable of self-development ... as to believe that He required a fresh act of intervention to supply the *lacunas* which He Himself had made'.[13] And Darwin's sole public champion in the USA, Asa Gray, head of the Herbarium at Harvard

> was a devout Christian man. All his life Asa Gray continued to maintain that by thus introducing law into the development of the species Darwin strengthened the argument of design. He wrote letters to Darwin trying to persuade him that he had indeed strengthened the argument from design.[14]

Reactions such as these were more widespread than was suggested by the rapidly spreading caricature of a contemporary battle between 'science' and 'religion'.

Nonetheless, there undoubtedly were those whose polarised reactions fed such a caricature and lent it some credence. Harriet Martineau, who had once been such an admirer of Malthus, wrote to her fellow secularist campaigner George Holyoake: 'What a book it is! – overthrowing (if true) revealed Religion on the one hand & Natural (as far as Final Causes and Design are concerned) on the other. The range & mass of knowledge take away one's breath.'[15] Her only reservations appeared to concern those of Darwin's sentences that gently implied theistic presuppositions. On the other hand, the now elderly priest Adam Sedgwick, former professor of Geology at Cambridge, responded in a way that was predictable, given his previous record. He had reacted violently to Robert Chambers's *Vestiges* some decades before and, while this reaction was no doubt partly to be attributed to the latter's faulty science, it was clear that what really provoked Sedgwick's ire was Chambers's earlier quoted conviction that 'the distinction usually taken between the physical and moral is annulled'. This continued to be his stumbling block 15 years later when confronted with *The Origin of Species*. Though he wrote friendlily to Darwin, his former pupil, he made clear that he read parts of the book 'with absolute sorrow, because I think them utterly false and grievously mischievous. You have *deserted* ... the true method of induction, and started in machinery as wild, I think, as Bishop Wilkins's locomotive that was to sail with us to the moon.' As Desmond and Moore observe:

> he accused Darwin of trying to sever the link between material nature and its moral meaning. Only this indication of divine love can keep the social fabric secure. 'Were it possible to break [the link], humanity, in my mind, would suffer a damage that might brutalize it, and sink the human race' into a cesspit.[16]

If Harriet Martineau and Adam Sedgwick represented the polarised reactions of belief and unbelief to *The Origin of Species*, their private reactions were soon to be given public expression in an exaggerated and caricatured form. Harriet Martineau's position was articulated by the much more rumbustious and confrontational Thomas Huxley, renowned agnostic scientist, while Sedgwick's views were expressed by the more poised and polished, but also more superficial and slippery, Samuel Wilberforce, Bishop of Oxford. Their face-to-face encounter at a public meeting of the British Association in Oxford in June 1860 has entered the folklore of the 'science and religion' encounter as embodying the titanic head-to-head nature of the clash between these two disparate fields of human life and endeavour. Owen Chadwick likewise said: 'This clash became the symbol of the entire Victorian conflict'; although he also reminds us: 'It did not become that symbol until near the end of the Victorian age, for though it was talked about privately, it did not become matter of public interest until the publication of Darwin's biography (1887) and still more of Huxley's biography (1900).'[17]

The eye-witness accounts of the confrontation are numerous and contradictory. Indeed, as time went on, the accounts of the ripostes between Huxley and Wilberforce became wilder and more sensational. The encounter gained its notoriety from its flippant tone and the knock-about character of the debate, rather than from its intellectual weight and substance. The nadir of this tone came when Wilberforce, apparently spontaneously and driven on by student laughter, asked whether the apes were on his grandfather's or grandmother's side. Huxley, later recounting the event to correct some of the more outlandish testimonies, said that while he would never have dreamed of conducting the debate along such lines, he would nonetheless meet the bishop on his own grounds:

> If then, said I the question is put to me would I rather have a miserable ape for a grandfather or a man highly endowed by nature and possessed of great means of influence & yet who employs these faculties & that influence for the mere purpose of introducing ridicule into a grave scientific discussion, I unhesitatingly affirm my preference for the ape.[18]

The encounter was certainly the stuff of sensation, but as countless historians have been at pains to point out, it is unreliable as a guide to the way in which the accord between science and religion came to unravel in the nineteenth century. We have already observed, with Chadwick, that it became a 'symbol' of the supposed 'clash' only when seen through a retrospective mist. And Young has argued that while the highly polarised nature of a clash was common in the minds of the general public, he says that, in the case of the intelligentsia:

> I find them making a subtle accommodation with the theory [of evolution] and adopting an attendant natural theology

> which, while it made God more remote from nature, made his rule grander at the same time that it left him much more a personal deity ... there is little evidence to show that any of the principal figures in the debate were antitheistic. By concentrating on Huxley and Tyndall historians have failed to see just how easily the theory of evolution was accommodated by some of the most sophisticated and subtle thinkers of the period.[19]

The picture that thus emerges is one of a variegated spectrum. At each end, we have those who believe that scientific advances have 'disproved' religion, and, on the other, we have those who reject these advances on the grounds that they are incompatible with revealed truth. Between these poles, we find forms of accommodation, and these themselves vary. Some viewed scientific advances entirely positively; rather than being seen as threatening to revelation, they are rather seen as being complementary to it and, indeed, advancing it. Others entertained a less intrinsically exalted view of the status of scientific discoveries, but nonetheless believed it essential that, for the sake of truth, some way of attaining an accord between these views of the world be found.

But while historians have no doubt been right to draw attention to the disparate ways in which the Victorian encounter between science and religion was negotiated, I nonetheless want to suggest that more important than these differences were the presuppositions that virtually all these responses shared. Whether rejecting religion, rejecting science or seeking some sort of accommodation between them, all such thinkers were agreed that a particular problem existed which they were each, in their different ways, seeking to address. Their conception of this problem was what, I suggest, they shared. For they all appear to be convinced that religion and science are merely different methods (in the minds of some, rival methods) of pronouncing on a *common* object: the origins, history, character and development of the natural world. This is perhaps brought most starkly into focus when we look at some of the attempts to harmonise discoveries in geology with the creation accounts in Genesis. Such attempts were widespread and popular, especially during the middle decades of the century. As Victor Shea and William Whitla point out, the harmonisers

> continued to attempt a fresh accommodation of the chronology of geology to that of Genesis. After the publication of Chambers's *Vestiges*, this controversy became one of the popular challenges of the day... For instance, the popularizer Mrs John Wright drew on Lyell, Buckland, Miller, and Bakewell to show that 'a close investigation of facts ... [will be] found to harmonize with the biblical statements of the character and works of God'.[20]

Once again, we are brought back here to the notion of a 'fusion' between science and religion, where the methodological and qualitative differences between the two discourses are erased. They are both seeking to do the same work of articulating the truth of a common object and so, where there is not direct accord, the encounter can only be conceived as constituting a clash which must be resolved by the rejection of one or the other, or the accommodation of one or both to the other.

It will be helpful at this stage to specify precisely what was at stake in this perceived clash. Whether the reaction was rejection or accommodation, why exactly was such rejection or accommodation deemed to be necessary? We observed at the outset that the challenge to theism presented by science was intimately linked to that presented by biblical criticism. The findings of scientists appeared to reinforce those of biblical critics to the effect that the Bible could not be regarded as being straightforwardly or entirely, or at all, as 'historical truth'. While this was certainly the case and while there were undoubtedly those who simply believed that 'Darwin had disproved the Bible', it has to be said that there was more at stake than this alone. Even those who were quite willing to accept the spiritual, non-historical, non-literal character of the truth of Scriptures still felt that the findings of science represented a 'challenge'. In what sense was this so?

John Hedley Brooke has summarised some of the key ways in which Darwin

> impinged on many facets of popular Christian doctrine: the nature of biblical authority, the historicity of the creation narratives, the meaning of Adam's fall from grace and (connected with it) the meaning of Christ's redemptive mission; the nature and scope of God's activity in the world; the persuasive force of the argument from design; what it meant for humankind to be made in the image of God; and the ultimate grounds of moral values.[21]

The force of these challenges to the nineteenth-century mind should not be underestimated, neither should it be suggested that for post-nineteenth-century minds these questions are entirely dissolved. But what emerges very clearly as a presupposition of many or most of these challenges is the sense that science and religion provide alternative, rival, competing accounts of essentially the same thing. They seem to assume that the author of Genesis and Charles Darwin were undertaking the same quest, but merely using different means and with different states of knowledge. In other words, it is taken for granted that science and religion are providing different answers to the same questions, and there is no sense that they might actually be providing different answers to *different* questions. There is scarcely any acknowledgement that theology might be doing something other than providing an account of natural history. In making this point, I do not mean to trivialise the force of the challenges identified by Brooke; I am not suggesting that they can all be straightforwardly 'overcome' by a more sensitive awareness of the qualitative difference between the domains of science and theology. If theology is to be in any sense 'engaged' with the world, these are challenges that it will need in some way to address. But this is different from the nineteenth-century conviction that if the two are to be reconciled, some unified, harmonised theologico-scientific explanation would need to be developed that could synthesise the insights of both. As Terry Eagleton has recently observed:

> Science and theology are for the most part not talking about the same kind of things, any more than orthodontics and literary criticism are. This is one of the reasons for the grotesque misunderstandings that arise between them… The quarrel between science and theology, then, is not a matter of how the universe came about, or which approach can provide the best 'explanation' for it. It is a disagreement about how far back one has to go, though not in the chronological sense. For theology, science does not start far back enough – not in the sense that it fails to posit a Creator, but in the sense that it does not ask questions such as why there is anything in the first place, or why what we do have is actually intelligible to us.[22]

Thus, properly understood, the argument between theology and science is a false one because they are not talking about the same things. Their discourses operate on different levels and with different subject matters. Of course, it may be that one will reject theology because one finds that discourse to be meaningless or unintelligible. But this is quite different from rejecting theology because it is *incompatible* with science. In principle, they cannot be incompatible because they are not operating in a common domain within which such incompatibility could arise.

Nineteenth-century thinkers, as we have seen, obviously thought otherwise, but this was because they were inheritors of those intellectual shifts that we analysed in earlier chapters. As we saw there, and as we rehearsed again at the outset of this chapter, the net results of those shifts was to place science and religion on a common epistemological plane, so that they became 'fused' into one single discourse. This is why, as we traced in Chapter 3, God became a 'thing', a 'being', an 'object' somewhat analogous to the objects of scientific investigation. This is also why, as we saw in the last chapter, the Bible came to be viewed increasingly as a reportage of literal history in the modern sense, somewhat analogous to mathematical or scientific textbooks. In light of this, we may come to understand why the challenge science presented to the truth of the Bible or to its understanding of creation was not so much a challenge to religion or to its theology as such; it was rather a challenge to a specifically *modern* understanding of that religion, and a *modern* rendering of its theology. We can thus say that science did indeed present a challenge to religion, but it is the *nature* of this challenge that has often been misunderstood. What science did was to challenge religion's own self-understanding and self-rendering. Science was right to think that theology was trespassing on its domain, but this was because theology had abandoned and evacuated its own distinctive and proper domain. It certainly challenged the modern self-understanding that religion then professed, but this should perhaps be reinterpreted as a challenge to religion to consider how it might be understood, interpreted and rendered otherwise. That it could indeed be interpreted otherwise is obvious; if the analysis we developed in earlier chapters is persuasive, we can see that the understanding of religion inherited by the nineteenth century was a modern innovation and was in no way integral to religion itself. Thus, even if a return to pre-modern theology is ruled out, it at least provides an instance of how theology might be rendered otherwise, in a way different to that of Enlightenment modernity.

It would be some time before these lessons would be learned. As the twentieth century proceeded, it became increasingly common to accept that religion and science are not directly competitive 'explanations' of the same things. And, in the second half of the twentieth century, there were increasing attempts to free theology itself from its modern legacy, as we shall consider further in Chapter 8. But, of course, old ways of thinking continue to linger. Terry Eagleton's comments, quoted above, were provoked by Richard Dawkins's perpetuation of a peculiarly nineteenth-century mentality. Eagleton says that theology does not

> see God the Creator as some kind of mega-manufacturer or cosmic chief executive officer, as the Richard Dawkins school of nineteenth-century liberal rationalism tends to imagine – what the theologian Herbert McCabe calls 'the idolatrous notion of God as a very large and powerful creature'. Dawkins falsely considers that Christianity offers

> a rival view of the universe to science. Like the philosopher Daniel C. Dennett in *Breaking the Spell*, he thinks it is a kind of bogus theory or pseudo-explanation of the world. In this sense, he is rather like someone who thinks that a novel is a botched piece of sociology, and who therefore can't see the point of it at all.[23]

Although old ways of thinking continue to exercise an allure, such that we can see instances of their persistence today, it is nevertheless the case that even in the nineteenth century they began to fade. We have seen that at the height of the clash between science and religion in the years after 1859, whatever the reactions to this perceived clash, there was generally a shared assumption that science and religion were providing rival, alternative hypotheses of the same physical realities. Thus, even those who wished to argue for the compatibility of science and religion felt constrained to do so by showing how they could be combined and intermingled into one synthesised account. Charles Darwin himself became increasingly aware of the folly and dangers of such an artificial synthesis. Although he had inserted into *The Origin of Species* several passages of an obviously theistic character, he came to regret this and removed at least some of them from later editions. But it is his motive for making these deletions that is of particular significance. Nick Spencer says that Darwin's frustration at his occasional use of the term 'creation', for instance, arose

> not because he had subsequently developed a well-formed idea about how life on earth had originated. He hadn't. Rather, he disliked blurring the lines between scientific and theological terms … his theory was scientific, standing or falling on those credentials alone, and he wanted to avoid anything that detracted from that.[24]

If this is so, it suggests that Darwin was becoming increasingly convinced that the 'fusion' between science and religion, which was such a feature of the early modern mentality, had now become unhelpful and damaging, both to science and to religion.

As the nineteenth century turned into the twentieth, others were reaching the same conclusion. Chadwick has pointed out:

> In 1900 men talked as though the conflict was over. The difficulties in the minds of the young were not scientific. A non-conformist of 1900 testified that his questioning young no longer assumed a conflict between science and religion, and that if they asked him about intellectual difficulties they often asked him about the textual criticism or the authority of the Bible. Some sighed that the conflict no longer raged, for peace was established because religion had abandoned, or was abandoning, an ancient claim to give truths about the physical world. Those who sighed preferred a territory where two sides competed for a no-man's land, to a territory where each side was left in possession of its own domain without influence upon the other. Some philosophical divines were left with a sense of dissatisfaction, at this division of the world into compartments, which they bequeathed to the twentieth century.[25]

If Chadwick is right, then the ramifications are significant. For what he is essentially suggesting is that the end of the nineteenth century began to witness the demise both of the accord between science and religion that had held sway since the dawn of modernity, and also the discord that briefly erupted between them in the nineteenth century. Already in 1900 there was emerging a recognition that, properly understood, science and religion were concerned with separate and distinct domains. The fusion between them that had been established and sustained throughout modernity was now being perceived as being mistaken and damaging to both. If, as Chadwick says, 'some philosophical divines were left with a sense of dissatisfaction, at this division of the world into compartments', this is unsurprising, for this division marked the end of the modern philosophical dream of articulating a unified, systematic, totalising account of reality, a dream that was intimately bound up with the modern fusion of science and religion.

This separation of science from religion has not been universally embraced. A century after the publication of *The Origin of Species*, some were still expressing 'dissatisfaction, at this division of the world into compartments'. Writing in the high-profile collection of theological essays *Soundings* (1962), John Habgood, a scientist–theologian and future Archbishop of York, wrote:

> Among the many fronts on which theology has been attacked or questioned, there now seems to be at least one on which a truce has been declared. Almost every book on the relation between science and theology bears witness to it. There are many who assure us that there are now no grounds for conflict between the two disciplines, and that they should never have been fighting in the first place.[26]

Habgood's article expresses concern at what he considers to be an undue complacency in this respect, but perhaps as significant as this concern is the fact that he felt moved to express it. The accord which Chadwick believes had been reached between science and religion by 1900, on the basis of a mutual recognition of their differences, was one that had clearly been perpetuated and enhanced throughout the twentieth century.

Certainly, there have been exceptions to this consensus, most notably in the 'Bible belt' of the USA, which continues to serve as the battleground for ongoing clashes between evolutionists and creationists. Prominent though these debates are in the American religious and political landscape, they are nonetheless exceptional rather than representative in the context of the Western world more generally. Furthermore, as Thomas Dixon has pointed out, the debates are largely the product of a contingent confluence of contextual factors. He says that they

> are the products of 20th- and 21st-century America. They simultaneously mimic and reject modern science and have become quite widespread in modern America through the convergent influence of a number of factors, including an advanced state of scientific development, a high level of

> religious observance, and a strictly enforced separation between church and state.[27]

The simultaneous mimicking and rejection of modern science was, as we have seen, characteristic of many of the 'science and religion' debates of the nineteenth century. Some of those who opposed science on religious grounds did so because they understood their religion in a peculiarly scientific way. The same is true of many of the proponents of creationism in America today and, to this extent, some of these debates do appear to the outside observer to have a peculiarly nineteenth-century flavour to them.

But for much of the rest of the Western world, as the nineteenth century turned into the twentieth, religion and science came to be seen as being, in Eagleton's words, as distinct as 'orthodontics and literary criticism'. With the recognition of this irreducible difference came also the conviction that the provision of any unitary account that could mediate between them was an impossible dream. In light of these developments, it is little wonder that, with a few high-profile exceptions, one would now be hard pressed to find many twentieth-century persons who would espouse atheism on the basis of the discoveries of science. In the twentieth century, there emerged a quite different and more strongly felt challenge to theistic belief, arising from that century's acute awareness of the reality of evil and suffering.

Chapter 7

Atheism, Evil and Suffering

In November 1849, an intelligent but obviously mentally anguished young man began to write a letter, the answer to which he hoped would bring him some relief. He was an undergraduate of Trinity College, Cambridge, and his experiences to date were obviously typical of his class and age:

> He had mastered the classics with ease at Rugby, and had taken full advantage at Cambridge of all the opportunities the university offers to an intelligent young man. He spoke at the Union, discussed the discovery of Saturn, and in the vacation went mountaineering and collected alpine plants in Switzerland.[1]

But for Fenton Hort, this would-be idyllic existence was disturbed by that mental phenomenon that we have seen to be more typical of the Victorian period than any other: doubt. But what makes Hort's doubt particularly interesting for our purposes is that it sprang not from recent discoveries in biblical criticism or the natural sciences, but from a specifically moral question. He was increasingly finding the Christian doctrines of heaven and hell to be repugnant and, more specifically, he was finding it difficult to credit the existence of a perfectly good God who would subject the souls of the unsaved (many of whom were self-evidently not intrinsically evil people) to the everlasting punishment of hell.

The would-be recipient of his letter was the renowned theologian F. D. Maurice, a professor at King's College, London. Although the undergraduate and the professor had never met, Hort's letter

> showed him to be a young man seeking for the truth. Maurice sat down and wrote to him at once, in his own execrable handwriting, a letter which runs to eight pages of print, and which, deciphered at length, became one of Hort's most precious possessions. For Maurice gave him the help he needed by telling him something of his own pilgrimage.[2]

Indeed, Maurice expressed the views for which he was later to become notorious: 'The Eternal Life is the perception of [God's] love, the capacity of loving… The Eternal punishment is the loss of that power of perceiving His love, the incapacity of loving. No greater damnation can befall any.'[3] Such views were ultimately to cost Maurice his London chair, but the convoluted story of that drama (intertwined as it was with his founding and central position within the fledgling Christian Socialist movement) would take us considerably beyond our immediate task. But what is important for our purposes is to note that Fenton Hort is emblematic of a considerable strain of doubt, unbelief and ultimately atheism, a strain of atheism that is founded on specifically *moral* concerns.

It should be said at the outset that 'moral atheism' may take two distinct, though related, forms. The first is of the kind we have just seen manifested in Fenton Hort; namely, an unbelief stemming from the perceived immorality of God or of God's character as attested by religious doctrines or the perceived immorality of some of these doctrines themselves. The second form emerges not directly from the perceived immorality of God, but from the perceived immorality of the world. The world we inhabit is seen to be a vale of evil, misery and suffering, much of it inflicted and experienced in an arbitrary and therefore unjust way. This perception is then taken as being good grounds for doubting that such a world could be the creation of an all-loving, all-powerful, all-good God. Though these forms of moral atheism are distinct, they are, of course, very closely related. For, in both cases, the central question is whether a morally perfect God would allow certain things to happen. Would a morally perfect God really condemn the vast majority of his creatures to endless punishment? Would a morally perfect God really create a world that appears to be riven by so much arbitrary evil and unjust suffering? Indeed, sometimes the two forms of moral atheism could appear as two sides of the same coin, as John Stuart Mill said of his father's unbelief, for instance:

> my father's rejection of all that is called religious belief, was not, as many might suppose, primarily a matter of logic and evidence; the grounds of it were moral, still more than intellectual. He found it impossible to believe that a world so full of evil was the work of an Author combining infinite power with perfect goodness and righteousness.

But furthermore, the God of Christianity was 'a being who would make a Hell – who would create the human race with the infallible foreknowledge, and therefore the intention, that the great majority of them were to be consigned to horrible and everlasting torment'.[4] Although it would be misleading if applied too rigidly, there is some truth in the observation that the first form of moral atheism (as a protest against the doctrine of everlasting punishment, for instance) was a quintessentially nineteenth-century phenomenon, while the second (arising from an overwhelming awareness of evil and suffering in the world) was predominantly a twentieth-century one. In order to understand why this is the case, we need to look at each of these forms of moral atheism in turn.

Of the first form, Don Cupitt has said: 'The moral revolt against Christian orthodoxy in early Victorian England was violent.' He cites S. T. Coleridge's *Aids to Reflection* (1825), in which Coleridge says that a believer may assent to certain doctrines which are beyond comprehension, but he will find it much more difficult to believe in doctrines that conflict with his sense of right and wrong, of his moral justice. The difficulty is further exacerbated when it is realised that such conflicts occur at some of the most important junctures in Christian doctrine: 'Such are the doctrines', says Coleridge, 'of Arbitrary Election and Reprobation; the Sentence to everlasting Torment by an eternal and necessitating decree; vicarious Atonement, and the necessity of the Abasement, Agony and ignominious Death of a most holy and meritorious Person, to appease the wrath of God'.[5] Indeed, it was moral revolt against the logic of such central doctrines that loomed large in the unbelieving diagnoses of such thinkers as Francis Newman, J. H. Froude and Mary Ann Evans (George Eliot). In a discussion of these thinkers, Howard R. Murphy discerns in their discourses a fundamental clash between the otherworldly salvation assumed by orthodox dogma and the Victorian 'meliorist ethic', with its emphasis on sustained earthly human effort. Don Cupitt concedes that this may have been part of the story, but for him much more important is a cluster of Victorian moral principles which he characterises as moral 'republicanism'. In an important passage worth quoting in full, he identifies this cluster of principles as

> the moral seriousness, the emphasis on the individual conscience, on liberty, on the reform of the content of the law and the way it was administered. It seemed wrong to the nineteenth century to punish a man for holding the wrong religious beliefs – but God apparently still did so. The purpose of punishment began to be seen as remedial – but God punished retributively and endlessly. Consider how the Victorians felt about the damnatory clauses in the Athanasian Creed. God seemed morally archaic. He could punish the entire race for one man's sin. The traditional argument that we were seminally present in Adam's loins cut no ice with the Victorians, who made a sharp distinction between the realms of nature and of morality, as we do. A son should not be punished for his father's offence, nor should the innocent be punished in order to expiate the

> offence of the guilty. The Victorians thought it a moral duty to believe that no one was quite beyond redemption: they did not like the doctrine of Reprobation, and if a Broad Church clergyman questioned the doctrine of eternal punishment he might, with Maurice, be reviled by the theologians, but he was sure of the sympathy of a large public of liberal-minded laymen.[6]

Theologians themselves felt the force of these objections and knew that they had to be addressed. Maurice was one of the most influential to do so, but he was by no means the only one. In *Essays and Reviews*, for instance, the challenge presented by biblical criticism was addressed by Rowland Williams and the discoveries in the natural sciences were accommodated by Baden Powell. But these two challenges, strong though they were, had by no means entirely eclipsed the moral objections. In Williams's own contribution, the part of his essay that caused him the most difficulties was that which dealt with Baron Bunsen's revisionary reading of the doctrine of the atonement. Williams characterised what was then taken to be the orthodox understanding of the atonement as a 'fiction of merit by transfer', and the phrase reverberated around the theological corridors of controversy.[7] Williams's manner of expression was too blunt for some, but he had nonetheless identified what theologians were coming to see as a real and growing danger. He knew that what had come to be the church's accepted teaching on the atonement was morally repugnant and he further knew that such teaching was difficult to justify in light of recent researches in biblical hermeneutics. This was one of those instances where biblical criticism and moral criticism seemed happily to coincide in the interests of Christian truth. Williams believed it his duty to point this out. It was revealing and significant, however, that a Victorian volume of essays dealing with contemporary challenges to the veracity of Christian faith could not but deal with the so-called moral objections. To have neglected to do so would have been too glaring an omission.

As the nineteenth century turned into the twentieth, however, the 'moral' objections to Christianity came to be expressed less in terms of the doctrines of heaven and hell, of the atonement and so forth, but more in terms of what would become universally known to generations of theological students as the 'problem of evil'. As we have observed, these two manifestations shared a common underlying impulse, but the problem was now given a new and distinctive inflection. The central question now became whether a world that was self-evidently filled with so much evil and suffering was compatible with or told against the Christian doctrine of God. Why did this shift occur? It is possible, I think, to identify at least four possible currents by which we may render this shift intelligible.

First, we might venture to suggest that Maurice, Jowett and others had, to a certain extent at least, succeeded in their aims. In the twentieth century, a figure like Fenton Hort – racked by anxiety over the moral probity of particular doctrines – was a much rarer bird. It seems that the Broad Churchmen had succeeded in their attempt to uncouple the truth of Christian belief in its totality from what eventually came to be seen as crudely literal understandings of particular doctrines. The transition is personified in many ways by the subsequent career of the author of the first essay in *Essays and Reviews*, Frederick Temple. Originally condemned as one of the 'seven against Christ', Temple subsequently went on to become Bishop of Exeter, Bishop of London and, finally, Archbishop of Canterbury. The route travelled by Temple from 'heresy' to Canterbury was one on which he had scarcely had to change any of his theological opinions. True, at the time of his elevation to Exeter, there had been a vociferous contingent of malcontents who had made their antipathy clear. But, by the time he ascended Augustine's throne in Canterbury Cathedral, scarcely a murmur of protest was to be heard. And in this experience, Temple typified his age. What was once deemed heretical had become not only acceptable but respectable and, indeed, orthodox. Christians now felt psychologically at ease with the rejection or reinterpretation of doctrines that had once appeared morally repugnant. Furthermore, sceptics and atheists respected their right to do so, and few now proclaimed their atheism on the basis of the apparent immorality of certain aspects of Christian doctrine.

A second factor that contributed to the shift was the explosion in mass communications in the twentieth century and the increased knowledge that this brought of the wider world beyond one's own national boundaries. This inevitably brought with it a much greater sense of how arbitrary and unjust were the experiences and distributions of evil and suffering on a global scale. Until then, it had been much easier to view evil as a matter of individual culpability and sinfulness. Suffering in the sense of economic or social deprivation was either seen as part of a divinely ordered hierarchy or, again, as a matter of individual culpability, from which one could liberate oneself with sufficient effort. But as knowledge of the wider world grew rapidly and tangibly for many people during the twentieth century, the notion of moral deserts in relation to evil and suffering became much more difficult to sustain. It became increasingly apparent that many impoverished and disadvantaged societies were victims of global circumstances quite beyond their control. Natural disasters – earthquakes, famines and droughts – as well as fatal diseases appeared to strike whole communities at a whim of nature. Newspapers and later television brought home in a very tangible way just how frequent and random such occurrences were. With evil and suffering being so ubiquitous in the world, striking individuals in an apparently arbitrary and unjust way, the notion of the world as a divinely created and ordered harmony supervised and sustained by a benevolent deity became, for many, increasingly difficult to credit. This became a much more pressing question, for believers and atheists alike, than any questions about the moral status of particular Christian doctrines.

A third development was the fact that the twentieth century experienced war and premeditated killing on an unprecedented scale. Indeed, it has justifiably been described as the century of 'man-made mass death'. Not only were there two World Wars, with an interval of only 21 years between them, but the second of them had also been bound up with the Holocaust, in which the extermination of an entire race of people had been attempted. The question of where God had been in the midst of these catastrophes was one that echoed down the century. In the Jewish tradition, the sense of divine abandonment was expressed in the emergence of a 'death of God' theology. The slaughter, carnage and mechanically efficient killing revealed the depths of depravity to which humanity had descended. Evil appeared to have been pointlessly unleashed, apparently without any divine intervention to mitigate its worst effects. Divine deliverance was experienced by many only in its absence.

Away from societal changes and events on the world historical stage, a fourth development occurred within the ranks of academic philosophy. The inter-war years of the twentieth century had been dominated by linguistic philosophy and logical positivism. These movements were generally sceptical of or denied outright philosophy's capacities to articulate metaphysical truths. Instead, philosophical efforts were devoted to analyses of linguistic usage and questions of meaning. In logical positivism, particularly, metaphysical claims were not just open to doubt, nor even were they deemed to be false; because they failed the test of the verification principle, they were deemed to be meaningless statements, to which truth or falsity could not intelligibly be applied. The classic statement of this position was, of course, A. J. Ayer's *Language, Truth and Logic* (1936). After the Second World War, however, such rigid dismissals came to be reconsidered. Metaphysical questions came back onto the philosophical agenda, provided that they were addressed with care, with the same high standards of logic, coherence and linguistic precision as had been developed by philosophy in the inter-war years. Philosophy pursued with such an agenda and in accordance with this methodology came to be known as *analytical* philosophy, and was to have an enormous impact on the practice of philosophy, especially in Anglo-American universities. With the rehabilitation of metaphysical questions came also the rehabilitation of the philosophy of religion. Analytical philosophy came increasingly to be applied to religious beliefs and doctrines, primarily with a concern with elucidating their meaningfulness or otherwise and, ultimately, their truth or falsity.[8]

Among the questions addressed by the philosophy of religion in the mid-twentieth century, the so-called problem of evil came to be one of the most widely discussed. It was formulated in its classic form by the Oxford analytical philosopher J. L. Mackie, in a widely cited article entitled 'Evil and Omnipotence' (1955).[9] It was a forceful articulation of the *logical* problem of evil, in that it argued that there was a straightforward logical inconsistency in maintaining simultaneously: a) that God exists and is omnipotent; b) that God exists and is perfectly good; and c) that evil and suffering exist in the world. For Mackie, there was no logical way of reconciling these three statements, given that a perfectly good God would will the eradication of evil and suffering, and that an omnipotent God would be able to put this will into effect. He was willing to accept that the problem would be 'solved' if it were to be accepted that God is not entirely good or that God is not omnipotent, but this would not then be the God in which the vast majority of theists believe. As it happens, Mackie went on in that same article to argue against the coherence of the notion of omnipotence as such, but it is for the statement of the logical problem of evil that the article has been most remembered. The argument itself was not, of course, entirely new. A version of it had been expressed previously by David Hume in his *Dialogues Concerning Natural Religion* (1779). But whereas Hume was a sceptic in relation to all metaphysical truths, Mackie and other analytical philosophers were prepared to accept that metaphysical truths could legitimately be reached, but denied that the existence of an omnipotent God in the face of evil and suffering was one of them.

Intrinsic to the methodology of analytical philosophy was the application of two tests: that of coherence and that of evidence. Corresponding to these two tests were two distinct versions of the problem of evil. Mackie, we have seen, expounds the *logical* problem of evil, which is derived from an application of the test of coherence. Others, however, have developed versions of the *evidential* problem of evil. This version of the problem concedes that there may, in principle, be ways in which God's omnipotence and goodness could be coherently maintained in the face of evil and suffering in the world. This would depend upon a plausible case being made as to why an omnipotent and loving God *might* be justified in permitting evil and suffering in the world without in any way compromising God's omnipotence or goodness. But, having granted this concession, the evidential version of the problem of evil then goes on to argue that, given what we know and experience of the world and the nature of the evil and suffering within it, it is highly *unlikely* or *improbable* that such a God exists. In other words, even if the doctrine of God in a world of evil and suffering were to pass the test of coherence, the evidence in the world (the magnitude and arbitrary nature of evil and suffering within it) makes it highly unlikely that it would pass the test of evidence. So for many analytical philosophers, the tests of coherence and evidence, when applied in the particular case of the problem of evil, provides a firm basis for the espousal of atheism (or agnosticism).

Inevitably, some analytical philosophers of religion have disagreed with these arguments and have attempted to provide arguments to justify the existence of an all-loving, all-powerful God in the face of evil and suffering in the world. Just as there are two versions of the problem of evil, so also there are two replies to it. The first merely attempts to demonstrate the coherence or logical possibility of asserting that there is a God who is omnipotent and perfectly good, while simultaneously acknowledging the existence of evil in the world. The philosopher most associated with this reply is Alvin Plantinga, and his method of establishing the logical coherence of these notions is by postulating that human beings have free will, and that it is this that accounts for evil and suffering in the world. It should be noted that Plantinga does not attempt to demonstrate that human beings do indeed have free will, nor even that it is probable that they have free will. All he is concerned to show is that it is logically possible that human beings have free will and, therefore, that it is logically possible for an omnipotent, good God to exist in a world of evil and suffering. As to whether human beings do indeed have free will and as to whether such a God does indeed exist, these questions can only be answered – if they can be answered at all – by moving on to the second philosophical test, namely that of evidence. So in one sense what Plantinga has established, philosophically, is relatively modest. But in another sense it is very significant, for, if his argument were to be accepted as valid, it would constitute a rejection of Mackie's formulation of the *logical* problem of evil.[10]

Other philosophers, however, are not prepared to rest content with a merely logical answer to the problem of evil. They are not satisfied simply to establish that it is logically possible for such a God to exist in a world of evil and suffering. They wish to go further and argue that there are good grounds for thinking that such a God exists in a world of evil and suffering, that one would be rationally justified in believing in such a God in the face of evil and suffering. Such philosophers would need to argue, for instance, that there are good grounds for supposing that human beings are free, that there are good reasons to suppose that such a God would wish human beings to be free, and so forth. In doing so, they have attempted to develop an 'answer' to the evidential problem of evil and thereby articulate a 'theodicy'. Foremost among such philosophers have been John Hick and Richard Swinburne, each of whom has developed his own distinctive theodicy or 'answer' to the problem of evil. Like Plantinga, Swinburne's argument rests upon the free-will defence, but he wishes to go further than does Plantinga. Assuming that God exists (and Swinburne believes that there are good independent arguments for supposing that God does), then such a God would have good reason for creating human beings with free will. But a necessary condition for the operation of such free will is that human beings should have knowledge of what constitutes good and evil, so that the choice between them might be genuinely free and therefore morally responsible. Such knowledge is provided by 'examples' in the natural world of good and evil, and it is this, for Swinburne, that accounts for 'natural' evil and suffering that arises from it (from such things as earthquakes, famines, droughts and so forth). So for Swinburne, if an omnipotent and perfectly good God exists (for which he thinks that a philosophical case can be made), God would have good reason for permitting both natural evil (as a necessary precondition of freedom) and moral evil (as a necessary outcome of freedom).[11]

John Hick's theodicy was most fully developed in his book *Evil and the God of Love* (1966).[12] It is close, in many ways, to

Swinburne's theodicy and the two models share several common features. But as is well known, Hick's develops certain ideas he believes to be found in the writings of Irenaeus. Hick accepts the reality of human freedom and the part that this plays in understanding the origins of the phenomena of evil and suffering. But for Hick this is not in itself sufficient. Among other things, it renders evil and suffering entirely 'accidental' and contingent, contrary to the divine will, but 'tolerated' by God in order to respect the greater good of human freedom. Hick wants to provide an account that makes evil and suffering more than just an accidental contingency. Drawing on Irenaeus's insight that human creatures are created in the image of God, but need to grow into the likeness of God, Hick introduces a teleological perspective whereby human beings have the potential to realise their true purpose, to grow in the likeness of God and, finally, to attain eternal blessedness. But this growth into spiritual maturity can only come through a 'testing' of the soul, through the way that it deals with and confronts trials and tribulations, evil and suffering. So, on this account, evil and suffering are not merely accidental, but are necessary preconditions for proper spiritual growth. As Kenneth Surin has commented:

> Hick wants to say that suffering constitutes the *means* by which human beings grow into a relationship with their creator. Suffering, in one degree or another, is thus the *sine qua non* of attaining the perfect bliss that will be ours at the consummation of history.[13]

So evil and suffering is 'justified' on this account as being a necessary precondition for spiritual growth and, furthermore, once the *telos* of this process has been reached, the sufferer will be 'compensated' by the eternal bliss that is finally reached; such suffering is 'redeemed' by its glorious end.

Needless to say, the versions of the problem of evil articulated by Mackie and Flew, as well as the 'replies' developed by Plantinga, Swinburne and Hick, have been exhaustively analysed, and both sides of the argument have been subject to detailed and searching criticisms. It is beyond the scope of this book to follow the contours of these debates. I do want to suggest, however, that what these theodicists and anti-theodicists, theists and atheists, share is, in many respects, more significant than what divides them. For one thing, it should be noted that there is no disagreement between them with respect to philosophical methodology. The procedure of analytical philosophy – with its tests for coherence and evidence with regard to metaphysical questions – is accepted by theodicists and anti-theodicists alike. Theodicists believe, as much as do anti-theodicists, that these philosophical tests are indeed indispensable. If theism, viewed in the context of evil and suffering, fails these tests, they know that the outcome cannot but be fatal for religion. This is why it is so important for theodicists to show that theism passes these tests. Demonstrating this in the specific context of evil and suffering is precisely what their theodicies seek to do.

But, as we have suggested in earlier chapters, the particular philosophical methodology employed with regard to discourse about God cannot but have implications for the specific conception of theism to which it gives rise. And, if theodicists and anti-theodicists agree on this methodology, we may further expect that they would agree on the conception of theism that is at issue here. However much anti-theodicists deny the existence of God and however much theodicists defend it, the *definition* of God that is at issue turns out to be shared by both of them. In other words, there is no disagreement as to the *conception* of God, the actual existence of which is either being affirmed or denied.

Furthermore, if this shared conception of God is one that is produced by a distinctively *modern* methodology, then we may further expect that the conception of God that emerges is itself a distinctively *modern* one. If this is indeed the case, then the implications could be considerable. We have seen in the preceding chapters that biblical criticism and discoveries in the natural sciences presented a challenge to theism primarily because of the distinctively modern conception of theism that was dominant at the time. Based on these precedents, therefore, the question that we shall be led to ask is whether the problem of evil is likewise only a problem for a specifically modern conception of theism.

Perhaps if theism were conceived otherwise, the problem of evil – and with it the impulse towards atheism – would disappear or at the very least be weakened. Let us therefore consider some of these questions in more detail.

In his own study of what he calls the crisis of Christianity's moral authority, from which we have already quoted, Don Cupitt suggests that many of the problems surrounding the moral criticisms of Christianity may be traced back to a too anthropomorphic conception of theism. It is this, more than anything else, he suggests, that gives rise to perceptions of the immorality of particular doctrines or indeed of Christianity as a whole, as well as to the problem of evil itself. He expresses this as follows:

> Are the immoralities the inevitable result of trying to tell an anthropocentric [Christian] story? I think so. A very clear example is God's aseity or self-sufficiency... The purpose, or *a* purpose, of religion always was and always will be to lead men away from suffering, restlessness, anxiety, and contrivance, to a state of tranquil bliss. Theistic religions represent God as enjoying such a state, and inviting believers to share in it. There is, I think, nothing *intrinsically* morally repugnant about such an ideal ... But as soon as you try to represent it anthropomorphically it at once becomes repugnant. God looks self-satisfied, indifferent, smug, complacent, callous. His imperious bliss seems hard-hearted... God had been thought too anthropomorphically.[14]

So according to Cupitt the problems of moral objections to Christianity, including that of the so-called problem of evil, are *created*, or at any rate heightened, by an overly anthropomorphic conception of God. And when this happens, the impulse towards atheism is doubly pressing. For one thing, the anthropomorphic theism in itself comes to appear crude, inadequate and unsustainable. For another, the problem of evil, with which it is intimately linked, gives one all the more reason for rejecting such a conception of God.

But without dissenting from Cupitt's analysis, it will be instructive to state more specifically what *kind* of anthropomorphic God is at issue here. Kenneth Surin has asked this question, and has answered it unequivocally:

> It is certainly no exaggeration to say that virtually every contemporary discussion of the theodicy-question is premised, implicitly or explicitly, on the understanding of 'God' overwhelmingly constrained by the principles of *seventeenth and eighteenth century* philosophical theism.[15]

But if this is so, then we need to add here some words of clarification. For have we not already suggested that the conception of God assumed in most philosophical discussions of the problem of evil is one that is derived from analytical philosophy? And have we not already also said that analytical philosophy is a result of developments within mid-twentieth-century Anglo-American philosophy? It should be said, however, that any perceived contradiction here is only apparent. For analytical philosophy should be viewed as a particular species of Enlightenment philosophy deriving from the seventeenth and eighteenth century, rather than a heterogeneous alternative to it. In a sense, analytical philosophy is an intensification and exacerbation of certain tendencies that were already present in seventeenth- and eighteenth-century philosophy.

Likewise, the conception of God produced by analytical philosophy is an intensification and exacerbation of certain features of the conception of God produced by Enlightenment philosophy. So, for instance, Surin says that

> the divinity of modern theism thus turns out to be '*a*' being (an implicit stress is invariably placed on the indefinite article), a rare and fascinating 'entity', possessing a number of clearly specifiable characteristics. Theism is then simply to be understood as a hypothesis about this most sublime 'entity'.[16]

If the defining characteristic of this Enlightenment conception of God is its anthropomorphism, then analytical philosophy's conception of God is entirely consistent with it, but intensifies and exacerbates this anthropomorphism. As we saw in Chapter 3, Swinburne's conception of God, for instance, is entirely consistent with Surin's abstraction, but with certain additional 'twists' – that God is a 'person' without a body, within time, whose knowledge of the future is limited, and so forth. And as we there noted, each of these twists takes God in an increasingly anthropomorphic direction.

But if this is so, then why does such an understanding of theism intensify – or, indeed, as some would argue, *create* – the problem of evil? Why does such a conception of God make the problem of evil such a formidable one in a way that it may not have been for earlier and other conceptions? In order to answer this question, let us return to the logical problem of evil, as formulated by Mackie. As we have seen, central to this rendering of the problem are God's omnipotence and goodness, which taken together appear to be logically inconsistent with the phenomena of evil and suffering in the world. While no orthodox theist would wish to deny that God is omnipotent or good, it is the *interpretation* of God's omnipotence and goodness that is central and at issue here.

These questions have been taken up and pursued in detail by D. Z. Phillips. His main objection to the way in which analytical philosophers understand God's omnipotence is as follows:

> The meaning of 'omnipotence' is not determined by reference to the religious context implied by the proposition 'God is omnipotent.' Instead, it is laid down by what Mackie calls quasi-logical rules. But where do these rules come from? They do not seem to belong to any context. Thus, we are told, in the abstract, that omnipotence means 'the ability to do whatever is not logically contradictory.' This meaning, though applied to God's case, does not depend on any reference to religion.[17]

In contrast, Phillips wants to ask what omnipotence means when applied and used in a specifically religious context. For instance, such quintessentially human activities as riding a bicycle, eating an ice cream or having sex are not logically contradictory activities. At the same time, however, they are not possible activities for God – not because his omnipotence is in some way limited, but because, according to the grammar and logic of religious discourse, it makes no sense to talk of God doing such things.

Phillips also asks whether it would make sense to think of God as being able to learn a language, and replies in the negative: 'To have a language is to have acquired it. I cannot possess it "all at once". Even if someone thought, absurdly, that one could, or that God could, the fact would remain that the language has not been learned.'[18] The example of learning a language brings us close to what is at stake here. If it makes no sense (according to the logic of religious discourse) to speak of God learning a language, then to what extent does it make sense to speak of God 'intervening' in the world in order to 'prevent' certain things happening, or in order to 'ensure' that things happen in a certain way. Speaking in such a way seems to assume that God undergoes a process of deliberation, that he makes a decision to act, that he puts this decision into effect, and so forth. But as soon as we begin speaking in this way, it should strike us just how anthropomorphically we are speaking of God, for we are thereby turning God into a 'being' with 'agency' – in other words, a being like us, albeit much bigger and more powerful. But what if we were to say that God *cannot* 'intervene' in the world in order to prevent certain things happening, or in order to ensure that things happen in a certain way – not because his omnipotence is limited, but because it makes no religious sense to talk of God doing these things? Phillips would say that to speak of an agent who *could* do these things is to construct the notion of a big person in the sky, and such a projection is, by definition, not God. And if this is so, what implications does this have for the problem of evil?

Let us probe this suggestion in a little more detail. One way of articulating what is happening here is to say that, in the classic statements of the problem of evil, we see a specific instance of the way in which modern and analytical philosophy effects an epistemological inversion of pre-modern theology. In very general terms, pre-modern theological epistemology began with divine revelation and used this to extrapolate to and illuminate human realities. Modern epistemology did precisely the opposite. It began with human realities (notions of rationality, logic and so forth), and then extrapolated from these in order to reach transcendent truths. But a great deal is at stake in this methodological inversion. When the epistemological starting point is divine revelation, then human realities and truths become, qualitatively, a secondary extrapolation in relation to it; in other words, human realities are created in the divine image. Contrariwise, when the epistemological starting point is human concepts and experiences, then divine realities and truths become, qualitatively, a secondary extrapolation in relation to them; in other words, divine realities are created in the human image. This goes a considerable way towards explaining the anthropomorphising tendencies in modern philosophy, and it also exposes what may well be the crux of the issue when it comes to modern inflexions of the problem of evil.

What I am suggesting here is that when exponents of the problem of evil speak of the 'problem' posed by God's supposed omnipotence and goodness in the face of evil, what really creates this problem are the definitions of 'omnipotence' and 'goodness' that are employed. For in a way that is entirely consistent with the modern philosophical epistemology just outlined, these definitions of 'omnipotence' are derived from what it means for human beings to have and to exercise power; in other words, divine power is being created in the image of human power. And the same thing happens with regard to divine goodness in relation to human goodness. Thus, what these thinkers – theodicists and anti-theodicists alike – appear to understand as divine power or goodness is of the same order or *quality* as human power or goodness, but possessed in a much greater *quantity*. So, for instance, in terms of defining divine power, the starting point is what it means for human beings to have power: the capacity to get things done, change things, prevent things, overrule others, impose one's will by force, and so forth. Working with such an understanding of human power, this notion is then 'extended' in quantitative terms in order to reach the conception of divine power that results. But what if divine power is not simply an inordinately greater quantity of human power, but a different kind and quality of power altogether? What if, even more radically but with considerable theological warrant, divine power were to be understood not as a greater quantity of human power, but as an *inversion* of it?[19] What if philosophers were to take seriously the specifically religious injunction of the prophet: 'My ways are not your ways, neither are my thoughts your thoughts, saith the Lord'? That this might be considerably closer to what is intended by religious discourse is indicated when it is remembered that excessive or unlimited (human) power is almost always viewed (within religious discourse, but also outside it) as being a bad thing. Power must always be 'checked', 'balanced', 'reined in' and so forth. Divine power, in contrast, is held to be an unequivocal good. Indeed, if God is 'simple', as orthodox theology claims, then divine power cannot somehow be at the expense of or in conflict with divine goodness. Divine power *is* divine goodness, and surely the only intelligible way of making sense of this is to see divine power as being a different quality, a different *kind* of power, to that of human power.

The same sort of analysis could be made of modern philosophy's understanding of divine goodness in relation to human goodness. It should be remembered in this respect that human goodness only gets its sense within, and is defined in terms of, a context into which human beings are 'thrown' – a context of finitude, contingency and luck, so that human goodness is always manifested in such a way that it is inseparable from deliberation, dilemma, discernment, moral anguish, decision and so forth.[20] But the goodness of God is nothing of this sort; it is marked and defined by no such contingencies. Indeed, according to religious discourse, it is difficult to specify in what precisely God's goodness consists. As Aquinas emphasised in his teaching on analogical language, we know that God's goodness bears some limited resemblance to human goodness, but further than that we cannot go. A great deal of mystery remains – a goodness that is abstracted from the context of moral contingencies in which our understanding of goodness gets its sense is very difficult to specify.

So God's goodness is not of the same order as human goodness; on the contrary, a goodness constrained by finitude, contingency and chance is a different quality of goodness altogether. If all of this is so, it may well be that the problem of evil is a very substantial problem indeed for the question of the existence of an 'extraordinarily big person'. But as for whether the problem of evil is anything like as substantial a problem for God is, as they say, an entirely different question.

D. Z. Phillips has done much to illuminate what I am attempting to articulate here. He says:

> God has no biography, no inner life as an agent among other agents, in which, on some days, he goes through agony, doubts, has second thoughts, regrets, and so on… God's relation to the world, the sense in which he is 'other than' the world is itself a spiritual relation, not one of power and control. If one takes seriously the notion of God as Spirit, one sees, at the same time, that God can give no more and no less than what that Spirit is. If this notion is embraced, the 'cannot' in the claim that God cannot prevent the Holocaust would be seen as a grammatical or logical 'cannot'. It marks what cannot be said within a given conception of God.[21]

If we were to take up Phillips's suggestive comments here, we may well say that, if someone were to ask why God did not prevent the Holocaust, this would be logically or grammatically akin to asking why Love did not prevent the Holocaust. We may well say that the latter question is strictly unanswerable, other than to say that the Holocaust occurred precisely because people turned profoundly and unequivocally away from Love. In the midst of those horrific experiences, it may be that some were sustained by their belief in Love, and that their experiences impelled them to believe in Love much more strongly than they had done hitherto. Equally, however, it may be that some were so broken and destroyed by these experiences that belief in Love became, for them, simply impossible. 'How could you believe in Love', they may well ask, 'if you had seen what I have seen and experienced what I have experienced?'. Both of these responses are humanly, philosophically and logically intelligible, and if one were to ask about ways of 'deciding' between them, of 'determining' which was right or correct, one would be at a loss to know quite what was being asked.

But in these last sentences, what if 'Love' were to be replaced with 'God'? Would this bring us nearer to the essence of religious discourse about God? And if indeed it does, do we not begin to see the absurdity of claiming that there is a logical incoherence in claiming simultaneously: 1) that Love is omnipotent; 2) that Love is good; and 3) that evil and suffering exist? Is there really any contradiction between these claims at all? If a contradiction does seem to arise when 'Love' is replaced by 'God', does this suggest that the problem lies more in the way in which God is being defined and understood?

At this point, theists and atheists alike may well object that this is to be overly reductive. Is this not a case of treading the well-worn path of humanist reductionism or non-realism by reducing God to Love? Theists may object that this gives rise to an inadequate understanding of God, and atheists may object that it side-steps too easily the difficulties intrinsic to the problem of evil. But my point here is not to pronounce on the extent to which God is or is not synonymous with Love. I am here setting aside questions of the extent to which God is 'more than' or 'other than' Love, and the various ways in which this might be the case. Rather, my analysis was simply intended to be a thought experiment to induce the reader to ask whether talk of God, properly understood, is *closer* to talk about 'Love' than it is to talk about an extremely big human being, or a person without a body, as Swinburne puts it. I am suggesting that indeed it is. And if unease still persists, we should remind ourselves that, according to canonical religious discourse, it is said that 'God is Love'. But nowhere is it said that 'God is an extraordinarily big human being' or that 'God is a person without a body'.

So we appear to be reaching a conclusion similar to those reached in the preceding two chapters. In the first, we said that the advent of biblical criticism only really carried with it an atheistic impulse in relation to a specifically modern (and anthropomorphic) understanding of God, and a modern (and literal) approach to scriptural hermeneutics. Likewise, in the second, we saw that discoveries in the natural sciences – and Darwin's evolutionary hypothesis in particular – impelled many towards atheism primarily because of the specifically modern conception of God that was then prevalent, and the specific understanding of the relationship between religion and science that this entailed. We now seem to be saying something similar with respect to moral objections to theism, relating particularly to the existence of evil and suffering in the world. The so-called problem of evil is only really a 'problem' for a quintessentially modern conception of God.

So is this all that is to be said: that if God were to be purged of all the modern anthropomorphic distortions by which he has been disfigured, the problem of evil would simply dissolve? This is certainly the direction in which our discussion has been moving. But it will be necessary here to add some words of qualification to the effect that things are not quite that simple. For in our thought experiment, in which we drew an analogy between talk of God and talk of Love, we saw that we could well imagine that one who had experienced the horrors of the Holocaust might well have been broken and destroyed to such an extent that belief in Love/God becomes, for them, simply impossible. We saw this to be an intelligible and understandable reaction, the reality of which cannot be dissolved away by any supposed 'overcoming' of the problem of evil. This is to say that, however much we may expose the problem of evil to be a false problem (resting primarily on an inadequate understanding of God and an inadequate understanding of the role of philosophy in relation to God), there may well still be those whose experience of evil or reaction to evil is such that, for them, belief in God is precluded, albeit not in the strictly philosophical way that we have here been criticising. In other words, there may well be a different *kind* of problem of evil from the one we have been criticising and, should this eventually give rise to atheism, a different *kind* of atheism from the one we have thus far been discussing.

Another indication that this may be so appeared in the aftermath of the Boxing Day Tsunami of 2004. This event was one of the most significant recent natural disasters, resulting in loss of life on an enormous scale, as well as considerable suffering for those who survived. As was the case after the Lisbon Earthquake of 1755, it led believers and others to ask questions about the role and presence of God in the midst of such disasters. In the aftermath of the event, the Archbishop of Canterbury, Rowan Williams, gained extensive national publicity by his suggestion that Christians not only would but *ought* to ask themselves serious questions about the role and place of God in the midst of such disasters. The suggestion was that Christians *ought* to be troubled by such occurrences and that it was entirely proper – even theologically proper – for their belief in God to be challenged. This was a significant intervention for, although Williams is well known to be an accomplished theologian, his approach to theology is by no means that of an analytical philosopher of religion such as Mackie or Swinburne. Indeed, he agrees with D. Z. Phillips and others that many of the so-called 'problems' in the philosophy of religion are false problems. On the basis of Williams's writings, it is obvious that he would not consider biblical criticism or scientific discoveries as being serious grounds for challenging belief in God. But for Williams there is obviously a different kind of problem of evil from the kind we have been criticising, presenting a different sort of challenge to that presented by biblical criticism or natural science, or the modern problem of evil. If this is so, then we need to ask two central questions. First, in what way does this different kind of the problem of evil challenge theism, if not in the way we have been discussing in this chapter? Secondly, if the problem is such as to induce atheism, what kind of atheism is this and in what way does it differ from the atheism we have thus far been discussing?

First of all, then, in what way does this different inflection of the problem of evil challenge theism? Part of the problem, indeed, returns us to the question of the relationship between God and Love, and, specifically, it arises from the theological reluctance simply to *equate* God with Love. Again, if this reductive move were made, the problem would be far less pressing. But the tradition has always wanted to say that if, in one sense, it is true that God is Love, there is also a sense in which God is more than Love, just as God is more than simply Goodness.

As well as being Goodness and Love, God is also believed to be the *source* of goodness and love, as well as of the world in which goodness and love are to be found. And this, in many ways, brings us to the crux of the problem. How is evil and suffering to be accounted for in a world that is the creation of a good and loving God? It should be noted that this is not strictly a philosophical or logical problem, a problem of coherence or of evidence, as discussed earlier. This is not a case of using the problem of evil as a means of determining the likelihood of the existence of God. Rather, the scenario we are raising here is one where an already committed believer is challenged to find ways of accounting intelligibly (in theological terms) for the existence of evil. In this sense it remains an internal challenge for the tradition itself. The notion of the Fall conventionally has been invoked at this point, as has the doctrine of evil as 'privation', which insists that evil is, strictly speaking, *nothing* – in ontological terms, it is simply the absence of good. But neither of these teachings entirely dissolves the problem. For there remains the question of why the human will, if it is created by and is naturally orientated towards God, should have 'fallen' in the first place. This is why John Milbank has referred to the phenomenon of the Fall as being 'strictly baffling'.[22] Mystery and bafflement are not in themselves sufficient to cause unbelief and, indeed, it may be said that they are necessary preconditions for any form of belief as such. Nonetheless, they should give the believer pause for thought, and this is perhaps something along the lines of what Rowan Williams was intimating.

But what of those who remain outside the tradition, whether as agnostics, atheists or otherwise? Such unbelievers may agree entirely that this question is not for them a philosophical or logical puzzle. They may well agree that this is entirely to belittle the question at hand. Neither would they necessarily believe the God they are rejecting to be of the modern anthropomorphic kind which we have seen to be so problematic. But the position of these atheists is more akin to the kind of reaction to the Holocaust we identified earlier: someone who has been so broken and battered by their experience of suffering, whether their own or that of others, that belief in Love or belief in God simply becomes an impossibility – *not* on the grounds of logic or coherence, but simply in itself and on its own terms; belief in God is not an 'option.'

It is important to clarify further the nature of the atheism or unbelief at issue here. We have identified those analytical philosophers who agree on the essential nature of the theist/atheist puzzle before them and who agree on the philosophical methodology by which it is to be resolved. We have seen too that there are those who reject this methodology and the conception of God that it entails, and who believe that this rejection opens the way for a more authentic belief in God, even in the face of evil. Now we have the phenomenon of those who likewise reject this methodology as being utterly inappropriate, but who are nonetheless unable to subscribe to theism.

It is in order to illuminate the character of this form of unbelief that we now turn to the form of atheism that has been so vividly and famously displayed in Fyodor Dostoevsky's *The Brothers Karamazov*, particularly in books V and VI. In this novel, we see staged an interaction between the two brothers Ivan and Alyosha, in which, as Ivan tells Alyosha, 'What I'm trying to do is to attempt to explain to you as quickly as possible the most important thing about me, that is to say, what sort of man I am, what I believe in and what I hope for – that's it, isn't it?'[23] In the course of this discussion, there emerges Ivan's infamous moral indictment of God. But Dostoevsky is careful to clarify what *type* of discussion this is – and, perhaps more importantly, what type of discussion it is not. In particular, he is keen to stress that his consideration of the question of God is not to be reduced to that of a philosophical puzzle, a logical riddle. This approach to the question is embodied in 'the Russian boys and their professors' who entertain themselves with these logical conundrums in their pub discussions: 'what are they going to talk about while snatching a free moment in a pub? Why, about eternal questions: is there a God, is there immortality?'[24]

In his important philosophical discussion of this novel, Stewart Sutherland has brought out the implications of this crucial clarification. He says that Dostoevsky

> is engaged upon a philosophical discussion of just what the conceptual issues are in any discussion of 'the problem of the existence of God.' He is rejecting one pattern of discussion which sees the issue between atheism and belief as one of two competing hypotheses about which we might speculate, pro or contra, adding up points in favour and points against, 'while snatching a free moment in a pub.' Whatever the difference between atheist and believer, it is being argued, it is not the difference between two speculative hypotheses which may or may not engage the emotions, may or may not affect the pattern of one's life, affect what, in Ivan's words, one 'lives by'.[25]

In place of such an account, Sutherland suggests: 'Ivan's atheism is to be seen in terms of a moral response to what the believer talks of as God's creation.'[26] It is in light of this that Ivan's well-known articulation of his 'protest atheism' is to be understood:

> Tell me yourself, I challenge you – answer. Imagine that you are creating a fabric of human destiny with the object of making men happy in the end, giving them peace and rest at last, but that it was essential and inevitable to torture to death only one tiny creature – that baby beating its breast with its fist, for instance – and to found that edifice on unavenged tears, would you consent to be architect on those conditions? Tell me, and tell the truth... It's not God that I don't accept, Alyosha, only I most respectfully return him the ticket.[27]

In his analysis of Ivan's atheism, Sutherland suggests that it operates at three levels. First and most obviously, there is the act of moral rebellion, of the kind that is evident in the passages just quoted. The rebellion is rooted in a sense of the sheer immorality of supposing that extreme suffering – especially of the innocent and children – will somehow be 'justified' by subsequent 'compensation' or 'redemption'. The second, more puzzling, level is manifested in Ivan's apparent acceptance of God but rejection of his world, as is evident when Ivan says: 'It's not God that I don't accept,... only I most respectfully return him the ticket.' Elaborating on this, Sutherland says that

> Ivan's 'acceptance of God' is based on utter revulsion not just of the arguments of the Russian boys but of the God whom these arguments are intended to persuade us to accept or deny. His acceptance of their God, whom he believes also to be the God of the orthodox believer, is from one respect to be seen as the bitter joke of a man whose moral outrage at the implications of such forms of belief and disbelief is intense to the point of distraction.[28]

It should be noted here that, according to Sutherland, Ivan's outrage would be as much directed against unbelief as against belief, were this unbelief to be reached by the same processes of logical inquiry as those of the 'Russian boys'. In other words, it is the manner of approaching this question that is here the target of Ivan's invective, rather than the particular outcome that is reached. Atheism of this kind is as much morally indicted as is theism.

The third level at which Ivan's atheism operates is encapsulated when Ivan insists that, *even if* redemption were attained and harmony prevailed, 'I would rather remain with my unavenged suffering and unsatisfied indignation *even if I were wrong*. Besides, too high a price is asked for harmony; it's beyond our means to pay so much to enter on it.'[29] As Camus and others have pointed out, a great deal is entailed by this 'even if'.[30] What seems to follow from it is that Ivan's atheism would not be invalidated, even if it could somehow be demonstrated that an 'entity' called God actually exists. Even if such a God indeed existed and salvation were a possibility, this would not affect the validity of Ivan's atheism; his moral responsibility would still be to reject that God and to refuse that salvation. What this reveals is that Ivan's atheism is not primarily – indeed, is not at all – a matter of believing that an entity called God does not in fact exist. Even if such an entity did exist, Ivan would still consider it his moral duty to proclaim his protest atheism.[31]

Interestingly, there is here a structural similarity with accounts of theism (other than the modern anthropomorphic ones) which we have occasionally been eliciting in previous chapters. We have seen that, according to certain strands of orthodox theology (strands that were obscured by modernity), theism is not defined solely, or primarily or at all, by the question of whether an entity called God actually exists. Indeed, we have seen that to talk of God as an 'entity' or 'a being', or to say of God that he 'exists', would be deeply problematic for much of the orthodox theological tradition. To speak of theism as commitment to the existence of a certain kind of being is highly misleading – possibly even blasphemous or heretical. Now, it seems, we have come across a form of atheism that is similarly not defined primarily, or at all, by the question of whether a particular being or entity exists. As Sutherland says:

> a study of Ivan Karamazov puts a crucial question about the importance attached to the proposition 'God exists' in the implied accounts of the difference between belief and unbelief. What is at stake here is the *conception* of the reality of God, not just the question of whether there is such a reality, but of what it amounts to, to talk of, and believe in or rebel against the reality of God.[32]

We have thus been led to a conception of atheism (as we have also raised the possibility of a conception of theism) that is not primarily defined, if at all, by the question of whether an entity or being called God actually exists.

Our route in this chapter has been somewhat more circuitous than that travelled in the preceding two, and it has led us into more complex terrain. In the preceding chapters, we saw that developments in biblical criticism and discoveries in natural science gave rise, historically, to an atheistic impulse, primarily because of the distinctively 'modern' conception of God that was at issue and/or the distinctively modern ways of determining the 'reality' of that God. It was suggested that it was this 'modern' conception of God that gave rise to the atheistic impulse rather than these supposedly external pressures. If God were conceived otherwise, the so-called challenges arising from biblical criticism and natural science seemed to disappear or, at the very least, were considerably weakened. We have observed a similar phenomenon with the so-called problem of evil, a problem we saw, again, to be largely the creation of the 'modern' conception of God at issue and the modern philosophical procedures for determining the 'reality' of that God. In this sense, the problem of evil is as much a false problem for theism as are those challenges presented by biblical criticism and scientific discoveries.

But our consideration of evil and suffering has led us also to a different conception of atheism; just as it raises again the possibility of a different kind of theism. These are forms of theism and atheism that are not defined primarily by the question of whether a being or entity called God actually exists. We have been led to conceptions of theism and atheism that are more subtle and complex than is often assumed. This raises also the question of how the disagreement between *these* types of theism and atheism might be addressed or negotiated. Clearly, the disagreement will not, in principle, be 'settled' by recourse to philosophical logic, tests of coherence or evaluations of evidence, because, for these forms of both theism and atheism, such 'tests', such 'evidence', are irrelevant. They would have been as irrelevant to Aquinas as they were to Ivan Karamazov. How this disagreement might, in practice, be negotiated, if at all, is beyond the scope of this book. But we have at least been led to see that it is not only the *conceptions* of theism and atheism that are more complex than is often supposed, but, further, that the routes by which people might be led to such espousals and the means by which such disagreements might be negotiated are likewise more complex. The notion that the question of theism *versus* atheism can be reduced to arguments, based on logic and evidence as to whether a 'being' exists, could be seen to be as distorting in relation to atheism as it is in relation to theism.

Chapter 8

The End of Modernity – The End of Atheism?

Although our investigations have taken us across diverse terrain, we have nonetheless been led to converging conclusions. In each chapter, we have repeatedly seen that atheism is itself a distinctively modern phenomenon. That is to say, it is constituted by modern philosophical presuppositions and is made intelligible by a modern epistemology. Furthermore, we have seen how the theism against which atheism reacts and in relation to which it negatively defines itself is likewise a specifically modern species of theism. We have thus come to see an intimate connection between three concepts: the whole philosophical and cultural edifice of *modernity*; the modern form of *theism* to which this gives rise; and *atheism*, which is, simultaneously, a product of modernity and a reaction against modern theism. Insofar as this is the case, it would seem that it is impossible to revise or remove any one of these three concepts without it having a significant impact on the other two. This observation is of particular significance in a cultural and intellectual milieu in which the 'end of modernity' is being frequently proclaimed. Indeed, over the last several decades, many have been the voices announcing the terminal decline of modernity across a diverse spectrum of academic disciplines and wider cultural forms of life. If there is indeed a sense in which modernity has 'ended' or is 'ending', our analysis in the preceding chapters would seem to suggest that this would carry potentially far-reaching implications both for the form of theism that was dominant within modernity and also for the atheism which so decisively rejected such a theism. Could it be, then, that the end of modernity brings in its wake the end of atheism? This is the question I set out to explore in what follows.

But before addressing the question of the end of modernity directly, it is important for us to consider some of the ways in which, in *late* modernity, theism and atheism paradoxically appeared to reach a surprising accord. Long rent by an antithetical and hostile relationship, theism and atheism suddenly found themselves to be partners in an unanticipated marriage. The result was what some considered to be a paradox, others an oxymoron: an inventive and transgressive theological project that proclaimed the gospel of a 'Christian atheism'. Although emerging from within the academy, its impact was felt way beyond campus boundaries. The cover of the 1966 Easter edition of *Time* magazine featured a plain black background on which was set three simple words in bright red lettering: 'Is God Dead?'. Within the magazine, the article itself began as follows:

> Is God dead? It is a question that tantalizes both believers, who perhaps secretly fear that he [*sic*] is, and atheists, who possibly suspect that the answer is no. Is God dead? The three words represent a summons to reflect on the meaning of existence. No longer is the question the taunting jest of skeptics for whom belief is the test of wisdom and for whom Nietzsche is the prophet who gave the right answer a century ago. Even within Christianity ... a small band of radical theologians has seriously argued that the churches must accept the fact of God's death, and get along without him.[1]

'*Even within Christianity*' ... the intriguing question being raised by the *Time* article was the possibility that even Christianity itself was now becoming atheistic. Perhaps the final 'truth' of theism was being revealed in and as the ultimate truth of atheism?

The *Time* article had been prompted by the publication of Thomas J. J. Altizer's book, *The Gospel of Christian Atheism* (1966).

The gospel it proclaimed was unequivocally a modern one directed at a specifically modern audience. Indeed, Altizer himself later came to refer to the presumed milieu within which and for which he was writing as being one of 'full modernity'. The conceptions of theism and atheism at play in his work, therefore, are within the mainstream of the tradition of modernity we have been tracing in earlier chapters. Central to his gospel was the notion of the death of God. Although frequently associated with Friedrich Nietzsche, the notion had been given prior philosophical expression in the work of G. W. F. Hegel, and it is the Hegelian treatment of the death of God that is most influential for Altizer. The dual modern and Hegelian character of Altizer's project has been summed up by Mark C. Taylor, when he says: 'Although consistently described as a "radical theology", Altizer's position is not, in fact, a novel departure from the Western religious tradition. To the contrary, his theological vision represents a reworking of Hegel's most basic insights.'[2] The fact that Altizer's vision derives primarily from an Hegelian rendering of the death of God is significant. As well as placing his project more firmly within the modern trajectory, it also allows him to question the conventional opposition between theism and atheism; for one of Hegel's most significant contributions to Western philosophy was to draw attention to the ways in which apparently separate and conflicting oppositions are, in fact, dialectically implicated. The ambiguity to which this gives rise partly explains why some commentators subsequently took Hegel's insights in an explicitly Christian direction, while others developed them down an explicitly atheistic trajectory. Others still have explored the ways in which Hegel eludes both categorisations, characterising his thought as being 'heterodox' in relation to the Christian tradition. Altizer exploits such Hegelian ambiguity in his suggestion that Christian theism and secular atheism should be brought together rather than held apart.

What was distinctive, then, about Hegel's understanding of the death of God? Thomas A. Carlson has helpfully summarised what he takes to be the two central interrelated meanings of the death of God in Hegel's thought:

> On the one hand, God is called 'dead' insofar as God can seem or remain thoroughly remote and thus unknowable; on this view, the enlightenment rationality that reaches a high point in Kant and the pietistic feeling so influential in a Jocobi or Schleiermacher would equally condemn God to the lifelessness that ensues from the abstraction of the unknowable, from a lack of determinate content... On the other hand, Hegel opposes this unknowable and thus lifeless God in terms of a second 'death of God.' On this second understanding, God empties or negates precisely his own abstraction or emptiness, moving out of his remoteness and unknowability in order thus actually and concretely to live.[3]

As Carlson goes on to note, these two understandings require and are made intelligible by each other. There is thus an 'undecidability' as to which conception ultimately 'prevails'. Is God 'really' absolute and transcendent, or is God 'really' incarnate and immanent?

Hegel can claim of course, with some credit, that Christianity itself teaches the error of seeing here an either/or choice that must be resolved. God the Father is absolute and transcendent, while God the Son is incarnate and immanent, and the doctrine of the Trinity teaches the simultaneous necessity of both. But the ultimate unity of Father and Son is something that must actually and concretely be 'realised', and this is the necessary role played by the resurrection. If the absolute and unknowable Father is 'negated' by his appearance and incarnation as the Son, this immanent appearance itself stands in need of negation. In other words, God the Son must die, there must be yet another death of God, which is realised at the crucifixion. Otherwise, God's status would be 'resolved' into immanence and God the Father and God the Son would still stand in need of reconciliation. This reconciliation is effected by the resurrection. In the resurrection, God's descent into finitude is itself overcome, there is a 'negation of the negation' and, having passed dialectically through these stages, ultimate reconciliation is achieved. God the Father and God the Son are now finally reconciled through God the Spirit. Hegel can thus regard the doctrines of the incarnation, resurrection and the Trinity as being 'true', but, it should be noted, only in the sense that they are true pictorial representations of ultimate philosophical truths relating to the nature of Absolute Spirit.

We can thus see that, for Hegel, there are several ways in which God 'dies', several distinct understandings of the death of God, and each of these understandings mutually implies and requires the others. What is significant about Altizer's creative reading of Hegel is that it privileges the second death of God in particular above the others. What Altizer prioritises in his gospel of Christian atheism is the sense in which 'God dies in his abstract transcendence and unmoving eternity so as to become temporally immanent and thus concretely known to this world and its history'.[4] It is this conviction that stands at the heart of Altizer's project. As to why this second understanding of the death of God should be privileged, Altizer believes this to be justified by the insights of Nietzsche, which he sees as prophetic in relation to the world we currently inhabit. In other words, we may say that, for Altizer, it is Nietzsche's understanding of the death of God that induces him to concentrate on and elevate Hegel's second understanding of the death of God as the negation of transcendence. Altizer himself put it as follows:

> If there is one clear portal to the twentieth century, it is a passage through the death of God, the collapse of any meaning or reality lying beyond the newly discovered radical immanence of modern man, an immanence dissolving even the memory or the shadow of transcendence. With that collapse has come a new chaos, a new meaninglessness brought on by the disappearance of an absolute or transcendent ground, the very nihilism foreseen by Nietzsche as the next stage of history.[5]

For Altizer, taking Nietzsche's insights seriously means repudiating Hegel's final 'negation of the negation', whereby Christ's death and descent into hell are overcome through the resurrection. On the contrary, for Altizer's gospel of Christian atheism, God's death in Christ is final and irrevocable. He says: 'The radical Christian proclaims that God has actually died in Christ, that this death is both a historical and a cosmic event, which cannot be reversed by a subsequent religious or cosmic movement.'[6] Given that Altizer accepts God's death in the most thoroughgoing and irreversible way, one may well wonder why this does not result in his abandonment of Christianity altogether and his espousal of an outright and unqualified atheism. Altizer's answer to this question seems again to be imbued with the spirit of Hegelianism, in that it rests on the conviction that Christian theism and secular atheism are thoroughly and mutually implicated. Thus, to see the relationship between them in terms of a straightforward either/or choice is profoundly misleading. He believes that the leading prophets of atheism are so imbued with Christian preoccupations that this cannot be ignored. Contrariwise, Christianity contains within itself the resources which enable it to come to a greater understanding of the process of its own demise.

Thus, he says that

> it cannot be accidental that so many of the more creative theologians of our [the twentieth] century have implicitly if unconsciously shared much of Nietzsche's vision ... and it would be difficult to deny the fact that Nietzsche's whole vision evolved out of what he himself proclaimed to be the death of the Christian God, and we shall attempt to show that this event can only be perceived by faith.[7]

Given that atheism has emerged out of Christianity, Altizer believes that a fully-developed Christian atheism will be able to shed more light on our current situation than a secular atheism which artificially attempts to forget its past and its origins. So Altizer's method is to appropriate Christian doctrines, teachings and narratives, interpreting them in a new way that both assumes and casts light upon what he takes to be our contemporary atheistic condition. Thus, for example, he says that

> a contemporary appropriation of the symbol of the Kingdom of God can ... make possible our realization of the

> gospel, or the 'good news,' of the death of God: for the death of God does not propel man into an empty darkness, it liberates him from every alien and opposing other, and makes possible his transition into what Blake hailed as 'The Great Humanity Divine,' or the final coming together of God and man.[8]

But the Christian doctrine that Altizer believes can be most fruitfully developed in support of his gospel of Christian atheism is that of *kenosis*. This is the teaching that in the incarnation God laid aside his transcendence and emptied himself of his divine power in order to be incarnate in Christ. This theme of the metamorphosis of Spirit into flesh is one that he believes both stands at the heart of the received Christian tradition and also serves to illuminate our current situation. But in order for it to be appropriated and religiously effective in the current atheistic ontology, the received tradition must also be creatively developed. He says:

> Insofar as the kenotic or negative movement of the divine process is a movement into the actuality of human experience, it can neither be isolated in a given time and place nor be understood as wholly occurring within a given moment. On the contrary, the actualization of the metamorphosis of the Word into flesh is a continual and forward-moving process, a process initially occurring in God's death in Christ, yes, but a process that is only gradually and progressively realized in history, as God's original self-negation eventually becomes actualized throughout the total range of human experience.[9]

Altizer goes on to argue that every attempt to make God transcendent, to posit the divine as being set over against the human, is in fact a refusal of the logic of the incarnation, as is also the notion that revelation has been given a decisive and final expression. On the contrary, revelation is itself always a forward-moving process, with its original expressions constantly developing into new forms. Thus, for Altizer:

> The death of God in Christ is an inevitable consequence of the movement of God into the world, of Spirit into flesh, and the actualization of the death of God in the totality of experience is a decisive sign of the continuing and forward movement of the divine process, as it continues to negate its particular and given expressions, by moving ever more fully into the depths of the profane. A faith that knows this process as a self-negating and kenotic movement, as both embodied and symbolically enacted in the passion of Christ, knows that it becomes manifest in the suffering and the darkness of a naked human experience, an experience banished from the garden of innocence, and emptied of a sustaining power of a transcendent ground or source.[10]

In Altizer's vision, therefore, we see the extent to which Christianity has ceded to atheism. Unequivocally, this is a rendering of Christian theology that is 'emptied of a sustaining power and source'. At the same time, however, this resolutely atheistic ontology is best understood, experienced and negotiated through a thoroughly and appropriately reinterpreted Christian practice.

Altizer, however, is not the only theologian to have preached a gospel of Christian atheism. In the UK, from 1980 onwards, a similar but distinct project was to be developed by Don Cupitt. The relationship between the respective projects of Altizer and Cupitt is an interesting one that is composed of both convergences and divergences. Cupitt described his project as a 'Christian non-realism' rather than as 'Christian atheism', and this is significant for at least two reasons. First, it indicated Cupitt's formative background in the mainstream tradition of analytic philosophy of religion, with its foundational dualism between 'realism' and 'anti-realism'. Second, it was indicative of Cupitt's desire to disrupt the tendency, inherited from that very tradition, of seeing theism and atheism as being absolute and polar opposites. His early work set out to explore the possibilities of a *religious* theism purged of objective metaphysics, which, as a result, could be viewed as a form of *philosophical* atheism. In other words, in metaphysical terms, Cupitt was as atheist as was Altizer, and indeed Cupitt himself described his own work as being 'objectively atheous'. But he thought that an effective Christian theism did not depend upon the objective existence of a divine object, entity or being. Rather, Christian theism should be reinterpreted as belief in or commitment to God as the highest spiritual ideal that embodies our highest religious and spiritual values.

One result of this was that Cupitt's Christian non-realism, at least in its earlier stages, required much less drastic doctrinal revisionism than did Altizer's Christian atheism. Whereas we have seen Altizer to have radically reinterpreted doctrines of the incarnation, kenosis and so forth, Cupitt suggested that much of the content of doctrinal, spiritual and ethical teaching could be left intact, but with the whole now interpreted in a non-realist (non-literal, non-objective) fashion. When evacuated of its objective metaphysics and thus understood in a non-realist way, Cupitt suggested that Christianity not only continued to operate remarkably effectively, but even became religiously and spiritually purer as a result. Many of the differences between Altizer and Cupitt may be understood in terms of their respective philosophical and theological influences. Whereas Altizer was inspired by Hegel, Nietzsche and Blake, Cupitt looked rather to Kant, Kierkegaard and the Buddha. Furthermore, the paradoxical and counter-intuitive marriage of Christian theism with metaphysical atheism was heightened in Cupitt's case by the fact that he was an ordained and practising priest of the Church of England.[11]

Like Altizer, Cupitt's starting point was the decline of objective theism and, again like Altizer, this decline was understood to be a direct result of the advent and consummation of modernity. Cupitt says that the traditional realist understanding of God – God as 'an actually-existing independent individual being ... belongs entirely to traditional culture and must vanish with the changeover to the modern outlook'.[12] In other words, the objective realist understanding of God was formed within and is only really intelligible within a traditional or pre-modern world-view. The coming of modernity brings with it all sorts of changes in cosmology, theories of knowledge, social institutions and notions of selfhood and autonomy. These changes are so complete and thoroughgoing that it is difficult to see how the realist conception of

God is still possible and intelligible in the modern world. Should this be doubted, Cupitt would point to the 'almost apocalyptic event [of] the great defection from God that has gathered pace over the past two centuries or so'.[13] Furthermore, confidence in the philosophical arguments for the existence of God has gradually weakened and belief in the existence of an objective divine reality has waned. Thus far, Cupitt would appear to be at one with the mainstream tradition of modern atheism or agnosticism.

But he goes on to make two important observations, which converge in their practical outcome. First, in spite of the undeniable decline of institutional and doctrinal religion in the West, there is still a human need, perhaps even stronger than before, for some form of religious or spiritual commitment and practice. As Cupitt observes:

> the typically modern pressure for thoroughgoing 'liberation' can easily issue in an anarchic freedom that rejects all structure and becomes quite contentless. A freedom that is in no way directed by a spirituality does not know what to do with itself and does not know where it is going... We need a spirituality to direct our freedom and make it fruitful, so that human lives can gain something of the nothing-wasted integrity and completeness of a work of art. When lives are rounded off in that way, death loses its sting.[14]

Secondly, Cupitt says that, contrary to what is traditionally thought, the efficacy of religion – and Christianity in particular – as a salvific form of spiritual practice does not in fact depend upon the existence of an objective metaphysical God. On the contrary, Christianity may still be practised as an internalised religious requirement with complete commitment, without it being authorised by and founded upon an objective God. Indeed, Cupitt goes further, suggesting that Christianity may not only dispense with the notion of an objective God, but may even *profit*, religiously and spiritually, from doing so. This suggestion is derived from what he perceives to be the central Christian imperative towards disinterestedness.

At this point, of course, Cupitt reveals his deep indebtedness to Kant, for whom disinterestedness is a necessary precondition for a moral act as such. For Kant, any action undertaken with a view to some motive, reward or goal, other than the fulfilment of the act itself, destroys disinterestedness and, with it, the moral worth of the action. A moral action is one undertaken for no reason, purpose or motive other than for the sake of the fulfilment of the moral law. Cupitt wholeheartedly endorses this principle, although in doing so he does not believe himself to be adopting an exclusively Kantian moral principle. On the contrary, he believes that Kant's teaching on disinterestedness merely made explicit what had always been a central stream of the Christian tradition, for Christianity has always taught the necessity of overcoming base egotism and of attaining the highest degree of self-transcendence. But this religious imperative was always in danger of being undermined (and sometimes was undermined) by the conception of God as an objective, personal being, and this danger was further heightened when accompanied by doctrines of heavenly rewards and hellish punishments. Even where doctrines of heaven and hell are not paramount, talk of doing things to 'please' or 'appease' an objective, personal God would seem to undermine the spiritual purity of absolute disinterestedness. For Cupitt, there is an inherent tension between disinterestedness and objective doctrinal claims, which appears repeatedly through the historical development of the theological tradition. He argues that if disinterestedness is to be taken utterly seriously, this would seem to demand the overcoming of an objective God and, indeed, a realist understanding of religious doctrines more generally. On this reading, there are strong *religious* reasons for abandoning the objective reality of God.

This does not entail taking leave of God *per se*, however. On the contrary, God continues to be 'the beginning and end of the religious life'. Cupitt says that

> God is the central, unifying symbol of the religious life. The unconditional religious requirement ('the will of God') is an autonomous inner imperative that urges us to fulfil our

> highest possible destiny as spiritual, self-conscious beings emerging from nature. The requirement is *not* purely immanent, because it is not merely a demand that we fulfil the immanent teleology of our own present natures; on the contrary, it requires self-transcendence and victory over nature. Hence the appropriateness of the symbol of a transcendent being who imposes it; and he not only imposes it but also represents the goal towards which it directs us, for God is depicted as being already sovereign over nature ('the creator of the world'), with the highest degree of spirituality and self-awareness ('life, spirit'), freedom and love.[15]

Thus, God is a central and unifying symbol or ideal that 'exists' insofar as that ideal is appropriated and enacted (and thereby made 'real') in a particular religious life. Cupitt sees a precedent for such an understanding in the writings of Kierkegaard, for whom 'the religious demand is not something inferred from facts about the external world. It establishes itself autonomously and inwardly within the self as an inescapable claim upon the self.'[16] As for whether such a God exists objectively outside the context of a particular and lived religious life, Cupitt insists that such a question

> is of no religious interest. There cannot be any religious interest in any supposed extra-religious reality of God, and I have argued all along that the religious requirement's authority is autonomous and does not depend upon any external imponent. The authority of the religious requirement has to be autonomous and intrinsic in order that it may be fully internalized, imposed by us freely upon ourselves and made our own... So it would seem that religion forbids that there should be any extra-religious reality of God.[17]

Cupitt insisted that he continued to speak of God and to pray to God, and that God was the most central and unifying element of his religious life. As such, he considered himself to be – in specifically religious terms – a 'theist'. At the same time, however, he considered such theism to be perfectly compatible with an ontological and metaphysical commitment to atheism. As we have seen, for Cupitt, religious theism almost seems to demand a metaphysical atheism.

So in the thought of Altizer and Cupitt, we witness the apparent reconciliation of theism with atheism, in which they are no longer viewed as being diametrically opposed alternatives. Both thinkers provide distinct visions of how a 'religious atheism' may be conceived. In noting this, however, it is important to probe further into the precise nature of this reconciliation. Perhaps the most prominent feature of their respective visions is the shared assumption of an atheistic ontology. Insofar as religion is reconciled with atheism, this is effected *within* a context of 'objective' atheism that is assumed rather than questioned. For Altizer, this atheistic situation can only be properly understood in the rays of light cast by a Christian analysis. For Cupitt, Christianity can best be understood and practised by 'bracketing' the question of objective theism, and may even be enhanced by assuming a backdrop of objective atheism. This ontological prioritising of atheism is entwined with an epistemological and sociological prioritising of *modernity*. Altizer, we have seen, writes for and within a cultural setting he characterises as 'full modernity',[18] and Cupitt too claimed to be developing a religious vision and practice for the modern world.

Admittedly, in Cupitt's case, the picture is complicated by the fact that, after the publication of *Taking Leave of God* (from which my characterisation of his religious non-realism has been drawn), he was increasingly influenced by Derrida and other continental thinkers, with the result that his conception of a modern autonomous consciousness gave way to a much more fluid conception of subjectivity. Nevertheless, even after this move had been made, Cupitt continued to insist on an ontological monism and immanence, frequently proclaiming that 'nothing is hidden', thus betraying the enduring influence of the 'modern' episteme.[19] In spite of their disruption of the opposition between theism and atheism, therefore, it would appear that Altizer and Cupitt confirm rather than question the analysis that has been developed in the preceding chapters. That is to say, their respective visions manifest a deep complicity between modernity and atheism. Their ontological privileging of atheism is bound up with an explicit or implicit commitment to the conditions of modernity. Thus, the emergence of such phenomena as 'Christian atheism' or 'Christian non-realism' does not question – but indirectly confirms – our contention that the inner logic of modernity seems inevitably to culminate in atheism.

Mark C. Taylor was among the first to criticise Altizer for remaining bound up in and committed to a modern philosophical paradigm, and he was also among the first to take theology in a specifically postmodern direction. Given the close link we have repeatedly exposed between modernity and atheism, it would seem that any attempt to move beyond modernity would be likely to have potentially very significant ramifications for atheism itself. If modernity and atheism are as deeply implicated and as mutually founding as we have been arguing, this would suggest that any attempt to question the hegemony of modernity would also thereby be an attempt to question the privileging of atheism. In the work of Taylor, we find this precisely to be the case.

Although Taylor has long acknowledged his indebtedness to Altizer, his fundamental criticism of Altizer – developed in numerous ways over the years – is that his thought remains too *modern*. This is particularly evident when Taylor says that Altizer's

> commitment to so-called high modernism and his overt hostility to postmodern consumer culture blinds him to the significant changes that have taken place in the last quarter century… It is as if history literally ended in the mid-sixties and everything that has transpired since has been the eternal return of the same.[20]

More specifically, Taylor sees in Altizer's work the embodiment of a specifically modern desire: 'Modern culture expresses a deep and abiding longing for the presence of the present and the present of presence,'[21] a longing which we have seen to be abundantly satisfied in Altizer's work. (The same, of course, is also true of

Cupitt's work, with its commitment to a thoroughgoing monism and immanence.) Taylor says that

> Altizer clings to the *identity* of identity and difference. This privileging of identity makes it possible for him to affirm the recovery of presence ... origin becomes presence in and as the total presence of the end. Absence, in other words, is not irreducible but is the momentary difference that secures the identity of presence and the presence of identity.[22]

But for Taylor, this modern insistence is problematic, not least because it refuses to learn the most central lessons taught by Nietzsche:

> The presence of *parousia* and its necessary condition, history, are 'shadows of God' which, Nietzsche observed, are only slowly dispelled. Altizer prolongs these shadows. The 'primary' 'representative' of the death of God has not carried the death of God far enough. As a result of his abiding belief in total presence, Altizer is still caught in the web of Western onto-theology that is unravelling around him.[23]

But what does it mean for Taylor to say that Altizer has not carried the death of God far enough?

At this point, it will be instructive to return to Nietzsche's original proclamation of the death of God, as mediated through the parable of the madman in *The Gay Science* (1882). This much quoted parable opens as follows:

> Have you not heard of that madman who lit a lantern in the bright morning hours, ran to the market place and cried incessantly, 'I seek God! I seek God!' As many of those who do not believe in God were standing around just then, he provoked much laughter. Why, did he get lost? said one. Did he lose his way like a child? said another. Or is he hiding? Is he afraid of us? Has he gone on a voyage? or emigrated? Thus they yelled and laughed. The madman jumped into

> their midst and pierced them with his glances. 'Whither is God' he cried. 'I shall tell you. *We have killed him* – you and I. All of us are his murderers.'[24]

At the conclusion of his discourse, the madman realises that his hearers are uncomprehending and dumbfounded; they were

> silent and stared at him in astonishment. At last, he threw his lantern on the ground, and it broke and went out. 'I come too early,' he said then; 'my time has not come yet. This tremendous event is still on its way, still wandering – it has not yet reached the ears of man ... This deed is still more distant from them than the most distant stars – *and yet they have done it themselves*.'[25]

What may we take to be the central message of the parable of the madman? Clearly, to understand the madman's primary concern as being to announce the 'advent of atheism' would be too egregious a misreading, for it would render much of the rest of the parable senseless. His hearers already 'do not believe in God', so if the madman's message had simply been one of atheism, his hearers would have responded with an indifferent shrug of the shoulders rather than with stares of incomprehension. What is it, then, that the madman's audience do not understand; what is it that 'has not yet reached the ears of man'? The answer is to be found at the centre of the madman's discourse, when he exclaims on the *implications* of the act – the murder of God – that his hearers have themselves committed:

> All of us are [God's] murderers. But how have we done this? How were we able to drink up the sea? Who gave us the sponge to wipe away the entire horizon? What did we do when we unchained this earth from its sun? Whither is it moving now? Away from all suns? Are we not plunging continually? Backward, sideward, forward, in all directions? Is there any up or down left? Are we not straying as through an infinite nothing?[26]

It would seem, then, that the death of God has the most radical implications that leaves nothing unchanged, and it is this that the madman's hearers, the atheists, those who have killed God, do not yet realise or understand.

For Nietzsche, it is a profound illusion to suppose that when God dies, everything else remains unchanged. On the contrary, the 'entire horizon' gets wiped away; the earth gets 'unchained' from its sun. More particularly, we may extrapolate, many of those notions and beliefs held dear by modernity – truth, progress, history, absolute presence (to name but a few) – are likewise 'wiped away' and 'unchained'. It would be an illusion to suppose that when God dies such notions as truth, progress, history and absolute presence continue unaffected; they may remain insecurely in place for a while, but they are ultimately 'shadows of the dead God' and are destined to dissipate like the God whom they shadow. Although it may not immediately be obvious, they are all profoundly theological notions that depend upon the secure foundation that God provides. When God dies, many of our other cherished beliefs and values die too. Thus, the madman's hearers seem to represent many of our present-day secular atheists who seem to assume that although God is dead, 'truth' remains alive and well. If the madman were to return today, he might well find, yet again, that he has come too soon.

If the death of God brings with it the death of metaphysical truth, then we have also to ask what this implies for atheism, which is, in most of its manifestations, an objective metaphysical truth claim; namely, that God does not exist. It would seem that the death of God paradoxically entails also the death of atheism, for it may well be argued that atheism, like metaphysical truth, is a shadow of the dead God. Atheism thus belongs to that twilight mental world in which it is supposed that, when God dies, all our other cherished notions and beliefs may continue intact. If Nietzsche was the first thinker in the West to herald the end of modernity, he is also the thinker who shows us why the end of modernity may bring with it also the 'end of atheism'.

Returning to Taylor's criticisms of Altizer, we can now see why Taylor believes that Altizer has not escaped from the shadows of the dead God and why he has not taken the death of God far enough. In insisting on the ontological truth of atheism, in his confidence in the consummation of history, and in his belief in the realisation of absolute presence and total immanence, Altizer gives credence to modern truths that the death of God should render unstable. It is in order to escape the shadows of the dead God that Taylor believes we must look elsewhere towards more explicitly postmodern thought. If Altizer responds to the absolute transcendence of orthodox theology by asserting the absolute immanence of Christian atheism, Taylor asks:

> What does the alternative of transcendence and immanence leave out? Is there a nondialectical third that lies between the dialectic of either/or and both/and? Might this third be neither transcendent nor immanent? Does this neither/nor open the time-space of a different difference and another other – a difference and an other that do not merely invert but actually subvert the polarities of Western theological reflection? To begin to respond to such questions, we must try to think the unthought and perhaps unthinkable difference, which I name with the improper name 'altarity,' by rethinking the death of God. Instead of leading to the total presence constitutive of the complete realization of both God and humanity, the death of God calls into question the very possibility of fulfillment by forever deferring the realization of presence.[27]

So, for Taylor, dissolving transcendence into immanence is to remain under the shadows of the dead God. This is because one has not seriously questioned the priority of the *dualism* between transcendence and immanence which is itself an effect of the God that is being declared dead. One will have merely inverted rather than subverted this dualism. The task, therefore, is to think beyond transcendence and immanence by imagining that which is forgotten or repressed by the dualisms of modernity, and which simultaneously serves as the necessary precondition (in the manner of a transcendental or quasi-transcendental) for those very dualisms. In attempting to think this thought which had been left unthought by modernity, Taylor found the early writings of Jacques Derrida to be an invaluable resource.

For Taylor, the significance of Derrida's thought lay in its interrogation of the dualistic oppositions by which modern thought and reality have been 'mastered'. Writing many years later in the wake of Derrida's death, Taylor said that

> the guiding insight of deconstruction is that every structure – be it literary, psychological, social, economic, political or religious – that organizes our experience is constituted and maintained through acts of exclusion. In the process of creating something, something else inevitably gets left out. These exclusive structures can become repressive – and that repression comes with consequences. In a manner reminiscent of Freud, Derrida insists that what is repressed does not disappear but returns to unsettle every construction, no matter how secure it seems.[28]

In countless studies, Derrida undertook painstaking readings of philosophical, literary and other texts to demonstrate how this quasi-phenomenon could repeatedly be discerned, albeit indirectly. For Taylor, deconstruction had important theological roots and implications that had not always been fully realised. This was partly because Derrida himself had always been careful to distinguish his work from the theological enterprise, even though, as he himself admitted, his mode of expression frequently appeared to echo that of negative theology. But for Taylor, deconstruction could only properly be understood in the context of debates about theology and the death of God, whilst deconstruction also had important theological ramifications that could no longer be ignored. Indeed, Taylor's central claim was that 'deconstruction is the "hermeneutic" of the death of God'.[29] In other words, Derrida's necessarily tortuous but also enlightening deconstructive enterprises ought to be viewed as a practical enactment of the implications of the death of God, the implications that the madman's hearers in Nietzsche's parable had so signally failed to understand.

Far from the death of God necessarily culminating in atheism, therefore, it should rather be understood as culminating in deconstruction, which itself exposes and seeks to think beyond the very dualism between theism and atheism. For Taylor, this created unexplored possibilities for a postmodern theology which sought to take full cognisance of the insights of deconstruction. These possibilities were explored by Taylor in his seminal book, *Erring: A Postmodern A/Theology* (1984). Taylor's creation of the neologism 'a/theology' was significant. It indicated that he was distancing his enterprise from that of theology (with its assumption of an ontology of *theism*) and also from that of 'atheology' (with its assumption of an ontology of *atheism*). What is of central importance here is the slash (/) that marks the point of undecidability between theism and atheism, between theology and atheology. This undecidability is not one of paralysing indecision; rather, it points towards an errant and liberating wandering in that shifty terrain that lies between and beyond theism and atheism, and the other dualistic binaries of modernity. In exploring and wandering through this terrain, Taylor draws attention to the ways in which so many of the founding concepts of modernity have a concealed theological foundation. Inevitably, therefore, and as we intimated earlier, the death of God has enormous ramifications beyond the confines of theology itself.

Indeed, for Taylor, the death of God brings with it also the disappearance of the Self, the end of History and the closure of the Book. But as we have seen Taylor to have pointed out in relation to Altizer, it is not enough simply to negate these concepts, which would be to remain caught up in the very structures of thought of which they are emblematic. He quotes J. Hillis Miller, who says: 'To put a minus sign instead of a plus sign before the elements of Western culture is not to liberate oneself from them but to remain entirely bound within their net.'[30] The task, therefore, is not simply to negate these concepts of God, Self, History and Book, but to imagine how they might be re-envisaged and re-inscribed beyond the limits of their simple affirmation or negation. This is what it means to insist on the slash (/) of a/theology.

But just as Taylor believed Altizer's rendering of the death of God to be incomplete and insufficiently radical, so too Taylor in turn has been criticised for failing to deliver the full rigour of the slash (/) of undecidability that he himself deemed to be necessary. In an important review of *Erring*, John D. Caputo made precisely this point, arguing that Taylor's 'hermeneutic of the death of God' too often slips into an 'hermeneutic of nihilism'.[31] Rather than maintaining the slash (/) between theology and nihilism, Taylor too often appears, in practice, to subordinate the former to the latter, or, as Caputo himself puts it, he appears to allow 'the theological to dissipate without remainder in a world of random play and bottomless chessboards'.[32] In Caputo's own work, most notably *The Prayers and Tears of Jacques Derrida* (1997) and *The Weakness of God* (2006), he attempts to deliver that which Taylor had promised. Whereas Taylor had drawn on Derrida's early work from the 1960s and 1970s, Caputo has engaged with Derrida's later work of the 1980s and 1990s, a period in which Derrida became much more explicitly concerned with religion as such. In drawing out more fully the explicitly theological implications of this work, Caputo has developed a religious and philosophical sensibility which is neither straightforwardly theistic nor straightforwardly atheistic. It appears to be a religious and philosophical disposition that is between and beyond the modern dualism between theism and atheism.

Whatever one makes of the disagreement between Taylor and Caputo, it can nevertheless be seen that, in the work of both, the end of modernity does indeed bring with it the end of atheism. As we have seen, this does not mean that, for them, the end of modernity opens the way towards a simple return of theism. That would be to remain caught within the dualistic logic of modernity. But it is that very dualism between theism and atheism that is here called into question. So the end of modernity may be seen to bring in its wake the 'end of theism' and the 'end of atheism', or, perhaps better, it points to a future that lies beyond the dualistic oppositions of modern metaphysics, a future that is *neither* theistic *nor* atheistic.

Some contemporary thinkers, however, have wanted to go further still, making the seemingly audacious claim that the death of God and the end of modernity actually open the way for a return of orthodox theism. Although at first sight such a claim may appear paradoxical and even logically perverse, one can actually begin to make sense of it in light of the analyses developed in earlier chapters. We have seen that in modernity a new conception of God emerged, a conception that was quite distinct from the conceptions of God that had prevailed hitherto. It is thus claimed that the God whom Nietzsche declares dead is precisely this modern God. As the last thinker of modernity or the first thinker of post-modernity, Nietzsche proclaims the death of the God of modernity. For such thinkers, Nietzsche's death of God is to be welcomed, for *this* God was always an idol, and the death of *this* God allows for the return of an authentic, non-idolatrous conception of God. Understood thus, Nietzsche becomes an accomplice of authentic theology rather than its enemy.

The thinker who has been most associated with this line of argument is the French philosopher and theologian Jean-Luc Marion. For Marion, the modern God is an idol because the conception of the divine is limited to what the human gaze can conceptualise and represent. He says:

> The concept, when it knows the divine in its hold, and hence names 'God', defines it. It defines it, and therefore also measures it to the dimension of its hold. Thus the concept on its part can take up again the essential characteristics of the 'aesthetic' idol ... and allows it to freeze the divine in a concept, an invisible mirror. Notably, the 'death of God' presupposes a determination of God that formulates him in a precise concept; it implies then, at first, a grasp of the divine that is limited and for that reason intelligible... It is on the basis of this concept that the critique exerts its polemic.[33]

Thus, the death of God entails the death of a 'God' formulated conceptually in a particular way, that of modern metaphysics. But if this is so, it implies also that atheism

> is worth only as much as the concept that contains it. And, as this concept of 'God' accedes to the precision that will render it operative only by remaining limited, one must say that a conceptual atheism can assure its rigor, demonstrativeness and pertinence only because of its regionalism; not *in spite of* it, *but indeed because of* it: regionalism indicates that for the term, by definition undefined, of God, the concept substitutes some precise definition, 'God', over which, through the determining definition, understanding will exercise its logic. Thus the conceptual atheisms imply the substitution for *God* of a given regional concept – called 'God'; therefore they bear only on concepts each time fostering this 'God' that they announce.[34]

Marion's point here is, of course, entirely consistent with that made in our earlier chapters, in which we claimed that modern atheism is constituted by the rejection of a specifically modern God. With the eclipse of modernity, we see also the eclipse of this modern God, with the result that modern atheism comes increasingly to appear as a chimera, trenchantly denying a concept that few now would wish to affirm, not even many of those who wish to define themselves as theists.

But if the modern God is now being eclipsed, what is it that contemporary theists – those, like Marion, who have taken leave of the modern idolatrous conception of God – affirm? As Marion suggests, this question is extremely difficult to answer in any unequivocal sense for the very good reason that God cannot easily be conceptualised – to contain God by the definition of a particular 'concept' would again be to turn him into an idol. The challenge that is faced here is nothing less than the challenge to think without and outside of ontological difference. But does not this attempt in fact render thought in itself impossible? And if God must be thought, God 'can meet no theoretical space to his measure'. But perhaps, Marion suggests, the difficulty of thinking outside of ontological difference 'directly suit[s]' the impossibility of thinking God as such.[35] He says that one name remains feasible:

that of *agape*. Why love? Because it 'still remains, paradoxically, unthought enough to free, some day at least, the thought of God [under erasure] from the secondary idolatry'.[36] But even ascribing to God the name of *agape* must still be tempered by the cultivation of a disciplined and difficult silence. The cultivation of such a silence is difficult, not least because:

> Silence, precisely because it does not explain itself, exposes itself to an infinite equivocation of meaning. In order to keep silent with regard to God, one must, if not hold a discourse on God, at least hold a discourse worthy of God on our silence itself.[37]

But this keeping of silence is not, of course, an end in itself. One keeps silence in order to *receive* something, and this is inseparable from the faith that God exposes himself to thought. As Marion says:

> Keeping our silence, in order precisely by this reserve to honor that which we would designate by silence – in other words, in this case, God – this would become thinkable only if God exposed himself to thought. The retreat of our eventual silence implies an absolute point of reference around which a respectful desert might grow.[38]

Arising from this, there are two possible misconceptions which must be guarded against. First, it would be a mistake to say that Marion simply equates God with love, if love be understood as a human, finite phenomenon. The love as which God gives himself exceeds and transcends everything, including human love and including Being. Secondly, it would be a mistake to dismiss Marion's thinking on God as hopelessly empty and abstract were one to make that judgement without taking into account the importance for Marion of biblical revelation, the ecclesiastical location of all such reflection, including, most notably, the central location of the Eucharist. Indeed, Marion would agree that all such reflection would be hopelessly abstract were it not for that location and were it not for the conviction that God gives himself to be received. What we can see from this all too brief characterisation, however, is how far removed Marion's thinking of God is from a conception of God as a 'being' who 'exists'. It is precisely this latter conception that Marion takes to be an idol and which, he believes, must be declared dead.

Marion is by no means the only contemporary theologian whose thinking about God has been moving along these lines. In particular, a movement known as 'radical orthodoxy' has been very influential in contemporary Anglo-American theology in thinking about God anew, freed from the shackles of modernity, which, it would agree with Marion, has the practical result of turning God into a finite idol. John Milbank, the most influential theologian of radical orthodoxy, has done much to promote what he believes to be a non-modern, non-idolatrous conception of God. His conception of God differs from that of Marion in several important respects. The detail of his criticism need not detain us here, although it will suffice for us to note that Milbank thinks that Marion's turn from modernity has not gone far enough, rather than that he is moving in the wrong direction.[39] Building on his reading of Thomas Aquinas, Milbank argues that the true subject matter of metaphysics is the created Being of created beings. But God, who is the source and creator of Being and beings, is not himself subject to Being and is therefore outside the jurisdiction of metaphysics. Consequently, Milbank says that 'the domain of metaphysics is not simply subordinate to, but completely *evacuated* by theology, for metaphysics refers its subject matter – "Being" – wholesale to a first principle, God, which is the subject of another, higher science, namely God's own, only accessible to us via revelation.'[40]

God is therefore not only *not* a 'being', he is also *not* subordinate to, *nor* contained by, the Being of beings. The whole panoply of metaphysical procedures – rational argument, empirical evidence, experiential inference and so forth – simply cannot apply to God. If they are, they are treating God as an 'object' or 'thing' within the realm of Being, and the conclusion of such an investigation will inevitably be that such an 'idol' does not exist.

In the broad contours of their thinking about God, Marion and Milbank should be understood as being representative rather than exceptional in contemporary theology. We find clear echoes of their analyses in numerous other influential contemporary theologians. Fergus Kerr, for instance, has emphasised that 'God is clearly not "a person"'. Drawing, like Milbank, on the thought of Aquinas, he says that 'Aquinas's God is no supreme entity at the top of a hierarchy of substances'. He probes Aquinas's often overlooked question of whether we should treat the word 'God' as a verb, and, in doing so, he emerges with an image of God 'which many would regard as extremely strange and even alienating'. For Aquinas, God, it seems, is best identified in 'a cluster of verbs'; God is conceived of 'as sheer activity, *energeia* – the blissful activity of a triad of action-based relations'. Such a conception, Kerr avers, far from being a 'reassuring foundation', brings us 'dangerously, comically' close to Derrida's non-concept of *différance*.[41]

Rowan Williams, too, has been consistently concerned with rejecting the modern framework that would present us with an either/or choice between God as 'a personal being' who 'exists' (modern theism), and the denial of such a 'being' (modern atheism). In the context of a discussion of Cupitt's work, he says:

> There are long-standing uncertainties about the rightness or adequacy of treating God as an object, an individual to whom acts and properties can be straightforwardly ascribed... We are fascinated by selves as we understand them, and so find it practically impossible to conceive of a relation to God which is not comparable to a relation to a self – an ensemble of impressions, memories, emotions, reactions.[42]

In order to resist this temptation – a temptation to which the mainstream of modern theology and philosophy succumbed, Williams looks to Wittgenstein, who compares talk of the 'existence' of God to talk of the 'existence' of colour. Clearly, talk about the existence of colour does not mean that the speaker believes that there is a particular 'object' or 'being' called 'colour' that 'exists':

> The question, 'what difference does colour make?' cannot be answered with reference to some particular; and there is no graspable 'essence' of colour abstracted from its role in our perceiving. Its essence is its existence: what we mean by colour as such is established only by the fact of its all-pervasiveness in our discourse. And so with God... What distinguishes God-talk from the language of colour ... is that the former sets the *whole* business of our knowing and perceiving against the measure of an all-inclusive vision and all-inclusive affirmation; it is part of the process of coming to love the world-as-a-whole by a growth towards (or into) a perspective like that.[43]

So although we would not wish to say that colour is an object, being or thing that exists, neither would we want to say that there is no such thing as colour. It would be highly misleading to suppose that we must be forced into this either/or antinomy, an antinomy that, for Williams, is equally misleading when applied to the question of God.

Elsewhere, Williams also gestures towards a conception of God that seems to have something in common with Kerr's characterising God as being more a verb than a noun. For Williams, too, it seems that the least misleading way of understanding God is as an 'act'. Asking whether 'God' conceived as an 'object with a history' can really be understood to be God at all, he says:

> The meaning of 'God' as displayed in the history of Israel and the Church has to do with the historical realities of transformation and renewal of such scope that they only be ascribed to an agency free from the conditions of historical contingency, and one that challenges rather than endorses what claims to be the heights of moral and spiritual attainment. And it is out of this meaning of God that there gradually develops the fully articulated doctrine of God characteristic of patristic and medieval theology: the

> unconditioned *act* of self-diffusion and self-sharing upon which all things depend – with the important corollary that this act is 'simple', it is what it is without the admixture of elements or constraints from beyond itself, and so is entirely at one with itself, consistent and faithful.[44]

Enough has been said here to give some indication of the way in which contemporary theologians are conceiving of God after the death of (the modern) God. Marion, Milbank, Kerr and Williams by no means agree on all aspects of theology and their methodologies certainly differ in some important respects. But they are all agreed that the God of modernity, the emergence of which we traced in earlier chapters, was an idol. And they are all agreed that Nietzsche was right to declare that God dead, just as they are agreed that the task of thinking about God *after* modernity is best inspired by the thinking about God that took place *before* modernity. It is also important to observe that Marion, Milbank, Kerr and Williams are by no means exceptional mavericks in contemporary theology. On the contrary, they are broadly representative of a very significant, if not the dominant, stream of theology in recent years.

Whether an atheist (who is such on the basis of a denial of what Marion would call an idolatrous God) would be persuaded by such an understanding of God is another question. One can imagine such an interlocutor replying rather in the manner that we saw Don Cupitt to do when he complained of Aquinas that he appears to be 'striving after vacuity'. In other words, Marion's way of envisaging God might appear to some to be empty and vacuous, which is to say that the conception would mean nothing to them; that they would be unable to make any sense of it. At the heart of such a reaction, we see coming to light the phenomenon of atheism as understood by a philosopher like D. Z. Phillips. Speaking of such an atheist, Phillips says:

> It is not that he sees what it means to say that God exists, but simply does not believe that he does. Rather, he cannot

> see what it means to say that God exists. He is not saying, 'I happen to believe that God does not exist, but, of course, he might have'. Rather, he is saying that God *cannot* exist, because to talk of 'existence' in this context simply does not mean anything. Atheism, then, denies *the possibility* of believing in God, for to believe that God exists is to try to say what cannot be said.[45]

Phillips here gives us an indication of what an intelligible form of atheism might look like after the end of modernity. We have seen that the end of modernity carries with it the death of (the modern) God, and also, therefore, the death of (modern) atheism. Modern theism and modern atheism get their sense within a shared modern framework within which the theist affirms, while the atheist denies that a 'personal being' called God exists. But the end of the modern framework itself entails the death of such a God; this is the revolution we saw Nietzsche to have inaugurated.

After modernity, therefore, the disagreement between theist and atheist can no longer revolve around the question of whether a personal being called God exists, for both are agreed that the end of modernity is inaugurated by Nietzsche declaring such a God to be dead. We have seen that, after modernity, theologians are attempting to recover a conception of God that is far removed from the modern (and they believe idolatrous) conception of God. They speak of a God beyond or without being, a God who bestows existence but who doesn't himself exist, a God whose reality is far removed from what we understand to be reality in the physical world. In such a context, an atheist who continues to proclaim that a personal being called God does not exist would seem to be shooting at an illusory target. For we have seen that such theists in this context would agree that such a God does not exist; such a God is, after all, merely an idol. So the disagreement between a theist and atheist can no longer be located here.

But we *can* imagine someone saying that a God beyond or without being is a vacuous concept. Such a person would be able to make no sense of such talk; it would be unintelligible to him, mean nothing to him. After modernity, I am suggesting, this is what it would mean to be an atheist. But if this is so, we can see that the disagreement between theist and atheist can no longer be understood to be a disagreement about a matter of 'fact'. 'Facts' belong to the realm of this creaturely world, and a non-idolatrous God cannot be spoken of as if he were a fact. After modernity, both theist and atheist should be able to agree on this. The question of the 'existence of God' is no longer a 'factual' question that can be settled by worldly criteria such as rational argument or physical evidence. The question of God now becomes a question of finding meaning and intelligibility in a specifically spiritual reality, God, and not so doing. A *spiritual* reality is not one that can be settled as a matter of fact; if it could, it would no longer be spiritual, but temporal, and thus no longer God. As Phillips says, if God is conceived in this way and his *spiritual* reality is taken seriously, 'then finding God would be finding this spiritual reality. Struggling to believe would be struggling to find it. Rebellion would be defying or hating this spiritual reality.'[46]

So does the end of modernity bring with it the end of atheism? Emphatically yes, if by atheism we mean a specifically modern atheism, the emergence and history of which we have been tracing throughout this book. We have seen that the advent of modernity gave rise to a specifically modern form of theism that was quite distinct from theisms that had prevailed hitherto. Coterminous with this was the rise of a modern atheism, which constituted itself in its reaction against and denial of such a modern theism. The end of modernity was inaugurated by Nietzsche's proclamation of the death of God, which is the enactment of the death of metaphysics, which brings in its trail both the death of modern theism and the death of modern atheism. In this sense, the end of modernity does indeed bring in its wake the end of atheism.

But clearly this does not mean that, with the end of modernity, there will be a universal submission to the sway of theism. If anything, there are more non-theists now than ever before. Indeed, it is possible to imagine a reader being persuaded by the entire analysis of this book, and all of its arguments, while still remaining unpersuaded by theism in any guise, whether pre-modern, modern or post-modern. But insofar as such readers have taken cognisance of the end of modernity, and insofar as they accept that the God of modernity is rejected as much by contemporary theologians as by modern atheists, the *nature* of their atheism will be different from that which dominated in modernity. Accepting that the notion of God as a being who exists is now no longer at issue, and accepting that the question of God is not a factual one that can be settled by rational argument or empirical evidence, such atheists would be constituted as such by their conviction that the God of whom contemporary theologians speak is a vacuous concept that is unintelligible to them, and which has no real meaning in their life, whether this be cause for regret or celebration. This is the kind of atheism towards which we have been gesturing towards the end of this chapter and the last, a kind of atheism that is no longer an artefact of modernity.

Of course, full-blown modern atheists continue to exist and, indeed, have become increasingly vociferous in recent years. Richard Dawkins and Christopher Hitchens, for instance, continue to reject a God that we have seen to be characteristically modern. They reject such a God because they believe that rational argument and scientific evidence point overwhelmingly to the 'truth' of atheism. But insofar as they believe atheism to be a 'truth' that can be shown to be probable by rational argument and scientific evidence, they reveal themselves to be still standing under the shadows of the dead God.[47] In which case, perhaps the real problem with the outlook shared by Dawkins, Hitchens and the other 'New Atheists' is not that it is atheistic, but that it is not atheistic enough.

Notes

Introduction

1 See Richard Dawkins, *The God Delusion* (London: Bantam Press, 2006), Sam Harris, *The End of Faith: Religion Terror and the Future of Reason* (London: Free Press, 2006), Christopher Hitchens, *God is Not Great: How Religion Poisons Everything* (London: Atlantic Press, 2007), and Michel Onfray, *In Defence of Atheism: The Case Against Judaism, Christianity and Islam* (London: Serpent's Tail, 2007).

2 See Charles Taylor, *A Secular Age* (Cambridge, MA: The Belknap Press of Harvard University Press, 2007).

3 Michael Allen Gillespie, *The Theological Origins of Modernity* (Chicago: University of Chicago Press, 2008), p. 5.

4 Ibid.

5 Andreas Huyssen, 'Mapping the Postmodern', *New German Critique* 33 (1984), p. 10. I have replaced the terms 'modernism' and 'postmodernism' here with the terms 'theism' and 'atheism'.

Chapter 1 The 'Appearance' of Atheism in Modern History

1 See Charles Taylor, *A Secular Age* (Cambridge, MA: The Belknap Press of Harvard University Press, 2007).

2 Jan N. Bremmer, 'Atheism in Antiquity', in Michael Martin (ed), *The Cambridge Companion to Atheism* (Cambridge: Cambridge University Press, 2006), p. 11.

3 Michael J. Buckley, *At the Origins of Modern Atheism* (New Haven: Yale University Press, 1987), pp. 9–10.

4 Michel de Certeau, *The Possession at Loudun*, trans. Michael B. Smith (Chicago: University of Chicago Press, 2000), p. 101.

5 For a discussion of witchcraft in an English context, see Jonathan Lumby, *The Lancashire Witch Craze: Jennet Preston and the Lancashire Witches, 1612* (Lancaster: Carnegie, 1995).

6 Buckley, *Origins of Modern Atheism*, p. 249.

7 Ibid.

8 Ibid., p. 250.

9 See, for instance, Frank Tallett, 'Dechristianizing France: The Year II and the Revolutionary Experience', in Frank Tallett and Nicholas Atkin, *Religion, Society and Politics in France since 1789* (London: Hambledon Press, 1991), pp. 1–28.

10 For further discussion of this, see John P. Clayton, *Religions, Reasons and Gods: Essays in Cross-Cultural Philosophy of Religion* (Cambridge: Cambridge University Press, 2006), especially Chapter 2, 'Thomas Jefferson and the Study of Religion'.

11 Buckley, *Origins of Modern Atheism*, p. 10.

12 Adrian Desmond, *Huxley: The Devil's Disciple* (London: Michael Joseph, 1994), p. 373.

13 Ibid., pp. 374–5.

14 Ibid., p. 375. Desmond suggests that this was because the new term had many advantages: 'It switched the emphasis to the scientific method and its sensual limitations... He portrayed agnosticism not as a rival "creed," but as a method of inquiry... His was a sect to end all sects: an attempt to clamber on to a higher moral plane, to escape the priests and paupers, Comtists and Christians. Agnosticism was a many-coloured philosophical cloak, allowing [Huxley] to mask his deep doubt and engage in moral brinkmanship.'

15 For a primary account of these events, see the 'Judgment on Appeal: The Attorney General v Bradlaugh, 1885', in James R. Moore (ed), *Religion in Victorian Britain*, Vol. 3: *Sources* (Manchester: Manchester University Press, 1988), pp. 360–9.

16 Buckley, *Origins of Modern Atheism*, pp. 10–11.

17 Horace Mann, 'H. Mann on the Religious Census, 1853', in Moore (ed), *Religion in Victorian Britain*, Vol. 3, p. 315.

18 Hugh McLeod, for instance, has commented that 'working-class churchgoing seems to have been considerably higher than was recognised by some middle-class observers, such as Horace Mann, the author of the famous official commentary on the 1851 census. It was also somewhat higher than was suggested by the censuses, which counted attendance on a single day, and so missed some of those who attended regularly, but not every Sunday.' *Religion and Society in England, 1850–1914* (Basingstoke: Macmillan, 1996), p. 65.

19 Mann in Moore (ed), *Religion in Victorian Britain*, Vol. 3, p. 316.

20 Owen Chadwick, *The Victorian Church*, Vol. 1 (London: A & C Black, 1966), p. 333.

21 Pierre Pierrard, *L'Eglise et les Ouvriers en France (1840–1940)* (Paris, 1984), p. 236. Quoted in Thomas Kselman, 'The Varieties of Religious Experience in Urban France', in Hugh McLeod (ed), *European Religion in the Age of Great Cities 1830–1930* (London: Routledge, 1995), p. 165.

22 Kselman, 'The Varieties of Religious Experience in Urban France', p. 165.

23 Buckley, *Origins of Modern Atheism*, pp. 28–9. Quotation from John Henry Newman, *Apologia pro vita sua* (New York: Norton, 1968), p. 188.

24 See Stephen Toulmin, *Cosmopolis: The Hidden Agenda of Modernity* (Chicago: University of Chicago Press, 1990), pp. 157–8.

25 Buckley, *Origins of Modern Atheism*, p. 28.

26 See, for instance, Steve Bruce, *God is Dead: Secularization in the West* (Oxford: Blackwell, 2002).

27 See Grace Davie, *Religion in Britain since 1945: Believing without Belonging* (Oxford: Blackwell, 1994).

28 See Paul Heelas and Linda Woodhead, *The Spiritual Revolution: Why Religion is Giving Way to Spirituality* (Oxford: Blackwell, 2005), and Paul Heelas, *Spiritualities of Life: New Age Romanticism and Consumptive Capitalism* (Oxford: Blackwell, 2008).

29 See, for instance, Mark C. Taylor, *Hiding* (Chicago: University of Chicago Press, 1997), *About Religion: Economies of Faith in Virtual Culture* (Chicago: University of Chicago Press, 1999), *After God* (Chicago: University of Chicago Press, 2007), and Graham Ward, *Cities of God* (London: Routledge, 2000) and *True Religion* (Oxford: Blackwell, 2002).

Chapter 2 The Development of Atheism in Modern Thought

1 See, for instance, Lubor Velecky, *Aquinas' Five Arguments in the Summa Theologiae* (Kampen: Pharos, 1994). It should be noted that Velecky's work is representative of a wider movement in recent theological scholarship.

2 The debates between John Milbank, Nicholas Lash and Wayne J. Hankey give a sense of some of the issues at stake here. See Nicholas Lash, 'Where Does Holy Teaching Leave Philosophy? Questions on Milbank's Aquinas', *Modern Theology* 15 (1999), pp. 433–44, John Milbank, 'Intensities', *Modern Theology* 15 (1999), pp. 445–97, and Wayne J. Hankey, 'Why Philosophy Abides for Aquinas', *The Heythrop Journal* 42 (2001), pp. 329–48.

3 Martin Luther at the Diet of Worms, in Henry Bettenson (ed), *Documents of the Christian Church* (London: Oxford University Press, 1947), p. 285.

4 Richard H. Popkin, *The History of Scepticism from Erasmus to Descartes* (Assen, Netherlands: Koninklijke Van Gorcum & Comp. NV, 1960), p. 3.

5 Ibid.

6 René Descartes, *Meditations on First Philosophy*, trans. John Cottingham (Cambridge: Cambridge University Press, 1996), p. 17.

7 Karl Barth, *Church Dogmatics* III/1, ed. G. W. Bromiley and T. F. Torrance, trans. J. W. Edwards, O. Bussey and Harold Knight (Edinburgh: T & T Clark, 1958), p. 362.

8 Mark C. Taylor, *Erring: A Postmodern A/Theology* (Chicago: University of Chicago Press, 1984), p. 22.

9 For further discussion of this, see John P. Clayton, 'The Otherness of Anselm', in *Religions, Reasons and Gods: Essays in Cross-Cultural Philosophy of Religion* (Cambridge: Cambridge University Press, 2006), pp. 161–80.

10 J. Hillis Miller, *Poets of Reality: Six Twentieth-Century Writers* (New York: Atheneum, 1969), p. 3, quoted in Taylor, *Erring*, p. 22. Jean-Luc Marion has similarly claimed that the objects 'proved' to exist by arguments for the existence of God are idols, and therefore not God at all. We shall return to look at Marion's analysis in Chapter 8.

11 John Locke, *An Essay Concerning Human Understanding* (1690) (Oxford: Clarendon, 1975), p. 314.

12 For a detailed explication of this suggestion, see Michael Allen Gillespie, *Nihilism Before Nietzsche* (Chicago: University of Chicago Press, 1995).

13 David Hume, 'Dialogues Concerning Natural Religion (1789)', in *Principal Writings on Religion Including Dialogues Concerning Natural Religion and the Natural History of Religion* (Oxford: Oxford University Press, 1993), p. 106.

14 David Hume, *An Abstract of a Treatise of Human Nature* (1740), quoted in Ernest Campbell Mossner, *The Life of David Hume* (Oxford: Clarendon Press, 1970), p. 127.

15 Ibid., p. 126.

16 Immanuel Kant, *Prolegomena to Any Future Metaphysics* (1783), trans. Paul Camus, rev. James W. Ellington (Indianapolis: Hackett, 1977), p. 5.

17 Immanuel Kant, *Critique of Practical Reason*, trans. Lewis White Beck (New York: The Liberal Arts Press, 1956), p. 137.

18 G. W. F. Hegel, *The Phenomenology of Spirit*, trans. A. V. Miller (Oxford: Oxford University Press, 1977), p. 11.

19 Ibid., p. 49.

20 Ludwig Feuerbach, *The Essence of Christianity*, trans. George Eliot (New York: Harper & Row, 1957), p. 26.

21 Karl Marx, *Capital*, Book I in Karl Marx and Friedrich Engels, *On Religion* (Atlanta: Scholars Press, 1982), p. 135.

22 It has been common to present Friedrich Nietzsche as the thinker who brought atheism to its final fruition. But this is misleading. For Nietzsche, 'truth' was an effect of theism, and the death of the latter entails also the death of the former. Insofar as atheism represents a truth claim, it is as problematic as is theism. Both theism and atheism, therefore, are

casualties of Nietzsche's death of God. I shall return to this point in more detail in Chapter 8.

Chapter 3 The God that Modern Atheism Rejects

1 On the theme of 'domestication' and for a wider discussion of some of the themes addressed in this chapter, see William C. Placher, *The Domestication of Transcendence: How Modern Thinking about God Went Wrong* (Louisville: Westminster John Knox Press, 1996).
2 Don Cupitt, 'Kant and the Negative Theology', in Brian Hebblethwaite and Stewart Sutherland (eds), *The Philosophical Frontiers of Christian Theology: Essays Presented to D. M. MacKinnon* (Cambridge: Cambridge University Press), p. 57.
3 Thomas Aquinas, *Summa Theologiae*, Vol. 3, trans. Herbert McCabe (London: Blackfriars, 1964), p. 67.
4 Michel de Certeau, 'Is there a Language of Unity?', *Concilium* 6 (1970), p. 91.
5 Aquinas, *Summa Theologiae*, 1a, 13, 11. Quoted in Cupitt, 'Kant and the Negative Theology', p. 58.
6 David B. Burrell, *Aquinas: God and Action* (London: Routledge & Kegan Paul, 1979), p. 67.
7 See Don Cupitt, 'The Doctrine of Analogy in the Age of Locke', *Journal of Theological Studies* 19 (1968), pp. 186–202.
8 Cupitt, 'Kant and the Negative Theology', p. 58.
9 John Hick, *Death and Eternal Life*, 2nd edn (London: Macmillan, 1985), p. 24.
10 For further discussion of this, see Steven Shakespeare, 'A Hiding to Nothing: Cupitt and Derrida on the Mystery Tour', in Gavin Hyman (ed), *New Directions in Philosophical Theology: Essays in Honour of Don Cupitt* (Aldershot: Ashgate, 2004), pp. 101–16.
11 Charles Taylor, *A Secular Age* (Cambridge, MA: The Belknap Press of Harvard University Press, 2007), p. 231.
12 Amos Funkenstein, *Theology and the Scientific Imagination: From the Middle Ages to the Seventeenth Century* (Princeton: Princeton University Press, 1986), p. 25.
13 Ibid., pp. 77–80.
14 Ibid., p. 25.
15 See Michael J. Buckley, *At the Origins of Modern Atheism* (New Haven: Yale University Press, 1987), Chapters 2 and 3.
16 It is important, however, not to disguise the differences between the theism of thinkers such as More, Malebranche and Clarke on the one hand, and that of contemporary analytical philosophers such as Swinburne on the other. In particular, as Funkenstein reminds us (*Theology and the*

Scientific Imagination, p. 24), however 'material' and 'temporal' was God's body, this did not necessarily entail anthropomorphism, which More, for instance, emphatically rejected. In Swinburne's theism, in contrast, anthropomorphic features come to the fore.

17 Richard Swinburne, *The Coherence of Theism* (Oxford: Clarendon, 1977), p. 71.

18 Richard Swinburne, *Is There a God?* (Oxford: Oxford University Press, 1996), p. 4.

19 See ibid., p. 9.

20 Ibid., p. 8.

21 Cupitt, 'Kant and the Negative Theology', pp. 58, 59.

22 Ibid., pp. 63, 64.

23 John Milbank, *The Word Made Strange: Theology, Language, Culture* (Oxford: Blackwell, 1997), p. 11.

24 Nicholas Lash, 'Ideology, Metaphor and Analogy', in Brian Hebblethwaite and Stewart Sutherland (eds), *The Philosophical Frontiers of Christian Theology: Essays presented to D. M. MacKinnon* (Cambridge: Cambridge University Press, 1982), p. 78.

25 Funkenstein, *Theology and the Scientific Imagination*, p. 116.

26 John Hick, *An Interpretation of Religion* (Basingstoke: Macmillan, 1989), p. 244.

27 J. L. Mackie, *The Miracle of Theism: Arguments for and against the Existence of God* (Oxford: Clarendon, 1982), p. 109.

Chapter 4 The Theological Origins of Modern Atheism

1 Hans Urs von Balthasar, *The Glory of the Lord: A Theological Aesthetics*, Vol. V: *The Realm of Metaphysics in the Modern Age*, trans. Oliver Davies et al. (Edinburgh: T & T Clark, 1991), p. 12.

2 Thomas Aquinas, *Summa Theologiae*, Vol. 3, trans. Herbert McCabe (London: Blackfriars, 1964), p. 67.

3 Balthasar, *Glory of the Lord*, p. 10.

4 John Duns Scotus, *Philosophical Writings*, ed. and trans. Allan Wolter (Edinburgh: Nelson, 1962), p. 5.

5 Balthasar, *Glory of the Lord*, p. 16. My emphasis.

6 Duns Scotus, *Philosophical Writings*, p. 2.

7 Gerard Loughlin makes this distinction in the context of a discussion of John Hick's conception of God. See Gerard Loughlin, 'Prefacing Pluralism: John Hick and the Mastery of Religions', *Modern Theology* 7 (1990), p. 39.

8 Éric Alliez, *Capital Times: Tales from the Conquest of Time*, trans. Georges Van Den Abbeele (Minneapolis: University of Minnesota Press, 1996), p. 200.

9 Catherine Pickstock, *After Writing: The Liturgical Consummation of Philosophy* (Oxford: Blackwell, 1997), p. 123.

10 See William C. Placher, *The Domestication of Transcendence: How Modern Thinking about God Went Wrong* (Louisville: Westminster John Knox Press, 1996), pp. 71–4. I am particularly indebted to Placher's reading of Cajetan.

11 See Edward A. Bushinski's introduction to Thomas de Vio, Cardinal Cajetan, *The Analogy of Names and the Concept of Being*, trans. Edward A. Bushinski, 2nd edn (Pittsburgh: Duquesne University Press, 1959), p. 7.

12 David B. Burrell, *Aquinas: God and Action* (London: Routledge & Kegan Paul, 1979), p. 55.

13 Placher, *Domestication of Transcendence*, p. 72.

14 de Vio, *Analogy of Names*, p. 11.

15 See ibid., pp. 14, 22–3.

16 Ibid., p. 15.

17 Ibid.

18 Ibid., p. 20.

19 Ibid., pp. 24, 25.

20 Nicholas Lash, 'Ideology, Metaphor and Analogy', in Brian Hebblethwaite and Stewart Sutherland (eds), *The Philosophical Frontiers of Christian Theology: Essays presented to D. M. MacKinnon* (Cambridge: Cambridge University Press, 1982), p. 78. The distinction between analogy and metaphor is also discussed by Janet Martin Soskice in Metaphor and Religious Language (Oxford: Clarendon Press, 1985), pp. 64–6.

21 de Vio, *Analogy of Names*, p. 26.

22 Ibid., pp. 27, 28.

23 Ibid., p. 54.

24 Placher, *Domestication of Transcendence*, p. 74.

25 Balthasar, *Glory of the Lord,* Vol. V, pp. 23–4.

26 Francisco Suárez, *Disputationes metaphysicae*, disp. 1, sec. 1, no. 19, quoted in Balthasar, *Glory of the Lord*, Vol. V, p. 24. My emphasis.

27 Jean-Luc Marion, 'The Essential Incoherence of Descartes' Definition of Divinity', in Amélie Oksenberg Rorty (ed), *Essays in Descartes' Meditations* (Berkeley: University of California Press, 1986), p. 306.

28 Ibid., p. 25.

29 See Pickstock, *After Writing*, p. 123.

30 Charles Taylor, *A Secular Age* (Cambridge, MA: The Belknap Press of Harvard University Press, 2007), p. 271.

31 Alliez, *Capital Times*, p. 218.

32 See ibid., p. 201.

33 Ibid., p. 226.

34 Ibid., p. 225.

35 Ibid.
36 For a critique of such an analysis, see Richard Cross, 'Where Angels Fear to Tread: Duns Scotus and Radical Orthodoxy', *Antonianum* 76 (2001), pp. 1–36.

Chapter 5 Atheism and the Rise of Biblical Criticism

1 Stephen Toulmin, *Cosmopolis: The Hidden Agenda of Modernity* (Chicago: University of Chicago Press, 1990), p. 34.
2 Amos Funkenstein, *Theology and the Scientific Imagination: From the Middle Ages to the Seventeenth Century* (Princeton: Princeton University Press, 1986), p. 346.
3 David Newsome, *The Victorian World Picture: Perceptions and Introspections in an Age of Change* (London: Fontana, 1998), pp. 227–8.
4 J. N. D. Kelly, *Early Christian Doctrines* (London: A & C Black, 1977), p. 70.
5 Ibid., p. 71.
6 Ibid.
7 Ibid., p. 73.
8 Ibid., p. 74.
9 Charles Gore, 'The Holy Spirit and Inspiration', in Charles Gore (ed), *Lux Mundi* (London: John Murray, 1890), pp. 357–8.
10 See Charles Taylor, *A Secular Age* (Cambridge, MA: Harvard University Press, 2007), p. 271.
11 See Alan Ford, *James Ussher* (Oxford: Oxford University Press, 2007), and James Barr, 'Why the World was Created in 4004 BC: Archbishop Ussher and Biblical Chronology', *Bulletin of the John Rylands University Library of Manchester* 67 (1984), pp. 575–608.
12 See Nick Spencer, *Darwin and God* (London: SPCK, 2009), p. 42.
13 Benjamin Jowett, 'On the Interpretation of Scripture', in *Essays and Reviews: The 1860 Text and Its Reading* (Charlottesville: University of Virginia Press, 2000), p. 504.
14 Ibid., p. 502.
15 For a biography of Colenso, see Peter Hinchliff, *John William Colenso, Bishop of Natal* (London: Nelson, 1964).
16 John William Colenso, *The Pentateuch and Book of Joshua Critically Examined*, Vol. I (London: Longman, 1862), pp. vii–viii.
17 Ibid., p. xxvi.
18 Ibid., pp. 123–4.
19 Owen Chadwick, *The Victorian Church*, Vol. II (London: A & C Black, 1970), p. 91.
20 Colenso, *Pentateuch and Book of Joshua*, p. 141.
21 Chadwick, *Victorian Church*, Vol. II, p. 113.

22 Owen Chadwick, 'The Established Church under Attack', in Anthony Symondson (ed), *The Victorian Crisis of Faith* (London: SPCK, 1970), p. 96.
23 Gerard Loughlin, *Telling God's Story: Bible, Church and Narrative Theology* (Cambridge: Cambridge University Press, 1996), p. 123.
24 Rowan Williams, *On Christian Theology* (Oxford: Blackwell, 2000), pp. 47–8.

Chapter 6 Atheism and the Rise of Science

1 Owen Chadwick, *The Victorian Church*, Vol. II (London: A & C Black, 1970), p. 1.
2 John Hedley Brooke, *Science and Religion: Some Historical Perspectives* (Cambridge: Cambridge University Press, 1991), p. 7.
3 See Noel Annan, *The Dons: Mentors, Eccentrics and Geniuses* (London: Harper Collins, 1999), Chapter 2.
4 Michael J. Buckley, *At the Origins of Modern Atheism* (New Haven: Yale University Press, 1987), p. 193.
5 Leslie Stephen in F. W. Maitland, *The Life and Letters of Leslie Stephen* (London, 1906), pp. 150–1, quoted by Jeffrey von Arx, 'The Victorian Crisis of Faith as Crisis of Vocation', in Richard J. Helmstadter and Bernard Lightman (eds), *Victorian Faith in Crisis: Essays on Continuity and Change in Nineteenth-Century Religious Belief* (Basingstoke: Macmillan, 1990), p. 281, note 16.
6 David Newsome, *The Victorian World Picture: Perceptions and Introspections in an Age of Change* (London: Fontana, 1998), p. 198.
7 Robert M. Young, 'The Impact of Darwin on Conventional Thought', in Anthony Symondson (ed), *The Victorian Crisis of Faith* (London: SPCK, 1970), p. 14.
8 Adrian Desmond and James Moore, *Darwin* (London: Michael Joseph, 1991), p. 117.
9 Ibid., p. 118.
10 Adrian Desmond, *Huxley: The Devil's Disciple* (London: Michael Joseph, 1994), p. 193.
11 Young, 'Impact of *Darwin*', p. 16.
12 Quoted in Young, ibid., p. 17.
13 Quoted in Desmond and Moore, *Darwin*, p. 477.
14 Chadwick, *Victorian Church*, Vol. II, p. 19.
15 Quoted in Desmond and Moore, *Darwin*, p. 486.
16 Ibid., p. 487.
17 Chadwick, *Victorian Church*, Vol. II, p. 10.
18 Quoted in Desmond, *Huxley*, pp. 278–9.
19 Young, 'Impact of Darwin', p. 23.

20 Victor Shea and William Whitla (eds), *Essays and Reviews: The 1860 Text and Its Reading* (Charlottesville: University of Virginia Press, 2000), pp. 87–8.
21 Brooke, *Science and Religion*, pp. 281–2.
22 Terry Eagleton, *Reason, Faith and Revolution: Reflections on the God Debate* (New Haven: Yale University Press, 2009), pp. 10–11.
23 Ibid., p. 6.
24 Nick Spencer, *Darwin and God* (London: SPCK, 2009), p. 82.
25 Chadwick, *Victorian Church*, Vol. II, p. 35.
26 John Habgood, 'The Uneasy Truce between Science and Theology', in Alec R. Vidler (ed), *Soundings: Essays Concerning Christian Understanding* (Cambridge: Cambridge University Press, 1962), p. 21.
27 Thomas Dixon, *Science and Religion: A Very Short Introduction* (Oxford: Oxford University Press, 2008), p. 83.

Chapter 7 Atheism, Evil and Suffering

1 Florence Higham, *Frederick Denison Maurice* (London: SCM Press, 1947), p. 83.
2 Ibid., pp. 83–4.
3 Quoted in Higham, ibid., p. 83.
4 John Stuart Mill, *Autobiography* (1873), Chapter II. Quoted in Don Cupitt, *Crisis of Moral Authority*, 2nd edn (London: SCM Press, 1985 [1972]), p. 13.
5 S. T. Coleridge, *Aids to Reflection* (1825), 'Aphorisms on Spiritual Religion': Bohn edn. (1901), p. 103. Quoted in Cupitt, *Crisis of Moral Authority*, p. 21.
6 Cupitt, *Crisis of Moral Authority*, p. 22.
7 Rowland Williams, 'Bunsen's Biblical Researches', in *Essays and Reviews: The 1860 Text and its Reading* (Charlottesville: University of Virginia Press, 2000), p. 196.
8 See Richard Swinburne, 'The Value and Roots of Analytical Philosophy of Religion', in Harriet Harris and Christopher J. Insole, *Faith and Philosophical Analysis: The Impact of Analytical Philosophy on the Philosophy of Religion* (Aldershot: Ashgate, 2005), pp. 33–45, especially pp. 34–6.
9 J. L. Mackie, 'Evil and Omnipotence', *Mind* 64 (1955), pp. 200–12. The article has subsequently been reprinted in numerous anthologies. A developed version, incorporating responses to critics, may be found in *The Miracle of Theism: Arguments for and against the Existence of God* (Oxford: Clarendon, 1982), Chapter 9.
10 See Alvin Plantinga, *God, Freedom and Evil* (London: Allen & Unwin, 1974).
11 See Richard Swinburne, *The Existence of God* (Oxford: Clarendon, 1979).
12 John Hick, *Evil and the God of Love* (London: Macmillan, 1966).

13 Kenneth Surin, *Theology and the Problem of Evil* (Oxford: Basil Blackwell, 1986), p. 95.
14 Cupitt, *Crisis of Moral Authority*, pp. 28–9.
15 Surin, *Theology and the Problem of Evil*, p. 4.
16 Ibid., p. 5.
17 D. Z. Phillips, *The Problem of Evil and the Problem of God* (London: SCM Press, 2004), pp. 10–11.
18 Ibid., p. 12.
19 This suggestion is taken up and greatly developed by John D. Caputo in his *The Weakness of God: A Theology of the Event* (Bloomington: Indiana University Press, 2006).
20 On this, see Bernard Williams, 'Moral Luck', in *Philosophical Papers 1973–80* (Cambridge: Cambridge University Press, 1981), pp. 20–39.
21 Phillips, *Problem of Evil*, pp. 226–7.
22 John Milbank, *Being Reconciled: Ontology and Pardon* (London: Routledge, 2003), p. 8.
23 Fyodor Dostoevsky, *The Brothers Karamazov*, trans. David Magarshack (Harmondsworth: Penguin, 1958), p. 274.
24 Ibid., p. 273.
25 Stewart Sutherland, *Atheism and the Rejection of God* (Oxford: Basil Blackwell, 1977), p. 28.
26 Ibid.
27 Fyodor Dostoevsky, *The Brothers Karamazov*, trans. Constance Garnett (London: Heinemann, 1948), pp. 251–2. I have here followed Sutherland in quoting from the Garnett translation.
28 Sutherland, *Atheism and the Rejection of God*, p. 33.
29 Dostoevsky, *Brothers Karamazov*, trans. Garnett, p. 251.
30 While numerous scholars have agreed on the significance of this 'even if' for Ivan's atheism, there is no unanimity as to how this should be interpreted. Sutherland himself dissents from Camus at this point, and my own formulation here is somewhat different to that developed by Sutherland.
31 It is worth noting that just as Ivan Karamazov articulates a 'moral atheism' that is not directly defined by the question of God's 'existence', so also there is an 'immoral atheism' that is likewise not defined by the question of God's 'existence'. Alenka Zupančič has suggested that this is precisely what we find in the character of Don Juan: 'What is utterly unthinkable in this universe is that someone who does not doubt the existence of God should live his life *regardless of Him*. Yet this is the very stance that Don Juan assumes.' 'Kant with Don Juan and Sade', in Joan Copjec (ed), *Radical Evil* (London: Verso, 1996), pp. 105–25, p. 107.
32 Sutherland, *Atheism and the Rejection of God*, pp. 37–8. My emphasis.

Chapter 8 The End of Modernity – The End of Atheism?

1 'Toward a Hidden God', *Time*, 8 April 1966, p. 82. Quoted in Mark C. Taylor, *Disfiguring: Art, Architecture, Religion* (Chicago: University of Chicago Press, 1992), p. 155.
2 Taylor, *Disfiguring*, p. 155.
3 Thomas A. Carlson, *Indiscretion: Finitude and the Naming of God* (Chicago: University of Chicago Press, 1999), pp. 23–4.
4 Ibid., p. 25.
5 Thomas J. J. Altizer, *The Gospel of Christian Atheism* (London: Collins, 1967), p. 22.
6 Ibid., p. 103.
7 Ibid., pp. 23–4.
8 Ibid., p. 107.
9 Ibid., p. 108.
10 Ibid., p. 110.
11 It should be noted that Cupitt's project has mutated considerably over the years. In particular, the non-realism has extended itself beyond the religious realm, becoming philosophically all-pervasive, while the accompanying religious vision has gradually become less explicitly Christian. Furthermore, Cupitt's personal philosophical canon has expanded to encompass Nietzsche, Derrida and numerous other continental thinkers. In this discussion, I am concentrating on his early version of Christian non-realism, as first articulated in his book *Taking Leave of God* (London: SCM Press, 1980). For a discussion of the evolution of Cupitt's thought over the years, see my 'Introduction' to Gavin Hyman (ed), *New Directions in Philosophical Theology: Essays in Honour of Don Cupitt* (Aldershot: Ashgate, 2004), pp. 1–15.
12 Cupitt, *Taking Leave of God*, pp. 15, 20.
13 Ibid., p. 16.
14 Ibid., p. 2.
15 Ibid., pp. 94–5.
16 Ibid., p. 67.
17 Ibid., p. 96.
18 For example, 'full modernity has known our apocalyptic ending as the death of God, an ultimate ending of our deepest ground, and therefore an ending that could only be an apocalyptic ending', *The Contemporary Jesus* (London: SCM Press, 1998), p. 13. The term 'full modernity' recurs throughout the book.
19 See, for instance, *The Last Philosophy* (London: SCM Press, 1995). As Graham Ward has commented of Cupitt and other radical theologians, 'Each theology aims to eradicate difference or otherness because of the philosophical monism of their commitment to a general "life-force".

They each interpret Nietzsche's Eternal Recurrence as the dissolution of identity and difference and this flies in the face of postmodernism, where difference is lionized.' Graham Ward, 'Postmodern Theology', in David F. Ford (ed), *The Modern Theologians* (Oxford: Blackwell, 1997), p. 592.

20 Taylor, *Disfiguring*, p. 158.

21 Ibid., p. 50.

22 Mark C. Taylor, 'Altizer's Originality', *Journal of the American Academy of Religion* 52 (1984), p. 582.

23 Ibid., p. 583.

24 Friedrich Nietzsche, *The Gay Science*, 125, in *The Portable Nietzsche*, ed. Walter Kaufmann (Harmondsworth: Penguin, 1976), p. 95.

25 Ibid., p. 96.

26 Ibid., p. 95.

27 Mark C. Taylor, 'The End(s) of Theology', in Roger A. Badham (ed), *Introduction to Christian Theology: Contemporary North American Perspectives* (Louisville: Westminster John Knox Press, 1998), p. 261.

28 Mark C. Taylor, 'What Derrida Really Meant', *The New York Times*, 14 October 2004.

29 Mark C. Taylor, *Erring: A Postmodern A/Theology* (Chicago: University of Chicago Press, 1984), p. 6.

30 J. Hillis Miller, 'Theology and Logology in Victorian Literature', in *Religion and Literature: The Convergence of Approaches*, supplement to *Journal of the American Academy of Religion* 47 (1979), p. 354, quoted in Taylor, *Erring*, p. 10.

31 See John D. Caputo, 'Review of *Erring: A Postmodern A/Theology*', in *Man and World* 21 (1988), pp. 108–26.

32 John D. Caputo, 'Atheism, A/Theology and the Postmodern Condition', in Michael Martin (ed), *The Cambridge Companion to Atheism* (Cambridge: Cambridge University Press, 2006), p. 277.

33 Jean-Luc Marion, *God Without Being: Hors-Texte*, trans. Thomas A. Carlson (Chicago: University of Chicago Press, 1991), p. 29.

34 Ibid., pp. 29–30.

35 Ibid., p. 45.

36 Ibid., p. 47.

37 Ibid., p. 54.

38 Ibid., p. 57.

39 See John Milbank, *The Word Made Strange: Theology, Language, Culture* (Oxford: Blackwell, 1997), Chapter 2.

40 Ibid., p. 44.

41 Fergus Kerr, 'Re-Reading Aquinas in Derrida's Wake', in Gavin Hyman (ed), *New Directions in Philosophical Theology: Essays in Honour of Don Cupitt* (Aldershot: Ashgate, 2004), pp. 95–8.

42 Rowan Williams, '"Religious Realism": On Not Quite Agreeing with Don Cupitt', *Modern Theology* 1 (1984), pp. 3–4.
43 Ibid., pp. 15–16.
44 Rowan Williams, *On Christian Theology* (Oxford: Blackwell, 2000), p. 21. My emphasis.
45 D. Z. Phillips, *Introducing Philosophy* (Oxford: Blackwell, 1996), p. 144.
46 Ibid., p. 145.
47 One final note of clarification is necessary here. We have said that the 'death of God' entails the death of the God of metaphysics, which can perhaps be understood as clearing an opening for an alternative conception of God, other than the God of metaphysics. Similarly, if, as we have suggested, the 'death of God' entails also the death of truth, the 'truth' that dies here is the modern metaphysical understanding of truth as 'correct representation', discoverable through reason and science. But this could again be understood as clearing an opening for an alternative understanding of 'truth', which is not constrained by that which modernity has deemed it to be.

Bibliography

Alliez, Éric, *Capital Times: Tales from the Conquest of Time*, trans. Georges Van Den Abbeele (Minneapolis: University of Minnesota Press, 1996).

Altizer, Thomas J. J., *The Gospel of Christian Atheism* (London: Collins, 1967).

——, *The Contemporary Jesus* (London: SCM Press, 1998).

Annan, Noel, *The Dons: Mentors, Eccentrics and Geniuses* (London: Harper Collins, 1999).

Aquinas, Thomas, *Summa Theologiae*, Vol. 3, trans. Herbert McCabe (London: Blackfriars, 1964).

Arx, Jeffrey von, 'The Victorian Crisis of Faith as Crisis of Vocation', in Richard J. Helmstadter and Bernard Lightman (eds), *Victorian Faith in Crisis: Essays on Continuity and Change in Nineteenth-Century Religious Belief* (Basingstoke: Macmillan, 1990), pp. 262–82.

Balthasar, Hans Urs von, *The Glory of the Lord: A Theological Aesthetics*, Vol. V: *The Realm of Metaphysics in the Modern Age*, trans. Oliver Davies et al. (Edinburgh: T & T Clark, 1991).

Barr, James, 'Why the World was Created in 4004BC: Archbishop Ussher and Biblical Chronology', *Bulletin of the John Rylands University Library of Manchester* 67 (1984), pp. 575–608.

Barth, Karl, *Church Dogmatics* III/1, ed. G. W. Bromiley and T. F. Torrance, trans. J. W. Edwards, O. Bussey and H. Knight (Edinburgh: T & T Clark, 1958).

Bettenson, Henry (ed), *Documents of the Christian Church* (London: Oxford University Press, 1947).

Bremmer, Jan N., 'Atheism in Antiquity', in Michael Martin (ed), *The Cambridge Companion to Atheism* (Cambridge: Cambridge University Press, 2006).

Brooke, John Hedley, *Science and Religion: Some Historical Perspectives* (Cambridge: Cambridge University Press, 1991).

Bruce, Steve, *God is Dead: Secularization in the West* (Oxford: Blackwell, 2002).

Buckley, Michael J., *At the Origins of Modern Atheism* (New Haven: Yale University Press, 1987).

Burrell, David B., *Aquinas: God and Action* (London: Routledge & Kegan Paul, 1979).

Cajetan, Thomas de Vio, *The Analogy of Names and the Concept of Being*, trans. Edward A. Bushinski, 2nd edn (Pittsburgh: Duquesne University Press, 1959).

Caputo, John D., Review of *Erring: A Postmodern A/Theology*, in *Man and World* 21 (1988), pp. 108–26.

——, *The Weakness of God: A Theology of the Event* (Bloomington: Indiana University Press, 2006).

——, 'Atheism, A/Theology and the Postmodern Condition', in Michael Martin (ed), *The Cambridge Companion to Atheism* (Cambridge: Cambridge University Press, 2006).

Carlson, Thomas A., *Indiscretion: Finitude and the Naming of God* (Chicago: University of Chicago Press, 1999).

Certeau, Michel de, 'Is there a Language of Unity?', *Concilium* 6 (1970), pp. 79–93.

——, *The Possession at Loudun*, trans. Michael B. Smith (Chicago: University of Chicago Press, 2000).

Chadwick, Owen, *The Victorian Church* (London: A & C Black, 1966, 1970).

——, 'The Established Church under Attack', in Anthony Symondson (ed), *The Victorian Crisis of Faith* (London: SPCK, 1970), pp. 91–105.

Clayton, John P., *Religions, Reasons and Gods: Essays in Cross-Cultural Philosophy of Religion* (Cambridge: Cambridge University Press, 2006).

Colenso, John William, *The Pentateuch and Book of Joshua Critically Examined*, Vol. I (London: Longman, 1862).

Cross, Richard, 'Where Angels Fear to Tread: Duns Scotus and Radical Orthodoxy', *Antonianum* 76 (2001), pp. 1–36.

Cupitt, Don, 'The Doctrine of Analogy in the Age of Locke', *Journal of Theological Studies* 19 (1968), pp. 186–202.

——, *Taking Leave of God* (London: SCM Press, 1980).

——, 'Kant and the Negative Theology', in Brian Hebblethwaite and Stewart Sutherland (eds), *The Philosophical Frontiers of Christian Theology: Essays Presented to D. M. MacKinnon* (Cambridge: Cambridge University Press, 1982), pp. 55–67.

——, *Crisis of Moral Authority*, 2nd edn (London: SCM Press, 1985 [1972]).

——, *The Last Philosophy* (London: SCM Press, 1995).

Davie, Grace, *Religion in Britain since 1945: Believing without Belonging* (Oxford: Blackwell, 1994).

Dawkins, Richard, *The God Delusion* (London: Bantam Press, 2006).

Descartes, René, *Meditations on First Philosophy*, trans. John Cottingham (Cambridge: Cambridge University Press, 1996).

Desmond, Adrian, *Huxley: The Devil's Disciple* (London: Michael Joseph, 1994).
—— and James Moore, *Darwin* (London: Michael Joseph, 1991).
Dixon, Thomas, *Science and Religion: A Very Short Introduction* (Oxford: Oxford University Press, 2008).
Dostoevsky, Fyodor, *The Brothers Karamazov*, trans. Constance Garnett (London: Heinemann, 1948).
——, *The Brothers Karamazov*, trans. David Magarshack (Harmondsworth: Penguin, 1958).
Duns Scotus, John, *Philosophical Writings*, ed. and trans. Allan Wolter (Edinburgh: Nelson, 1962).
Eagleton, Terry, *Reason, Faith and Revolution: Reflections on the God Debate* (New Haven: Yale University Press, 2009).
Feuerbach, Ludwig, *The Essence of Christianity*, trans. George Eliot (New York: Harper & Row, 1957).
Ford, Alan, *James Ussher* (Oxford: Oxford University Press, 2007).
Funkenstein, Amos, *Theology and the Scientific Imagination: From the Middle Ages to the Seventeenth Century* (Princeton: Princeton University Press, 1986).
Gillespie, Michael Allen, *Nihilism Before Nietzsche* (Chicago: University of Chicago Press, 1995).
——, *The Theological Origins of Modernity* (Chicago: University of Chicago Press, 2008).
Gore, Charles (ed), *Lux Mundi* (London: John Murray, 1890).
Habgood, John, 'The Uneasy Truce between Science and Theology', in Alec R. Vidler (ed), *Soundings: Essays Concerning Christian Understanding* (Cambridge: Cambridge University Press, 1962), pp. 21–41.
Hankey, Wayne J., 'Why Philosophy Abides for Aquinas', *The Heythrop Journal* 42 (2001), pp. 329–48.
Harris, Sam, *The End of Faith: Religion Terror and the Future of Reason* (London: Free Press, 2006).
Heelas, Paul, *Spiritualities of Life: New Age Romanticism and Consumptive Capitalism* (Oxford: Blackwell, 2008).
—— and Linda Woodhead, *The Spiritual Revolution: Why Religion is Giving Way to Spirituality* (Oxford: Blackwell, 2005).
Hegel, G. W. F., *The Phenomenology of Spirit*, trans. A. V. Miller (Oxford: Oxford University Press, 1977).
Hick, John, *Evil and the God of Love* (London: Macmillan, 1966).
——, *Death and Eternal Life*, 2nd edn (London: Macmillan, 1985).
——, *An Interpretation of Religion* (Basingstoke: Macmillan, 1989).
Higham, Florence, *Frederick Denison Maurice* (London: SCM Press, 1947).
Hinchliff, Peter, *John William Colenso, Bishop of Natal* (London: Nelson, 1964).
Hitchens, Christopher, *God is Not Great: How Religion Poisons Everything* (London: Atlantic Press, 2007).

Hume, David, *Principal Writings on Religion Including Dialogues Concerning Natural Religion and the Natural History of Religion* (Oxford: Oxford University Press, 1993).

Huyssen, Andreas, 'Mapping the Postmodern', *New German Critique* 33 (1984), pp. 5–52.

Hyman, Gavin (ed), *New Directions in Philosophical Theology: Essays in Honour of Don Cupitt* (Aldershot: Ashgate, 2004).

Jowett, Benjamin, 'On the Interpretation of Scripture', in Victor Shea and William Whitla (eds), *Essays and Reviews: The 1860 Text and its Reading* (Charlottesville: University of Virginia Press, 2000), pp. 477–593.

Kant, Immanuel, *Critique of Practical Reason*, trans. Lewis White Beck (New York: The Liberal Arts Press, 1956).

——, *Prolegomena to Any Future Metaphysics* (1783), trans. Paul Camus, rev. James W. Ellington (Indianapolis: Hackett, 1977).

Kelly, J. N. D., *Early Christian Doctrines* (London: A & C Black, 1977).

Kerr, Fergus, 'Re-Reading Aquinas in Derrida's Wake', in Gavin Hyman (ed), *New Directions in Philosophical Theology: Essays in Honour of Don Cupitt* (Aldershot: Ashgate, 2004), pp. 85–99.

Kselman, Thomas, 'The Varieties of Religious Experience in Urban France', in Hugh McLeod (ed), *European Religion in the Age of Great Cities 1830–1930* (London: Routledge, 1995), pp. 165–90.

Lash, Nicholas, 'Ideology, Metaphor and Analogy', in Brian Hebblethwaite and Stewart Sutherland (eds), *The Philosophical Frontiers of Christian Theology: Essays presented to D. M. MacKinnon* (Cambridge: Cambridge University Press, 1982), pp. 68–94.

——, 'Where Does Holy Teaching Leave Philosophy? Questions on Milbank's Aquinas', *Modern Theology* 15 (1999), pp. 433–44.

Locke, John, *An Essay Concerning Human Understanding* (1690) (Oxford: Clarendon, 1975).

Loughlin, Gerard, 'Prefacing Pluralism: John Hick and the Mastery of Religions', *Modern Theology* 7 (1990), pp. 29–55.

——, *Telling God's Story: Bible, Church and Narrative Theology* (Cambridge: Cambridge University Press, 1996).

Lumby, Jonathan, *The Lancashire Witch Craze: Jennet Preston and the Lancashire Witches, 1612* (Lancaster: Carnegie, 1995).

Mackie, J. L., 'Evil and Omnipotence', *Mind* 64 (1955), pp. 200–12.

——, *The Miracle of Theism: Arguments for and against the existence of God* (Oxford: Clarendon, 1982).

Marion, Jean-Luc, 'The Essential Incoherence of Descartes' Definition of Divinity', in Amélie Oksenberg Rorty (ed), *Essays in Descartes' Meditations* (Berkeley: University of California Press, 1986), pp. 297–338.

——, *God Without Being: Hors-Texte*, trans. Thomas A. Carlson (Chicago: University of Chicago Press, 1991).

Marx, Karl and Friedrich Engels, *On Religion* (Atlanta: Scholars Press, 1982).

McLeod, Hugh, *Religion and Society in England, 1850–1914* (Basingstoke: Macmillan, 1996).

Milbank, John, *The Word Made Strange: Theology, Language, Culture* (Oxford: Blackwell, 1997).

——, 'Intensities', *Modern Theology* 15 (1999), pp. 445–97.

——, *Being Reconciled: Ontology and Pardon* (London: Routledge, 2003).

Moore, James R. (ed), *Religion in Victorian Britain*, Vol. 3: *Sources* (Manchester: Manchester University Press, 1988).

Mossner, Ernest Campbell, *The Life of David Hume* (Oxford: Clarendon Press, 1970).

Newsome, David, *The Victorian World Picture: Perceptions and Introspections in an Age of Change* (London: Fontana, 1998).

Nietzsche, Friedrich, *The Portable Nietzsche*, ed. Walter Kaufmann (Harmondsworth: Penguin, 1976).

Onfray, Michel, *In Defence of Atheism: The Case Against Judaism, Christianity and Islam* (London: Serpent's Tail, 2007).

Phillips, D. Z., *Introducing Philosophy* (Oxford: Blackwell, 1996).

——, *The Problem of Evil and the Problem of God* (London: SCM Press, 2004).

Pickstock, Catherine, *After Writing: The Liturgical Consummation of Philosophy* (Oxford: Blackwell, 1997).

Placher, William C., *The Domestication of Transcendence: How Modern Thinking about God Went Wrong* (Louisville: Westminster John Knox Press, 1996).

Plantinga, Alvin, *God, Freedom and Evil* (London: Allen & Unwin, 1974).

Popkin, Richard H., *The History of Scepticism from Erasmus to Descartes* (Assen, Netherlands: Koninklijke Van Gorcum & Comp. NV, 1960).

Shakespeare, Steven, 'A Hiding to Nothing: Cupitt and Derrida on the Mystery Tour', in Gavin Hyman (ed), *New Directions in Philosophical Theology: Essays in Honour of Don Cupitt* (Aldershot: Ashgate, 2004), pp. 101–16.

Shea, Victor and William Whitla (eds), *Essays and Reviews: The 1860 Text and Its Reading* (Charlottesville: University of Virginia Press, 2000).

Soskice, Janet Martin, *Metaphor and Religious Language* (Oxford: Clarendon Press, 1985).

Spencer, Nick, *Darwin and God* (London: SPCK, 2009).

Surin, Kenneth, *Theology and the Problem of Evil* (Oxford: Basil Blackwell, 1986).

Sutherland, Stewart, *Atheism and the Rejection of God* (Oxford: Basil Blackwell, 1977).

Swinburne, Richard, *The Coherence of Theism* (Oxford: Clarendon, 1977).

——, *The Existence of God* (Oxford: Clarendon, 1979).

——, *Is There a God?* (Oxford: Oxford University Press, 1996).

——, 'The Value and Roots of Analytical Philosophy of Religion', in Harriet Harris and Christopher J. Insole, *Faith and Philosophical Analysis: The Impact of Analytical Philosophy on the Philosophy of Religion* (Aldershot: Ashgate, 2005), pp. 33–45.

Tallett, Frank, 'Dechristianizing France: The Year II and the Revolutionary Experience', in Frank Tallett and Nicholas Atkin, *Religion, Society and Politics in France since 1789* (London: Hambledon Press, 1991), pp. 1–28.

Taylor, Charles, *A Secular Age* (Cambridge, MA: The Belknap Press of Harvard University Press, 2007).

Taylor, Mark C., *Erring: A Postmodern A/Theology* (Chicago: University of Chicago Press, 1984).

——, 'Altizer's Originality', *Journal of the American Academy of Religion* 52 (1984), pp. 569–84.

——, *Disfiguring: Art, Architecture, Religion* (Chicago: University of Chicago Press, 1992).

——, *Hiding* (Chicago: University of Chicago Press, 1997).

——, 'The End(s) of Theology', in Roger A. Badham (ed), *Introduction to Christian Theology: Contemporary North American Perspectives* (Louisville: Westminster John Knox Press, 1998), pp. 255–67.

——, *About Religion: Economies of Faith in Virtual Culture* (Chicago: University of Chicago Press, 1999).

——, 'What Derrida Really Meant', *The New York Times*, 14 October 2004.

——, *After God* (Chicago: University of Chicago Press, 2007).

Toulmin, Stephen, *Cosmopolis: The Hidden Agenda of Modernity* (Chicago: University of Chicago Press, 1990).

Velecky, Lubor, *Aquinas' Five Arguments in the Summa Theologiae* (Kampen: Pharos, 1994).

Ward, Graham, 'Postmodern Theology', in David F. Ford (ed), *The Modern Theologians* (Oxford: Blackwell, 1997), pp. 585–601.

——, *Cities of God* (London: Routledge, 2000).

——, *True Religion* (Oxford: Blackwell, 2002).

Williams, Bernard, 'Moral Luck', in *Philosophical Papers 1973–80* (Cambridge: Cambridge University Press, 1981), pp. 20–39.

Williams, Rowan, '"Religious Realism": On Not Quite Agreeing with Don Cupitt', *Modern Theology* 1 (1984), pp. 3–24.

——, *On Christian Theology* (Oxford: Blackwell, 2000).

Williams, Rowland, 'Bunsen's Biblical Researches', in *Essays and Reviews: The 1860 Text and its Reading* (Charlottesville: University of Virginia Press, 2000), pp. 181–232.

Young, Robert M., 'The Impact of Darwin on Conventional Thought', in Anthony Symondson (ed), *The Victorian Crisis of Faith* (London: SPCK, 1970), pp. 13–35.

Zupančič, Alenka, 'Kant with Don Juan and Sade', in Joan Copjec (ed), *Radical Evil* (London: Verso, 1996), pp. 105–25.

Index